Volga, Volga

Lesley Chamberlain was born in 1951 and grew up in South Wales where she developed an early passion for languages and travelling. After studying at Exeter and Oxford she lectured in Russian for a year. In 1977 she joined Reuters and later worked as a correspondent in Moscow during the Cold War, before returning to concentrate on her own writing. She has published *Food and Cooking of Russia* (1982), *In the Communist Mirror* (1990) and reviews regularly for the *Times Literary Supplement* and *The Times*. She lives in London.

Lesley Chamberlain

Volga, Volga

A JOURNEY DOWN
RUSSIA'S GREAT RIVER

PICADOR

First published 1995 by Picador

This edition published 1996 by Picador
an imprint of Macmillan General Books
25 Eccleston Place, London SW1W 9NF
and Basingstoke

Associated companies throughout the world

ISBN 0 330 33346 1

1 3 5 7 9 8 6 4 2

A CIP catalogue record for this book is available from
the British Library

Typeset by CentraCet Limited, Cambridge
Printed and bound in Great Britain by
Cox & Wyman Ltd, Reading, Berkshire

For Elizabeth

Acknowledgements

To my daughter Elizabeth for bearing up and letting me go, and others who made this journey possible, I am indebted. Maxine Symons was a good friend to both of us as always. Keith Williams at the British Library offered invaluable help. Natasha Perova and Nadezhda Burova in Moscow, and Alexei Slapovsky in Saratov, were lifelines. Thanks are also due to those who answered my queries by telephone. They include Dr Shirin Akiner at the School of Oriental and African Studies, University of London and individuals at:

  The World Conservation Monitoring Centre, Cambridge
  The Medical Council on Alcoholism
  Alcohol Concern
  Fiat U.K. Ltd

Contents

CONTENTS

There water gleams, there Venice vaguely shows. Look at that street – it runs to China straight, and yonder star above the Volga glows. Oh, swear to me to put in dreams your trust, and to believe in fantasy alone, and never let your soul in prison rust, nor stretch your arm and say: a wall of stone.

Vladimir Nabokov, *The Gift*

I told him: no nation is capable of making life so decidedly meaningless as us Russians.

Maxim Gorky, *My Universities*

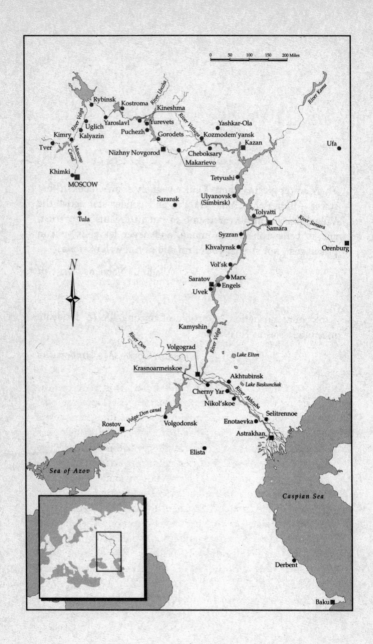

1

Introduction:
The Great Volga

T HE VOLGA RIVER, one of the world's great waterways, rises
northwest of Moscow and flows north, east and south
through the heart of Russia, before it finally reaches the
Caspian Sea. Centuries of poets, robbers, adventurers and tsars have
found inspiration and opportunity in its wide open spaces, occasional
steep banks and once model fecundity. Since medieval times the
Volga has protected Muscovy. In the mid-sixteenth century Ivan
the Terrible conquered it to expand and defend the Russian state.
Today it is still called the Russian mother, the provider, the Russian
homeland.

From source to mouth 3684km (2290 miles), it is the fifteenth-
longest river in the world – longer than the St Lawrence, the
Danube and the Orinoco, but dwarfed by the Nile, the Amazon, the
Mississippi and the three great rivers of Siberia. The British Isles
from John O'Groats to Land's End are a mere 856 miles long. The
Soviet dream was to create out of this promising accident of nature
the largest waterway in Europe, deep enough and wide enough
to bear a constant stream of freight barges connecting the Empire
from all points of the compass. But nature made the Volga a slow
and often shallow river, never sure of its direction. The sluggish
current, tending always to the right bank, would form islands of
flotsam and sand and endless marshy shallows. It was clear even in
tsarist days that only artificial means would enhance the river's
purposefulness.

Soviet Russia therefore made an old Russian dream come true.
It dug the Moscow canal and constructed the seven reservoirs which

1

have transformed a liquid sinew on the map into a chain of still wandering but now mainly deep water lines and jagged lakes. The modern Volga, a little shorter than it used to be, is 3187km (1980 miles) long measured from Moscow to the Caspian port of Astrakhan. At its height two decades or so ago it carried a sixth of all Soviet freight and millions of holidaymakers.

The achievement of the so-called Great Volga was political. The Volga now rose in Moscow, naturally an inland city enjoying only the modest resources of the Moscow river. But the most important consequences, at the cost of lives sacrificed to forced labour, were economic. The Great Volga linked the Soviet heart to six seas of the world. The 128km-long (80-mile) Moscow canal, Stalin's pet project from 1933 to 1937, which involved 'a special Navy' moving more than 200 million cubic metres of earth with only primitive machinery, linked the capital with the natural river and thus through to the Caspian. The Volga–Don canal of 1948–52 brought the Sea of Azov, the Black Sea and ultimately the Mediterranean into the network, while the Baltic canal, finished in 1964, opened the way to the Baltic and North Seas. The present-day Volga is an immovable memorial to Russian national ambition under Communism.

Many would say that it is also a monument to ineradicable folly. The rebirth of the Volga as a Soviet Russian river, an artificial, irreverent, man-centred creation in defiance of nature, has been immensely painful to all surrounding life, animal and vegetable. The fish have almost disappeared, the fertility of the riverside lands has drastically diminished, the landscape is blighted and the bathing dirty. Vast hydroelectric stations with ugly dams straddle the water, tumultuous locks manipulate the river level. Factory chimneys belch, sewage pipes spew. In the post-Communist years of free speech it is possible to spell out the desecration. Modify a sentiment of Lenin's that used to be plastered about the country: COMMUNISM IS SOVIET POWER PLUS THE ELECTRIFICATION OF THE WHOLE COUNTRY and you have, so far as the Volga is concerned, the contemporary demon: hydroelectrification.

Yet the writer Maxim Gorky noted how nineteenth-century Russians endlessly complained of the Volga's disruptive spring floods. When the Great Volga curtailed the floods, it seems they turned to complaining about the reservoirs. The Soviet Union had a poor reputation for preserving the environment, but it is not the only industrialized country to have committed ecological sins. The Rhine, the Thames and the Mississippi have also suffered. Meanwhile, over-fishing has depleted stocks in more than half the world's main fishing grounds: not just Volga fish are disappearing.

So the Volga is not a unique disaster. But it is tragic. Never perhaps has a river been so bound up with ideology and thus with the life of the Russian people. Its tragedy is uniquely eloquent. Gorky saw in its squandered shallows and unharnessed beauty a metaphor for the country's prodigal waste of human effort, and nowadays the Volga is even more obviously a metaphor for the dried-up source of seventy years of unnatural hope. It symbolizes Russia's unfathomable self-destruction under Communism.

2

Embarkation in a Time of Troubles

STALIN IMAGINED an ideal beginning to a Volga journey via the Northern River Station in Moscow. Having arrived in the dark from Moscow airport, I rehearsed this entrance next day. The Metro was full as usual of passengers encumbered with boxes and sacks and spare mechanical parts. To push and shove effectively, lacking a bosom or stomach of sufficient size, I should have brought my suitcase. Squashed, I rode the line crossing the city southeast to northwest and prayed for the end station to come soon. When I got out the chandelier-lit marble catacombs were impressive as always, though compared with Communist days messier and more animated, lined with buskers and beggars, pornography touts and religious revivalists. These were just some of the signs that Russia was undergoing a 'Time of Troubles'. That phrase is usually applied to the chaos between Ivan the Terrible's death and the Romanov succession, and again to revolutionary Russia this century, so I recalled it advisedly, knowing it didn't bode well.

Outside I crossed a wide, unmarked road without traffic refuges, an irregular dusty square without buildings, and passed a few ramshackle shopping kiosks smelling of dill and rotten milk – a sign of another kind of chaos, waste in a time of need. A track led through a small wood out on to another major road. 'River station?' I enquired hopefully, for nothing in Russia ever seems to be signposted, and many times a day I thank my personal gods that I speak the language. Someone nodded. Now I could see a tall statue of an Amazon holding a small sailing boat aloft and I knew I was heading in the right direction. She looked like the French

4

revolutionary spirit personified by Delacroix and popularized by French postage stamps. The age of Stalin loved this heroic style of womanhood as a symbol of political and military victory. A hellishly dark subway, alas, was the only way to reach her. The allegorical implication for humanity didn't strike me at the time. As a real woman I broke into a nervous trot. It was doubly good to be out the other side: I had survived – the same idea in Russian as 'getting across' – which gave me the absurd hope that Russia would also survive its troubled time.

The river station is grand because you don't so much enter it as process towards it, flanked by information boards like pages-in-waiting. But there the idyll stops, because the information doesn't function. Russians don't even stop to look, knowing it is impossible to buy a Volga cruise ticket without connections, bribes or at least substantial forethought. Still, I have my ticket, so I am free to contemplate the ideological scenery. Stalin set out the entrance to the Volga very nicely, part of a simplified world that might have been, and my job this morning seems to be to browse through the remnants of that broken romance.

The river station is of the same vintage as the Metro and the Amazon statue, the kind of architecture that Western visitors to Moscow usually admire so long as they neglect to make the connection with Stalin. It represents in stone all the thousands of wooden river stations of nineteenth-century provincial design which we would see along the Volga from its northerly tip in Rybinsk to Astrakhan in the south. Those wooden stations are charming and harmonious sights, with rows of regular rounded arches and slender-columned verandas. From above a single mezzanine window usually rises a pin-thin flagpole. Overall the impression, perpetuated from a paddle-steamer age shared by the Volga and the Mississippi, is of a docked miniature liner.

But the monument to Stalin's Moscow canal is more boastful and less alive. The flagpole has become a spire with a gold star aloft. Why it isn't red I don't know. The two broad sides of the building each sport twelve cracked coloured medallions in plaster bas-relief which only look from a distance like mosaics. Pictures for children, basic iconographic ideology, they show ships and boats and aquaplanes on the land side, Soviet achievements in transport and energy on the river side, and the Moscow Kremlin. With a building like this you can both feel the energy being squeezed out of the native cultural form and understand the power generated by the new. Stalin's age, whatever its political inhumanity, produced a 'classical' architecture which was strong and dignified by its clean lines and heroic proportions. I enjoyed this building.

So I regretted that, apart from the marble- and chandelier-furnished ticket office, the whole was crumbling. I looked with the melancholy with which one looks upon any broken life, upon any smashed grand ambition, at the decrepit pillared hemisphere at the far end of a grand land-bound craft. It might have been a banqueting room, but no one used it now. No longer a symbol of the ship of proletarian state, no longer betokening a new era of classical stateliness, the river station had come to resemble the ruins of a Roman temple.

Thus I began my trip in a mixture of admiration and melancholy, whilst struggling to find myself a place to stand and air to breathe, and I knew I was back in Russia. Otherwise, arriving by plane and taxi I might have been anywhere, and all I felt when crossing the gangplank of the *Nikolai Chernyshevsky* was relief at least to have made it to the canal. The plan was to take this Western-oriented ship to Nizhny Novgorod, about a third of the way down the river, and from there to transfer to an all-Russian boat, to make the contrast and complete the journey in the company of a Russian writer who had agreed to be my companion.

The *Chernyshevsky* was twelve years old, built in what used to be East Germany. It was the kind of comfortable pleasure boat beginning to be chartered by Western holiday firms now that a democratic Russia had opened its doors to the world. It astonished me with its size (four decks and a carrying capacity of around four hundred passengers) and stability and polish. Subconsciously I was expecting a wreck. At ten in the evening it was ablaze with lights that made the mock bronze fittings and the plastic-varnished pseudo-woodwork sparkle. Officers in the smart navy and cream uniform of the river fleet, the *Rechflot*, with epaulettes and braided cuffs, bestrode the red carpets. More humbly dressed sailors vaguely guarded the ship from unwanted shore visitors, and women staff in working overalls or night-time tracksuits fetched keys and linen and offered me a plate of eggs. I soon found out it was virtually the best river accommodation that Russia had to offer a Western traveller in 1993. The chartering company offered a traditional Russian Volga cruise as far as Nizhny Novgorod for Russians and foreigners, but with information and timetables and pictures, all normally rare commodities in this country.

I could afford to be on the top deck, given the low value of the rouble, and everything functioned smoothly in the small, neat, bright yellow cabin with bed, table, wardrobe and radio. The mixer tap was a movable hydra with a long neck, so that it could be hooked up to double as a shower. Outside on deck it was a mild, still August night, with only a faint freshness from the water to make the nostrils quiver. A fat, weighty, full moon hung portentously close over the dark trees in which the Amazon now slept astride. Pop music from the next boat enlivened the whole ex-Stalinist quayside. We were one of half-a-dozen cruise ships, moored side by side and one in front of the other like a pleasure village, with the bright lights of Moscow winking from across the city reservoir at Khimki, which is also the end of the canal. Tonight we would sleep in the capital, and at 5pm tomorrow, the hour all Volga cruises leave, we too would set sail.

With Moscow time three hours ahead of London, tomorrow came quickly after a deep sleep. In dock the ship had been functioning as a hotel to make the charter company extra money in a difficult summer. Someone banged erroneously on my door, thinking I was part of a group in transit: 'Breakfast!' I hauled myself up and out to eat semolina kasha with greengage jam and butter. There was cheese and ham for the hungry, and a plate of meat and potatoes. Refusing them gave me a chance to come to. I have a small two-breasted Amazonian body which wakes up quickly, often feels hungry and thrives on travelling, but couldn't eat all this.

I visited Russia in 1972, lived in Moscow for a year in 1979 at the height of the Cold War, and returned briefly in 1992, so much was familiar, including the immoderate intake of food. The breakfast table, despite the political upheavals of the last two years, still commemorated Soviet formality and low-taste quirkiness, with a creakily rotating cakestand incorporating condiments in a circular base, and small paper napkins quartered to a format useless for any greater task than blotting lipstick. Radio had changed, though. Gone were the solemnities of an heroic and sentimental life, in which the motherland was tearfully served to strains of Tchaikovsky. Consumer egotism and acquisitiveness had arrived, though their birth was premature and they lurched forward, having never learnt to toddle. Between bursts of rock and rap the city traffic news, sponsored by Sony, the Japanese electronics firm, was announcing which garages had petrol that day and some had none. After the ideological years everything was significant about the new life struggling to replace them. Advertisements revelled in the fetishism that the young Karl Marx abhorred about capitalism, urging people to acquire this and that to distinguish themselves from their neighbours. The same adverts sang the praises of money and share ownership, dancing gleefully round discredited totems. The capitalist vocabulary alone had immense value in bewildered post-Communist Russia. It carried a daemonic charge unattached to any corresponding way of life or moral code.

Theft, fraud and Mafia terror were rife. I knew that from newspapers, but I could not have imagined how gross a parody of all Soviet life would be the jingles that filled the air on the first day of my Volga trip. They represented a wholesale campaign to inspire ignoble and impossible goals: 'We help you attain your dreams. Buy a car from Holland! Get a flat in Moscow!' Those goals were certainly impossible for most people. It was a rare Russian who had enough to live on in those critical days of high inflation and proto-capitalist speculation. Only the few were already very rich, thanks to quick-thinking capital investment of old Communist funds, help from abroad, luck, talent, enterprise and finally, once again, crime. But the new would-be democratic politicians were rich, or that's what most people thought. They accused their leaders, from President Boris Yeltsin down, of filling their foreign bank accounts while the going was good, and of not being patriotic. *Après eux le déluge*.

So these were the Russians I was about to travel among:

millions of more or less apolitical victims of economic upheaval, thousands of revisionist ideologues, who still fancied themselves as those troublesome angels of nineteenth-century idealism, the working proletariat, hundreds of thousands of deposed Communist time-servers, thousands of new rich, and tens of thousands of new criminals. My point in distinguishing them only to collect them together again was simply this: all these people also love the river Volga, for the Volga is Russia. It is all things a Russian river can be to a patriotic native of the country.

To find that beautiful, contradictory, sad stream we finally left our Moscow mooring at 5.30 in the afternoon. Hanging over the rail I reflected that it was the complexity of Russia, the feeling that the mind was so tangled and the reality of institutions at once so stubborn and so rootless, that made me feel happy to be back. Over the ship's tannoy came energizing brass band music. The tune was 'Proshchanie Slavyanki', 'The Slav Woman's Farewell', the same tune which has for years sent young boys off to the army. A tall bouffante blonde in a short black and white polka dot 'ra-ra' skirt, stiffened with crinoline, and a bright pink blouse, who had posed on deck for birthday photographs with a bouquet of claret-coloured roses, waved goodbye to her mother. I got to know Olga by asking if I could take her photograph too. She was a journalist who had been sacked in Soviet days for writing positively about a nunnery. Now she ran a language school.

The tannoy followed up with a crackly taped radio broadcast on the joys of river travel, a hangover from the didactic society. I listened alone, on deck, sitting right under the loudspeaker, but the names of composers and writers and poets connected with the Volga escaped into the air. No Russians on deck could help. They hadn't got much out of seventy-two years of compulsory attention to pseudo-humanist pontifications, so why should they listen now?

The Chernyshevsky was moving at about 15km (10 miles) an hour, a good bit under its maximum speed. Liners like this, with two, then three, and nowadays four decks, have been plying the Volga since the private steamship companies were first established in the 1860s. The layout has remained the same since Chekhov's day, when in 1890 he set out along the Volga on the first leg of his long journey to the Pacific penal colony at Sakhalin. There are public rooms – a restaurant, a reading room, a big-windowed room with a piano – fore and aft, and cabins in between. The top class of travel has always been comfortable. I scoured the lower decks where mostly Russians had cabins at lower prices. The crew were housed at porthole level. Everywhere was clean – only the furnishings were plainer than in first class. Beyond 'Reception' lay a kiosk selling typical Russian treats: chocolate and sweet alcoholic drinks. A souvenir desk beside the restaurant had badges and postcards and some vases and fake 'French' perfume. So unattractive were these gifts that from a Western point of view the shop was redundant, I thought, though later I spotted an American wearing a peaked cap inscribed '*Rechflot*'.

There has never been much to do on a Volga cruise apart from reading and taking the air. Passengers ritually tramp round the ship from the rear sundeck to the always windy foredeck. It is quite a modern thing to sunbathe, though, and only the biggest ships have a specific sundeck. More traditional is to sit along the sides of the ship, outside the cabins, where there are upright chairs and aluminium tables, under a canvas awning, depending upon the weather. I sat there now, relaxed at being underway, and watched the scenery.

Stalin's Moscow–Volga canal, now just called 'Moscow', was too regular, with its concrete banks, to be wholly pleasing. Above the concrete the grass was tiered, and occasionally a few scrawny cattle grazed. A man had come with his bicycle and dog for a swim. All three were perched on the steep stone part of the embankment. The man removed his shoes and socks and the dog circled him excitedly. The canal water is cleaner than the river, it must be said; but also Russians, not spoilt for choice, are less fussy than people in the West.

After about two hours we reached a more open, natural-looking lake, with red-coloured sandy beaches and lyrically turned, wrought-iron moorings, surrounded by birch trees. In the early autumn people would dig under the trees for mushrooms. I knew because I used to come out here from Moscow to these artificially elaborated recreation spots. Westerners would drive, Russians would come by electric train or hydrofoil. One of a cluster of names on the map here said: Bay of Joy.

By nature the real Volga originates in the Valdai hills. Most dedicated guidebooks carry a picture of a small chapel among birch woods and marshes, where the sacred gush of water rises at Volgino Verkhovie in the Ostashkovo province of Tver. The princes of medieval Muscovy and their successors hallowed the birthplace of the river because the Volga determined the political might and geographical extent of their first state. Almost a thousand years later the Nazi Germans touched a sensitive national chord when they damaged the Volga chapel. Soviet soldiers quickly repaired the damage. The Volga in history kept pushing the Tartar back East and the Pole back West. It deserved to be celebrated. In 1649 Tsar Alexei Mikhailovich, the second Romanov, had a monastery built at Verkhovie, which means 'upper reaches'. It burned down, but there survives today that chapel amid the trees plus an ill-kept eighteenth-century church. Reborn Russian sentiment is campaigning to have the source of a great river treated with more respect than since the war, but I have no confidence this will happen soon. Russian people, however sentimental, are capable of startling contempt for history and life.

As for Tver, the nearest big place to Verkhovie, and renamed in Soviet times Kalinin, it has been deprived of much of its tourist trade by the Great Volga, though it still marks the beginning of the natural river's navigable course. Even in the nineteenth century, despite its charming old esplanades it was a thoroughly impoverished, sleepy place, as the playwright and Volga local Alexander Ostrovsky noted on a river journey in 1856. Today, with an irrecoverable medieval history, it is just one more ex-Soviet industrial town, specializing in engineering and textiles, and a port.

The water of the Volga canal soon flowed back within the confines of narrow concrete banks, becoming less picturesque as the light failed. The *Chernyshevsky* juddered and the engines

11

broke their silence as slowly we approached our first lock. It was at Iksha, and the first of a series of five which would raise our huge, flat-bottomed ship to the level of the real Volga. Everyone went up on deck. The solid concrete entrance arch looked like the sharp end of a giant four-poster bed or the gate of a miniature suspension bridge. It had a mural above it in high relief. All the canal locks are decorated, and one, according to a picture I have seen, has bronze models of old Volga sailing ships on its twin gateposts, so visually it is a pity that the ships mostly pass through the locks at night.

We are experiencing the beginnings of the Soviet Great Volga, as engineered by Stalin. It isn't possible *not* to keep thinking of that phenomenon called Stalinism. This canal built with forced labour is now a vital and successful part of Russian life. Many of the best-functioning parts of this country are built on the gratuitous, scandalous deaths of – to use Solzhenitsyn's figure – 60 million people. Stalin's architecture is orderly and ornate, and in a disorderly, disfigured country nothing has bettered it. So how is it possible to judge this Russia?

I cannot even quite regard place names like Bay of Joy as parody. For something tempts me about dreams of perfection. I've been wandering about Russia off and on for twenty years to trace the fate of a misguided perfectionist dream. And yet it is not so much the perfection as the dreaming of the dream that interests me now that I know the country and my older self better than my younger. Nor have I ever connected the perfect vision to any political system, but to a refinement of the human heart. So why come to Russia, then? The kind of answers which come to mind are: it's humbling, it's not a place for cynics, there was once a vision. Tonight when I first glimpsed the man and the dog going swimming the thought escaped me: life cannot be so bad if they are free and happy in nature on this calm evening. It was a wrong thought. Life could be dreadful. But Russia has this capacity always to inspire concern with the well-being of the inner man, its literature seeming to magnify the power of all humanist art.

*

We had dinner while the *Chernyshevsky* still sat in the concrete lock, so that for half an hour or so our view was of brute wall and green slime. The large dining room, with a tiny side entrance, occupied the whole of the front of the third deck and was surrounded by picture windows. Each table was laid attractively for six, with the usual black bread curling like shoe soles for having been cut too soon. Having ridden the Metro into Moscow with them earlier in the day, I sat next to Romanian-born Radu, who taught comparative literature in Paris, and his composed, elegant wife Anne, a geographer and historian. The conversation was hectic. Misha, a young Russian translator who had turned himself into a virtual Frenchman, and Yelena, a blonde Russian girl travelling alone, speaking only Russian, got caught in the crossfire when I asked Radu which country he regarded as his.

'None. I'm not a Romanian, I'm not a Frenchman, I don't have a country.'

It seemed to me that Radu longed to adopt Russia and I said so. Since he had left Bucharest in his early twenties this was his first taste of a recently Communist society, and he'd been enthusing about its spiritual quality all day. Like a 1970s' socialist – I told him – he wanted everything in Russia, from education to poetry, to be right where in the West it was wrong. We fought in French. Misha translated for interested Russians. Actually that generated more pathos. Radu loved Russia yet couldn't communicate, having deliberately failed Russian at school. Few in Eastern Europe then wanted to master intellectually the language of the political master. But now he couldn't talk to Yelena. He was domineering and irrational and I liked him hugely for baring his soul. '*Ya, Yelena, veliky durak!* I was a fool in the Russian class, Yelena. I never paid attention. What do you think, Yelena? I'm a fool, aren't I? Otherwise I could have talked to you.'

Hard to say what she thought, this shrewd, pleasant woman of twenty-four, who had recently opened a private business with her Italian boyfriend Mario. Its success meant she could afford this trip. As for Mario, they had sighted each other in Red Square and played a game of hide-and-seek around the big department store GUM before professing instant love. She and Mario now sold Russians petfood.

'Petfood? How can that be, Yelena? Most Russians don't have enough to feed themselves these days.'

'Oh, but they do. Many Russians have a lot of money to spend.'

Many? Some? I would like to see statistics which surely don't exist.

We finished our cabbage salad and pilaff and cheesecake. The Anglo-French contingent among us unanimously wanted coffee. We followed each other round the ship but it was too late for the café, too early for the bar. Then Misha remembered the samovar on the lower deck, an institution on Volga liners. There is always water at 80°C for hot drinks. He remembered someone had instant coffee. The restaurant gave us cups. So we went back and sat again after all the diners had gone. The coffee wasn't much, but victory in improvisation bonded us into a group. Russia perhaps does this to people: raises their emotional temperature and lowers their melting point.

Belatedly aware of the intense darkness outside, we went up on deck. Another tradition since steam days has been to cheer any passing Volga liners. Rowdy greetings came our way from a bonfire party on the shore. The Volga by night, even the canal, is thrilling when ships appear and disappear like mirages.

The inside of the ship flickered with more conventional and artificial excitement. The *Chernyshevsky* had a bar and ballroom on its top deck, the hallmark of its four-star status. Mainly young Russians with airs and graces learnt from transatlantic films were dancing to a Western-style disco band with a Russian repertoire partly sung in a kind of English. The bar remained Russian. It took forever to get served because every portion of chocolates or ice cream – Russians all seemed to buy an extra pudding in the bar – had to be weighed on an old-fashioned pair of metal shop scales like a tall sailboat. To drink there were coffee or sweet liqueurs or brandy or various direly artificial vinous concoctions, of which red sweet champagne from Bulgaria promised the least bad headache, someone said, but one sip suggested this prophecy was too hopeful. Smoke and noise polluted the atmosphere. It was hard for any of us to feel at ease, and Radu and Anne went to bed. Misha and I watched the dancing, periodically staring reproachfully at our undrinkable bottle. Among the jeans and high heels and heavy make-up one tall

14

slender girl with short black hair and a long easy olive jacket over pale straight trousers conformed to current Western taste. While we were watching her a couple of heavy-footed jivers fell headlong and the man, finding himself on top, stole a kiss. Unpleasant, I felt, such a gross display of possessiveness.

'I don't like these people! Look at the faces!' said Misha.

'Shall we dance, then?'

The singer was delivering a version of the 1993 hit 'Everything I Do I Do It for You'.

Misha was pale and too gentle, like a youth out of Turgenev. He told me he had spent hours in his room as a schoolboy reading and never joined the Soviet youth organizations. Later, when we sat down again, he half-whispered, half-shouted to make himself heard over the music: 'I must change my life. I don't make any friends here because I keep thinking I will go abroad.'

'You'll go, if you're determined enough,' I said. We walked reflectively on deck before sleep. Misha's position was just like Radu's twenty-three years before. He might go and live in the West, but how difficult it would be to survive, and at what psychological cost.

We spoke a mixture of French and Russian, Russian for me because I love the language and much of the joy of being in this country comes from wrapping myself in its generous, luxurious cloak, the cashmere of European tongues. Misha speaks French, for, like Radu, he already lives in a chosen land. Already there is this tension between them because of the potential similarity of their fates.

'Il est fou, ce monsieur. But you, you explore the Volga, you come to tell the world about Russia, you are my heroine.'

'Listen, Misha, this country is an assault course. I only like it because it taxes me. Oh yes, and I admire Russian literature. I want to see where it comes from.'

'And the Volga?'

'No one at home knows where it is.'

Misha looked faintly surprised, kissed my cheek goodnight, and as we approached my cabin door went off saying: 'Russia's an assault course. I like it!'

3

The Volga Flows
. . . Musically

THE REAL VOLGA joined us that night. On the morning of Tuesday, 10 August the water plashing beneath our bows was already two kilometres wide, with flat, distant, lightly populated green banks. This was the Uglich reservoir, and no nineteenth-century traveller would have recognized it as the river. It looked more like a sea. The day was already hot and many passengers were sunbathing on the spacious stern sundeck behind the captain's bridge. The deckchairs sagged so low that only the very agile ought to have used them. Others enjoyed the fresh air and the motion of the boat from upright chairs. A voice came over the tannoy, heralding a sight. Bikini tops were refastened; camera shutters clicked open and shut. We had reached Kalyazin, a small town much mentioned in old Volga voyages, and where Alexandre Dumas *père* began his Volga jaunt of 1858. Now, because of the Uglich reservoir Kalyazin lies under the water, and we saw only the bell tower of its old central church protruding, at an angle, smooth and white, like a sea-washed bone. My first foolish reaction was to feel incensed, my second was to find out what we were missing. It turned out to be not very much. Once there was a crenellated monastery, but even then Dumas was disappointed with his first glimpse from Kalyazin of his 'Queen of Rivers'. Moreover, the area was never specially pretty. The relics of the old town have been transferred to a museum.

Kalyazin was flooded because the natural Volga was too difficult to pass here. A 1911 Russian guide to the Volga by E. Lepeshinskaya and B. Dobrynin spoke of the river from around Tver down to Yaroslavl as

> pushing its way through vast depths of sand and clay, the result of ice age deposits. Beneath these the deeper-lying rock strata are entirely hidden from view. The banks become friable, and are already unable to withstand the destructive effect of the Volga, which leans towards the right bank, trying to enlarge its flow. It washes away the unstable glacial sediment. This sinks to the bottom and forms islands and sandbanks which create new impediments to shipping.

An Englishman, Laurence Oliphant, who made a Volga journey in 1853, found the sailors obsessed with these *perekaty*. Ships always anchored at night to be more certain of their course. Another English visitor, Maurice Baring, found the same slow routine in practice sixty years later.

The nineteenth-century Volga had its adjoining canal systems, the Mariinsky and the Tikhvinsky, now disused. But with the unquenchable twentieth-century need for a higher energy output to keep the Soviet nation warm and at work, plans of far greater magnitude had to be conceived, including not only more navigable waterways, but dams and power stations.

Still what galls nature-lovers is that the disfiguring hydroelectric stations, run at full capacity, have completely upset the ecological balance of the river. It was possible to clear villages and preserve old buildings by moving them to new sites, but the side-effects of so much hydro-engineering were not foreseen. Most obvious is the loss of fish. The changing water levels and the looming presence of the dams, together with the industrial waste which is not washed away by the now even slower flow of the river, have upset their reproductive cycles and also poisoned many of their existing number. There has also been land damage. The increased permanent extent of water has reduced available farmland or made what remains less fertile. The flood pastures of the Upper Volga, which supported cattle and a thriving leather industry, have disappeared altogether. This chronic disaster is not visible from the ships, but it is from the shores of Upper Volga towns. That is why no one speaks

17

without reservation of the reservoirs, such as this one before Uglich, which has swallowed Kalyazin.

The *Chernyshevsky*, though, glided on through the flat country-side, alternately aiming to please and instruct its guests in the art of admiring the river uplifted by art, the Volga Volga.

A t 11am there was a lecture in the music room about Volga music and folklore. The room was packed, despite the attraction of the sun outside. An ensemble of expert researchers and performers explained a collection of half-pagan, half-Christian part-songs. The songs told of the sowing and reaping of agricultural seed, of the influence of Volga waters upon the harvest, and of the sowing of the human seed. The lecturers were university staff on holiday, who began on a forced popular note by stressing the naughty romps in the lyrics. Children kept coming back and forth, slamming doors and shouting. The lecturers nobly continued talking about river pearls.

In former times Russian women wore highly embroidered costumes studded with river pearls to dance seasonal and social messages. These pearls, once called the Russian national stone, used to be found in more than one hundred and fifty Russian rivers in the seventeenth and eighteenth centuries, and some of the finest came from the Volga around Yaroslavl, about 200km (120 miles) downstream from where we were now sailing. This pearl-wearing reflected local wealth as well as costume. The German Baron Haxthausen, who travelled the Volga in 1847 to study the Russian economy, observed that even the poorest fisherwomen of the Upper Volga displayed at least three or four strings of real pearls around their necks, and the rich ones ten or twelve, plus a pearl-studded cap. Dense ornamentation on traditional costumes showed off wealth at the same time as it was required to stop evil spirits penetrating. The Volga also entered the dance in the characteristic long drooping sleeves of the women's blouses, which symbolized water. So there was an intimate, repeated connection between female nature and mother Volga. The pearls were also thought to mate, a pale reflection of the violent, tender and tragic human rituals so often described in the songs.

And what songs they were! Galina's and Olga's gratingly harmonious voices mimicked the flow of the wide river, and a little bird observing. Galina, with her large brown face and slanting Tartar eyes, explained that the water was nature and the bird human life. Another song related the fate of Tanyusha, a raped girl who killed herself and became a mermaid. Every summer on St John's Day (the feast of Ivan Kupala) she and the other mermaids had their revenge: they rose to ruin the lives of young men. Singing this song centuries ago young men jumped in and out of fire to show off their physical prowess, as old belongings were burnt and candles floated on the water. The whole ceremonial summer night ended in mass copulation, an excitement echoed in the song by stamping feet, or the rapping of a stick.

We lunched with those rasping tunes of the 'Volga Volga' in our ears, and passed through the immense lock to disembark at Uglich.

The small town on the birch-wooded right bank looked almost splendid, thanks to the blue and gold cupola of a church which immediately met the eye in brilliant sunshine against a blue sky. But it turned out that Uglich consisted of almost nothing else. Its few roads could be seen from the boat hugging the river, as if without the Volga's embrace the place would die.

A line of beggars, petty speculators and artful children, all selling tourist gimmicks, began from the staircase linking the ship's gangplank to the high wooded embankment and stretched over a kilometre back into the bare, dusty town square. Going ashore, we had to run this commercial gauntlet of appeals to our compassion, our poor taste, our foolishness – I couldn't decide which. The beggars were the old and the disabled, who couldn't live on a small pension in the face of rampant inflation and corrupt, irregular food supplies. Yelena had told me that prices were particularly high in Uglich shops because the goods were bought in Moscow and resold here. The speculators were young men who had heard that the capitalist West became rich through buying and selling for profit. The children were children, following in adult footsteps, wanting a bit of pocket money, harbouring TV-stimulated ambitions of T-shirts and German cars. The young men were selling watches produced by the local Chaika (seagull) watch factory, famous throughout Russia. I tried to find a map and bought some postcards for the equivalent of a dollar. A dollar wasn't much for me, but for a Russian it was a day's salary. The old women were selling berries and greengages by the tumbler, tomatoes, mushrooms, cucumbers and flowers. Up to five liners a day called at Uglich between 1 May and 1 October, and the local people descended like Volga seagulls at each ship's coming. There was much religious crossing of the breast and well-wishing at every transaction. Each visitor was cast in the role of potential Saviour.

Three hundred multi-coloured tourists in all, the Russians all knowingly with shopping bags (for the sellers have only their wares and sometimes a few pieces of flat paper to make a cone), snaked slowly into Uspensky Square, over a bridge across a muddy Volga tributary. The Uglich reservoir had dried up the rivulet and created a tranquil, sheltered mini-harbour where the big ships could not enter. On a stretch of sand naked children were playing and swimming and riding pedal-boats.

The square had long since lost the buildings which distinguished it in the seventeenth, eighteenth and nineteenth centuries – the Uspensky church and rows of stone-arcaded merchants' shops which traded knives, nails, leather, soap, meat, butter, and headscarves and woollen stockings. Like so many empty-seeming Russian historic towns, Uglich was dusty, formless and disorientating. On the water's edge stood the once splendid kremlin or citadel, a group of redbrick and white buildings, now without its encircling walls. The side elevations of the brick-built church of Dmitri the Bloody, whose blue and gold cupolas were visible from the river, were intricately decorated with ceramic tiles. The tiles, a speciality of the Upper Volga, were worth coming to see. But Uglich as a whole? Back to the left of Uspensky Square, against the wall of a grocery shop and a crude arts and crafts shop for tourists, local people were trading pickled mushrooms and cucumbers, jams, a single, days-old, dull-eyed carp, and a local variety of yellow-grey dried fish.

Uglich's history begins with the earliest Russian state, Kiev Rus. It existed before the state of Muscovy and witnessed the struggle against the Tartars to the east, who blocked Russian trade routes, and the struggle for power near at hand, when Tver and Moscow and Yaroslavl and Vladimir and Rostov were rival principalities. When Uglich became prominent in the late fourteenth century as Moscow's ally the kremlin was built as a religious, military and administrative centre. Trades and crafts took up their places outside its walls, and some ten monasteries were built in the surrounding area. Building in stone encouraged the painting of thousands of interior frescoes, of which today only relatively late and undistinguished examples remain in the kremlin complex.

But then in 1611 the Poles burned Uglich, and despite rebuilding it has been going downhill ever since. The fifteenth-century redbrick Palace of the Princes, the oldest extant building, which contains the kremlin museum, is an eloquent testament to a past talent for living: glazed tiles with fine historical and fabular motifs, tiled ovens, black pottery, carved furniture and wooden household objects, body warmers in fine fabrics, long velvet braided jackets, lace ruffs and embroidery. It also shows Soviet carelessness. A sign says the museum holds the pall of General Kutuzov, who fought against Napoleon and became the hero of Tolstoy's *War and Peace*, though no one knows where it is. Stolen perhaps.

The pervading emptiness of Russian provincial towns is partly the result of centuries of wooden building. Peter the Great even decreed that no provincial towns should build in stone. The rest is a mixture of economics and, lately, destructive ideology. Uglich was hit in the early nineteenth century when the Mariinsky canal routed ships from the Lower Volga and from the northwest via Rybinsk. Through disuse and neglect the river silted up so much that people could wade across. Only small-scale industries could flourish, and of those the important ones, processing agricultural produce, shrank to half their original number. The local people sought work elsewhere. Artists arrived in their place, to soak up the old-world atmospheric quiet. Historians followed, to catalogue and display and commemorate the past. Anton Chekhov's brother Mikhail, working in the town as a tax inspector but pursuing his main interests as a writer, journalist and theatre critic, was one of these; he formed a drama circle. There is something of the Cornish riviera about the whole of the Upper Volga, once more productive but now mostly dependent on the tourist trade.

Soviet power gave Uglich a boost. The hydroelectric station, a grand sight spanning the water, was one of the first on the Volga, finished in 1940. Factories were built, reviving the food processing industry and the production of high-precision minerals like the quartz on which the latest Chaika watches run. But at the same time the history which is Uglich's real claim to fame was expunged. Half the churches that were still remaining by the twentieth century were obliterated, and most of the rest have since rotted. The Pokrovsky monastery, which adorned pre-revolutionary postcards of the Volga banks, has disappeared under the reservoir. So that is the ghastly situation today.

Yet there is one real story which makes Uglich come alive. Pushkin learned it from the historian Karamzin, and the composer Mussorgsky learned it from both. That story is of the murder of Tsarevich Dmitri, the last son of Ivan the Terrible, which formed the background to Pushkin's drama and Mussorgsky's opera *Boris Godunov*.

The boy Dmitri, exiled to Uglich with his mother, was killed in 1591. A priest witnessed the death in the garden and sounded his church bell to spread the news. Dmitri's mother accused the Moscow boyar prince Boris Godunov, who stood to become tsar, of murder and Uglich rebelled. Godunov had his aide Prince Shuisky head an inquiry which found Dmitri to be the victim of epilepsy and the people and their bell guilty of treason. Tongues were cut, eyes put out, and many folk sent to Siberia. The bell was flogged and sent too, and only returned to Uglich three hundred years later, in 1892 – surely the longest exile in Russian history. Today the tour guides sound it once per group. It stands on show beneath a crude fresco of the fate of Dmitri. The most beautiful aide-memoire is a blue and yellow circular icon of the hallowed royal infant in black, painted in tempera on wood, clutching the same toy he was holding when slaughtered. This is the town crest.

In Russian crises the politics of the people is always at stake. Pushkin and Mussorgsky dug deep to try to understand. The common people were oppressed and fickle victims, but the tsar needed their approval as well as their fear. Boris, depicted by Pushkin and Mussorgsky as reluctant to accept power at the people's adulatory insistence, had their approval and lost it. He had to commit a terrible crime in order to concentrate his power. He died, conspired against and leaving chaos. Neither is dead, but similar things are said today about Russia's most recent leaders, Mikhail Gorbachev and Boris Yeltsin.

The Poles exploited Russia's Time of Troubles after Godunov's death, when famine, and the continuing connection of Godunov with Dmitri's murder, sparked a civil war. From Poland appeared the first of two famous false Dmitris, pretending to the Russian throne. The boyars killed the first after eleven months, replacing him with Shuisky who then, to win over the people, publicly admitted Godunov's complicity in the Uglich assassination and had the real Dmitri canonized.

Mussorgsky's score conveys what was really happening in those dark days. Shuisky is the wheedling tenor to Godunov's bass – the corrupt official who exploits a magnificent incidence of flawed greatness in a superior man.

There are plenty of Shuiskys in Russian politics today. And there are those who, however bizarrely, would say the West exploits the latest Time of Troubles to infiltrate its market philosophy, the way the Poles did then with their Catholicism. All one can do is stand here in the dust and heat and imagine the continuing drama pitching the people against the power-seekers, with all sides flying the colours of national pride.

Back in Uspensky Square a woman thrust flowers into my hands and insisted on not being paid. This *was* Russian pride, a token to say we are not beggars, moreover we even know how to cultivate our suffering. Two suntanned young boys, Sasha and Slava, whose command of English was astonishing for their eleven years, attached themselves to me. Sasha's T-shirt, called a *futbolka* in Russian, sported the designer name Dior. Slava had one announcing that great capitalist rank and Stalin nickname, Boss. 'Do you want to try fantastic Uglich ice cream?' they asked, wanting to know the price of ice cream in America. We toured the town with its low-rise apartment blocks and 'the falling down church' and they told me about their families. Slava's father managed a textiles shop, his mother worked in the watch factory. Sasha's stepfather bought and sold cars. Slava pointed to a distant balcony. 'Oh, look! Theez iz my grandmother.' They couldn't stop laughing.

23

Suddenly it was time to say goodbye. Sasha had admired my rollerball pen but I only had one. In fact all I had two of was dollars – a shameful present, but I gave it all the same. I had to run back to the *Chernyshevsky* and arrived with only three minutes to spare. The boys did well, though, because Radu, to whom I had told the story of the bell before we went ashore, came up behind and gave them dollars too.

I was momentarily thrown from my purpose. Like some invention of Nabokov, Radu had been trailing me and was shadow-writing the beginning of this book. Does this happen to male writers? It has more than once happened to me in this strange life. Now he taxed me for having gone off on my own. I only include this so my readers should know that women always have this extra dimension of life to deal with in whatever they do.

We sat after dinner in the music room, in the dark, which was the best way to watch the Volga slip by. Above us, nearer the prow, the captain also watched from his dark cockpit. Some Americans, one of whose number had gamely taken part in the folk song demonstration, another of whom wore the *Rechflot* cap, arrived in a gang and insisted on putting the lights on. They told jokes against the Russian airline Aeroflot, the domestic reputation of which is not good, and talked about the prices of things back home. Why do they have to behave in this dull and clannish way? Isn't Russia *special* to them?

A Polish woman, Regina, indulged us with chocolate and brandy and talked about love. Mercifully, Radu was absent. Misha was singing to his guitar. Most young Russian men sing and carry their guitars with them, especially on Volga holidays. People still make music here because of the lack of media entertainment, and of course the music embellishes the river. Yet not in a straightforward way, for this is real Russia, not an idyll in a Western mind. Misha's ballads expressed not a life close to nature, like the Volga folk songs, but one disinherited, in which the misfortunes of love were routinely entangled in daily urban squalor. His masters were the national hero Vladimir Vysotsky, who died tragically young in 1980; the poet Bulat Okudzhava; the immensely popular pre-revolutionary singer Alexander Vertinsky, famous for the song we know as 'Those Were the Days . . .'; and the Frenchman Jacques Brel. Regina then sang a quite different, *faux naïf* song made famous by the Russian artiste Ludmilla Zykina, starlet of the Brezhnev years. It went: 'From far off and far away the Volga river flows without bound and without end.'

She pressed home the message about love, having recently lost her son. I got a lump in my throat about a ghastly romantic mess I had left at home. Ahead of us on the river shone the bright distant lights of the *Feodor Shalyapin*, behind us trailed the *Maxim Gorky*. Every Volga liner is named after a writer or an artist or occasionally an historical figure. When they leave their harbour clusters they form convoys on the high water. Soviet culture was held together like this, by constant reinforcement of significant names, a substitute for belief.

4

Countryside and Ideology

NEXT MORNING, Wednesday, 11 August, was warm and sunny. The Volga, having reached its most northerly point at Rybinsk, had swung sharply south, following almost its natural course. Rybinsk, a medieval 'fish place', briefly changed its name to Andropovsk when Andropov succeeded Brezhnev's successor Chernenko as Communist Party leader. It was not a stopping place for the main tourist boats, though despite a great fire in the eighteenth century pre-revolutionary travellers found it attractive. From the top end of the Rybinsk reservoir the ships headed north up the Volga–Baltic canal, another creation of forced labour. All this had passed, together with Rybinsk's own Amazonian river statue heralding the lock gates, and the town of Yaroslavl, in the night.

After breakfast we were luckier, catching sight on the left bank of a visionary Kostroma. Lenin's hand, at a height to match the church cupolas, stretched out commandingly from this ancient town towards the Caspian Sea. Until not very long ago Lenin was in competition with the Amazonian women to lead this country. Now it has only its wonderful women left.

The broad Volga had become a charming sight. It flowed between gently undulating emerald banks and on these were clustered wooden villages, punctuated with silver onion domes. Some of the most famous nineteenth-century literary estates lie here. The poet Nikolai Nekrasov, who called the river his creative cradle, grew up in the village of Greshnevo, now renamed Nekrasovo. The houses, izbas and dachas, were pretty and probably without modern facilities. Misha, pulling up a deckchair, explained the difference: izba was a style of building with wood; dacha was any house, but usually wooden, mainly for holiday use.

The tannoy announced a Russian lesson for foreign guests. Radu and Anne went. I took the opportunity to search out the ship's library, which apparently existed, though I hadn't been able to find it. Vera Mikhailovna, one of our organizers, came with me, because strictly speaking it belonged to the crew. It was quite a discovery for someone like me, for whom ideas are quite as real as stone walls, and fall into disrepair and get used to build other things. Our ship was named *Nikolai Chernyshevsky*, after a Russian social democratic writer of the mid-nineteenth century. N. G. Chernyshevsky nurtured absurd views on literature and a misconceived desire to increase mass happiness. This library contained only his books. Vera Mikhailovna laughed. 'The Communists were hooligans. They used to force this stuff on people. We all had to read Chernyshevsky at school!'

Dissidents used to be branded hooligans. Now it appeared that the Communists were the ones who lacked social responsibility, because they forced children – and Volga sailors and travellers – to see the world in a false light. I admired Vera her quick turn of phrase, which summed up one aspect of the post-Communist situation. 'But you know, Lesley,' she added gravely, 'Chernyshevsky himself was a clever man. He tutored my great-grandfather.' Like many thoughtful Russians, Vera Mikhailovna knew that not everything once approved of should be automatically thrown away.

Back on the sundeck Radu hastened by, weaving through the bikinis and sun oil. Wrapped in a black leather jacket and cap and scarf, he looked as if he were braving a snowstorm. I hailed him as my comrade, quite out of tune with his circumstances. I told him the tale of the library and two deep vertical crevices cracked his forehead. We agreed this was a theme boat, the kind of phenomenon the contemporary West could only regard as parody.

Time now evaporated in pleasant conversations with new-style Russians. These were all people who had made the changes work for them. Olga catered for Russians' lack of confidence in their own language. A couple of middle-aged lovers who kept bumping into each other exuded friendliness, as if celebrating the fact that we all belonged now to the same sexy and fun world. He was in computers, she used to fix those unreal prices for groceries and housing which kept the average Russian happier under Communism than in the free market. The woman read a Cyrillic version of James Headley Chase while her man did press-ups. On other laps Jackie Collins rubbed spines with Alexandre Dumas, the same Dumas who had travelled this way a hundred and fifty years ago. Olga wasn't reading anything, but told me private tutors were again legal in Russia, after the Communist ban. There was a sense in which Chernyshevsky was himself back in fashion then, if not his books. Flora meanwhile, 'in international trade', devoured the Brothers Goncourt in translation. Russians haven't burst out of their old lives like released prisoners. It is more as if they have been washed up on a new shore. They have old habits and new circumstances to blend. Partly because of ideological distortions, including the mould-ing of reading habits around the classics, and the long exclusion of Western trash, partly because it is its own country, Russia has a unique cultural clock.

When we arrived in Plyos there was a buzz of what-shall-we-do-in-the-fine-weather. Several Russian volumes of Jackie Collins in translation closed in succession. Hire a rowing boat? Swim? These, I took it, were Russians who either had no interest in history or had already visited this little town, the origins of which dated back to the ninth century. For us foreign first-timers the sight of an almost Swiss-looking resort nestling in green hills was more alluring.

Immediately it had much more Instamatic appeal than Uglich, this place built at the confluence of the Volga and the local river Shokhonka and whose name meant long straight stretch of water or fishtail. The two forested hills between which the Shokhonka flows were high enough to be rare on the Upper Volga. The tree-lined low embankment beside the river, with benches overlooking, was a row of varied, two-storey stone buildings, mostly nineteenth-century. Beside the ship's gangplank a student was selling lacquered boxes in the local Palekh and Kholui styles. Everything in the museum catalogue he helpfully provided was, alas, so much better than what he had for sale. It included a tractor depicted as the centre of a fairy-tale, a beautiful version of the Soviet dream painted by the modern inheritors of the icon tradition. Meanwhile on the embankment postcard and fish sellers touted their wares. The smoked bream seller made more these days from letting tourists take his photograph. The oddly stocked shops behind sold everything from earrings to toiletries, bread to skis, and pretty much nothing at all. The food counters would have neither meat, sausage or cheese until Saturday, which was in four days' time. A small crowd had gathered to see what was being sold from the back of a lorry: books, imported instant coffee and tinned goods. Pop music blared out from a café which on closer inspection was an all-male establishment and filthy. Uphill from the river, white stone-built trading arcades where flour and grain had once changed hands dominated the old Market Square. A drunk lay asleep beside his vodka. Dubbed American films were showing in the cinema on the waterfront. I feared here was another Uglich, only prettier.

The coming of the railways did the most economic damage to Plyos, reducing its status as an important trading centre to that of a resort with a mere forty-five thousand inhabitants. The land around was never rich, but for centuries Plyos had had a flour mill, and its produce could be sold on. What remained were fish, but now they, sterlet especially, have been driven away by the pollution from the reservoirs. The industrial waste which is not washed away by the now even slower flow of the river has destroyed their habitat. All that are left are a few bream.

From the top of Cathedral Hill, reached by a green path lined with birch trees, we surveyed the motionless water of the Shokhonka. Here the water was mirror-bright, there it was green with moss, made stagnant by the reservoir system. Until recently this was called Freedom Hill. People were swimming and rowing boats down below. Dacha roofs stood out red amid dark green woodland. Beside us through a sparse copse ran children and grandmothers and goats. Little of Plyos's medieval history remained visible but up here its first wooden fortress had stood, a defence against the Tartars and later against those same Poles and Lithuanians who sacked Uglich.

It was like a private neighbourhood, this hilltop apart from the modern centre of Plyos, with chickens and chickweed and churches. In 1910 the local people erected a statue to Plyos's founder, Prince Vasily I of Moscow, son of Dmitri Donskoy who inflicted Russia's first key defeat on the Mongols at the battle of Kulikovo in 1380. Here for more than two centuries stood the Uspensky Orthodox church, Plyos's largest. In the Soviet period it was used as a tractor and motor workshop and its fate reminded me of those English churches around Southwold in Suffolk, so visibly butchered by Cromwell's Puritans. The Uspensky was struggling to regain a vestige of holiness, with men of the cloth milling about selling candles and icons and crucifixes. But it had been too much damaged by the removal of its historical patina.

'Do you believe in God?' our local guide Raisa, an immigrant from Tadzhikistan, splendid in a white dress, asked me. When I demurred she continued: 'I feel I ought to believe, now we are free, but I have read too much philosophy and psychology and history to make belief possible.'

'I think you put it exactly right,' I said.

'What do you believe in, then?' glowered a Holy Father selling those tin crosses which, worn with an unbuttoned shirt, post-Soviet men considered highly attractive to post-Soviet women that summer.

'Talking to people,' I replied. 'Trying to say what is so.'

Russia had this mania in 1993 for self-righteous, self-publicizing religion. Various forms of Christianity and sectarian worship were swarming around Russia after the death of Communism like so many false Dmitris after Boris, jumping at their opportunity. The radio waves were saturated with religious confessions and instruction. Everywhere we went, small choirs were singing in the churches for money. It would happen later that afternoon in Plyos. The church had climbed with great skill on to the capitalist bandwagon. I found it unpleasant and intrusive.

The Jewish Russian painter Isaac Levitan worked in Plyos. Of all painters, not one has better captured the moods of the Volga and the Russian countryside round about. Only through Levitan, who happened to be born in Lithuania, does the meaning of the Volga in Russian culture begin to be revealed. Uniquely sensitive to the moods and tones of this river landscape, he captured the humility of the Russian countryside, its plangent ordinariness, its very modest impact on the senses, compared with the dramatic coastlines of the Neapolitan peninsula and the cultivated extravagance of Monet's garden at Giverny, both of which he also knew. The quiet, unsentimental, precious picture of the Volga that Levitan engraved on Russian hearts was perhaps encouraged by literature. The theatrical impresario Sergei Diagilev said that nature in literature from Turgenev to Chekhov found its expression in Levitan, and it was Chekhov, a friend from their student days, who said that Levitan's work here constituted 'at last a smile' for him – and, one might say, for Russia too.

With his male companion and married mistress, all of them painters, Levitan lived by the river in a three-room rented 'house with an attic'. The mistress, also a pupil, was called Sofia Kuvshinnikova and historians don't doubt that she and Levitan were in love. They spent eight summers in Plyos, arriving by the first boat in May and leaving by the last in late September. Normally puritan Soviet critics approved of Kuvshinnikova, because she brought her young, moody lover – the age gap was thirteen years – to find calm and believe in his talent. The first year they came, in 1888, he was twenty-six, she thirty-nine.

When Chekhov stopped at Plyos in 1890 on his way to Sakhalin he specifically thought of his friend's tendency to gloom and need to smile. In doctorly fashion he wrote home: 'Levitan shouldn't live on the Volga. It puts gloom into the soul.' It was mischievous then to write to Kuvshinnikova that he had seen the house with the red roof. But already the writer in him was tempted. He drew on the Levitan–Kuvshinnikova affair for his story *The Grasshopper* the following year. Levitan was so insulted that he stopped speaking to Chekhov for two years.

Levitan painted wonderful, mostly unpeopled, pictures, though the best are not in the Plyos gallery. Olga passed us on our way to the dear little house which Raisa served up as her speciality for Plyos tourists, and said she was disappointed. You have to see the canvases in the Tretyakov Gallery in Moscow to know that, like

Caspar David Friedrich in Germany, Levitan stressed the majestic power of a nature which dwarfed the human contribution. *After the Rain, Plyos* (1889) and *Above Eternal Peace* (1894) are fine examples of his work; their beauty could dictate a volume on the Russian national soul. *A Fresh Wind. The Volga* (1895) captures the river in brisk, business-like mood by focusing on a moored barge in the bright morning in choppy blue water, while the awe-inspiring *Evening. Golden Plyos* (1889) speaks, quite Friedrich-like, of the Volga's poetic closeness to final things.

We adjourned to Raisa's for coffee. As usual there were no refreshments in a Russian town. Her wooden house beside the Volga had no running water or gas. An aesthetic refugee, she had chosen Plyos for its gracious exterior and the clean air by the – albeit dirty – river. I suppose that's what Levitan was too. Plyos also possessed this old neighbourhood, and many Russians now have a passion for all that is old, against that official Soviet love of the new which wilfully destoyed history. This area, where Levitan stayed and the museum now stands, used to be much further from the river, but the Nizhny reservoir, constructed in 1957, brought it close to the edge. Some fine buildings and the kind of busy foreshore visible in Levitan's paintings were lost then, but a few houses of a comforting age remain.

Raisa's apartment, reached by an indoor wooden staircase across a kind of loft area, had white walls enhanced by hanging red patterned carpets, flowers and books, and a brilliant white floor-to-ceiling tiled oven. Its two small rooms each contained a single bed. Raisa wanted to see a cleaner world and wore her white dress and painted her walls white to express that post-Soviet dream subliminally. She grew some fruit and vegetables and, the way all Russians do, pickled and bottled this and that. Seven of us sat round her kitchen table, drinking thimblefuls of vodka, sampling sweet tomatoes, cherry jam and marinated mushrooms. Radu, in his antiquated socialist-idealist way, was ecstatic to find that Raisa owned a bookshelf with books. Her sixteen-year-old son strummed a guitar to words by Vysotsky. I flicked through a book on Levitan in which Vysotsky and Tchaikovsky appeared as kindred spirits. For a short time it was possible to link almost everything of value which had happened so far on the Volga: the modesty of Levitan, the abrasive idealism of Vysotsky, Raisa's hopes for a cleaner world, her son's and Misha's hopes for a decent life, Radu's passionate search for a meaningful culture. As so often in Russia the intensity of the culture worked like an embrace, coming from every direction, and there was no time to become ironic and detached, as one might have done on reflection.

I so admired Raisa's healthy stand against Soviet Russia and her blazing white dress. That sense of personal ecology we can acquire to help us juggle nature and technology for maximum human benefit is virtually unheard of in Russia, where backwardness and lack of choice stifle it. The elements of personal ecology – diet, exercise, stress management, the desire for clean air and organic food – are Western fashion ideally underpinned by the idea that fine-tuning our physical needs gives us more self-control and therefore encourages our better selves. Psychology for the mind, personal ecology for the body, with both influencing the other, and morality, art and culture as relative superstructures on top of this foundation: is that not where our view of humanity has arrived? Relative, that is, insofar as they are *sayable*? On this voyage you will often see me acting upon this basic, actually ancient Epicurean wisdom: jogging along the Volga, exercising at the ship's rail, protesting when the food is bad, celebrating when it is good. One Russian woman I met, a few years older than me, said this was all too much self-love. My reply was that Russians go astray when they cultivate suffering excessively. A little more self-love here, individual and national, would not only preserve the female figure but also conserve history and buildings, watch over consumer standards and public health, and maintain, I am sure, a lovelier Volga.

We were still sitting at the kitchen table. A new member of our party, Nathan, so distinguished-looking in his sixties that he kept being asked if he were not the poet Okudzhava, grew pleasantly drunk on many thimblefuls. We all swapped addresses. Raisa's son couldn't sing, but went on trying.

5

The View from
the Bridge

ALREADY IT WAS a first last night. Tomorrow was Nizhny and I would not see Anne and Radu again. We dined early off tomato and onion salad, soup, rissoles and rice, and oladi (yeast pancakes) with tea. I put on the red dress which has accompanied many good occasions in my life. It was the only touch of glamour in a small suitcase which otherwise contained little more than jeans, shorts, a Swiss army knife, vitamin C, coconut oil and shampoo. Russia, I find, is like that. You don't know whether you're going to a ball or into the outback, so better cater for both but travel light. Things get stolen at the airport these lawless days. Last year I saw a British woman crying at the check-in when she wasn't allowed to take all her baggage by hand: 'Oh, God, I can't lose it all again.'

But tonight festivity was in the air. There was a good sense of voluntary belonging. All of us new acquaintances, more than half a dozen now, waved at each other on entering the dining room, recognizing that here lay a good time. We were very jolly even before Nathan produced a half-bottle of Côtes du Rhône saved from the aeroplane (fortunately he and I were the only drinkers). I would look back to this time on the *Chernyshevsky* as the Volga certainly, but only in miniature, only as an introduction to the great adventure, without its vexations and sadnesses, and therefore almost a holiday. Uglich and Plyos were quaint ports of call. Everything would change at Nizhny.

I might say with hindsight that how it would change could have been intuited in the view from the *Chernyshevsky*'s captain's bridge, for there on display at sunset were the real concerns of a river traveller: the mystery of the water, its moods, its resources, its craft, and the moods, resources and crafts of those who worked on it. Even to go and contemplate that, to break out of the pleasing society I had become part of, mixed in nationality, friendly, familiar, cooperative, I found hard, just as I have always been reluctant to begin journeys I knew would be difficult. But then I have this hankering for difficulty which goes deep, and Misha was at my elbow, determined that I should be a heroine. So here I made my third arrival at the Volga, as it were, that evening, tired and climbing the almost vertical metal steps to the bridge barefoot.

'Go on!' urged Misha. 'You must go up and talk to them.'

'The evening shoes will have to come off, then,' I called back reluctantly.

Mikhail, the first mate on watch from Plyos to Chkalovsk, gave a predictable account of his life on the river, speaking in the dark like a questionee on *Mastermind*. Did he love the Volga? Of course he did.

'I have been doing this job sixteen years. My mother was a *sturman* [navigator] who brought me on board when I was three months old. My father and my grandfather worked on the boats.'

'Your mother was a *sturman*?'

'Yes.' OK. Nothing unusual about that. Russian women have long been emancipated for certain jobs, from medicine to roadmending, anywhere they can be useful. Such emancipation has little to do with Western feminism, people boldly say now. Less then ten years ago many Soviet-fanciers pretended it did. In fact politics confuses what is at stake in the comparison. Work gives women dignity. Russian women have that in abundance. What they don't have is sexual liberation and 'new men'.

The cockpit was dark except for the last glimmer of natural light in the sky. The fading sunset evoked a faint gleam from the great twin brass cylinders of the steering wheel. It was like flying low in a plane over the water, we were so high up. Through the huge front wall of glass the view was panoramic, though the river was quiet. Bellbuoys bobbed in the broad water and lights winked on the shore. Mikhail explained that the river's depth was indicated from there by white triangular hoardings called *farvatery* (from the

German *Fahrwasser*, meaning a navigable channel). The ships also took their direction from the *farvatery*, which looked like the abandoned easels of giant painters packed up for the night.

A ship passed. The telephone rang. Mikhail was talking to his counterpart on that ship about their return journey from Astrakhan. They'd picked up a stomach bug. Everyone was ill. They'd picked up lots of fruit and vegetables from the south, too. Mikhail said he'd have two boxes of tomatoes. The control panel, all flickering needles and gauges, looked dull until, putting down the phone, he threw a switch which made it light up like a fairground. Now I could see a tall, broad-faced, well-looking man, one of those smart fellows in *Rechflot* uniform I had spotted in Moscow and not since. (Once a cruise is underway, the crew become invisible.)

It was a rare ship that passed, I observed. Did the traffic consist only of holiday liners?

There was the rub. Mikhail confirmed that proper goods traffic on the Volga in 1993 was exceptionally thin, with 40 per cent of the goods fleet idle. The post-Communist economic chaos had driven wide and deep. In addition to steeply risen fuel costs, suppliers had gone unpaid and therefore could not pay their shippers. Old markets for sand, salt, pebbles, coal, wood and oil had diminished or disappeared with the secession from the defunct Soviet Union of Ukraine and Belorussia. Poor interim organization of the industrial economy, resulting in processing plants not working, had instead encouraged the import of ready goods from outside Russia, leaving the great waterway almost redundant.

Mikhail was relatively unscathed. He had work and colleagues, who, as in the old system, half-righted the inefficient command economy by making individual corrections. Now they compensated for economic collapse by fetching provisions for each other. Such small-scale private enterprise was being practised all over Russia in 1993. The scale of it was a reversion almost to nineteenth-century ways, when peasants travelled the river, buying and selling goods by the sack.

'But what will happen when they privatize *Rechflot*?' I asked.

He put a hand to his face and rocked back and forth, pretending to weigh the question to which he knew that I knew there was no answer other than: 'Better the devil you know.'

The spectacle of decline, as evidenced by the slowed Volga, was hard for many Russians to contemplate after years of knowing their country to be a superpower. When I checked the 40 per cent figure with a journalist she said, with an odd degree of personal involvement: 'Ah, so you've noticed!' Mikhail was a man of few words, but others on my trip would be more vociferous in their collective shame. It was painful to be peering in at this hurt Russia.

In the morning the ship was stationary. I went up on deck and found us in mid-river, refuelling and surrounded by other boats and barges, many stacked with sweet-smelling birch logs. We had reached Chkalovsk, a new town focused on shipbuilding and repairs 150km (100 miles) upstream of Nizhny Novgorod. All along the right bank of the river were sawmills and bases of the timber industry. We had already passed their important centres in Yurevets and Puchezh. Before the river liners went over to oil early this century, they stopped often for wood to burn in the engine furnace. Travellers were woken at night by the repeated thud of timber on deck. The wood also occupied much space, though it provided lodgings under the stars for the lowest category of passengers. The sparks burnt the skin, but the smell of roasting sappy wood must have been intoxicating.

We glided on. Now the Volga moved between twin sandy banks with small beaches on both sides, ranks of rowing boats, the occasional church, and here and there a small plant dealing in sand or pebbles, with occasional workers passing on bicycles.

'Look, Viktor Nikolaevich, the kremlin is on fire!' The voice was Tartar-eyed Galina's, and the singers rushed from their impromptu practice session with a tape recorder beside the bar and hung over the deck rail. Nizhny was majestic from the water, incomparable with any other town along the Volga, but, busy talking to a woman emigrée returned to Russia for the first time, I had been too engrossed in the past to look. Now we all leaped up at Galina's cry. The evidently newly restored wooden roof of the White Tower of the ten-turreted Nizhny kremlin was blazing into the blue sky like a giant torch. No one seemed to care. No fire-fighting was in operation. Someone even spotted another tower that had burnt on a previous occasion. We docked as if this were just another ordinary place and went ashore. We had even arrived at a port without a name. The city authorities had taken down the Soviet name Gorky from the modern glass river station eighteen months ago, but couldn't afford a new one saying Nizhny. The matter was a local scandal.

Still, within hours of going ashore we knew the name was unimportant. Nizhny was not just another lost, anonymous Russian town. It had the strongest of identities, whether it was called Gorky after its most famous writer, or retained that resonant spondee plus a dactyl which the French writer Théophile Gautier claimed was his primary motive for making a trip there a hundred and thirty years ago. Nizhny Novgorod was a city with rank in the world. It was at last a city.

6

A Riot of Two Hundred Thousand Voices

NIZHNY STANDS on the right bank, where the Oka flows into the Volga, and its majesty derives from the contrast of a broad sweep of confluent water with a steep, high, wooded hill. From this Otkos the stone-built upper town gazes regally out to river, and the primitive and solid kremlin, built unusually on a slope, descends. The lower water is busy with ships, especially where the land forms a triangular wedge between the two rivers. This is called the Strelka, the arrow, and the Russian word is painted on the concrete-reinforced bank in huge red letters. Scores of ships and barges bringing goods to the old Nizhny Novgorod Fair used to moor along the Oka. The Alexander Nevsky Cathedral, an earth-coloured triangular church comprising five short towers culminating in small gold globes, was built in 1881 to preside over the Fair and dominates the Strelka side. Designed by Leonid Dahl, son of Russia's best-known lexicographer, it is not highly rated in the history of architecture but Nizhny would be markedly less spectacular without it. The nineteenth-century photographer Andrei Karelin assured the view near-immortality when he captured it in his Nizhny album.

The Fair was a feast for the senses. Travellers said it was a town in itself, with separate pavilions maintained by different nationalities in their particular style, churches financed by merchants, hotels and restaurants and a theatre. The white neo-classical Old Fair church, the Staroyarmarksky of 1822, survives, though not the Chinese pagodas, frequently remarked upon and pictured, which used to stand beside it. The Fair lasted for six weeks every July and

August, and was quite theatrical, decided the young Stanislavsky, carrying ideas with him to the Moscow Arts Theatre. To Gorky as a youth it was enough to stare at the Persians sitting cross-legged with their beards and coloured robes to dream of travel to the East. Merchants of every nationality and hue, including peasants from Siberia with the greasiest furs in the world, mingled with traders and customers from Europe. In the Fair's heyday, which lasted to the turn of the century, the density of boats made a pontoon from the Otkos side of town to the far Oka bank. A permanent bridge now spans the water. As so often with Russian reputations and Western travellers who test them, the Fair proved dirty on closer inspection and commercially uninviting. There were fleas in the beds and no bedclothes, and the food was atrocious. But the colour never failed. This was a meeting point for the world. Dumas spoke of the riot of two hundred thousand voices.

To look upon Nizhny and to read of its past is to recognize a great small city, quite entitled these days, with a population of one and a half million, to see itself as Russia's third capital. Since it was founded in 1221 it has three times come to the rescue of Moscow, a source of great civic pride. Two names bound up with that pride, Minin and Pozharsky, names which lead back to Russia's Time of Troubles, keep cropping up to endorse the city's independent identity. The upper town has its Minin Square, the Pozharsky monument and the Minin and Pozharsky obelisk. Kozma Minin, butcher to some, hero to others, started a voluntary campaign which in 1612 drew men from all along the Upper Volga into a force to save Moscow from imminent Polish attack. This was successfully done under the command of Prince Dmitri Pozharsky, Minin's general.

Nizhny could also claim that for three troubled centuries before Ivan the Terrible's conquest it acted as Moscow's shield against the Mongol Tartars to the east. A third, more recent distinction was to have raised an army in 1812 against Napoleon, once again with the combined forces of the men of the Upper Volga. Finally, Nizhny's patriotic citizens point out that it lies exactly in the centre of Russia.

The provincial, functional kremlin was first built in a typical mixture of wood and red and white brick in the early sixteenth century as a sober watchpost. Over it presides the sign of an elk, once said to have tapped with its antlers on a door to warn Nizhny's defenders of danger approaching. The kremlin descends the steep hill almost to the river; Catherine the Great greatly disliked its split-level, skew-whiff inelegance. The perimeter includes the much-restored church of the Archangel Michael, a token of Nizhny's brief medieval existence as an independent principality; a large, green, semi-wild open space; and an Eternal Flame commemorating thousands of dead in the last war. Legend has long rumoured an unlikely secret tunnel from the church to the Volga. But today only stone steps wend their way visibly towards the river, and they must have altered since a pre-revolutionary traveller called them grand. An exceptionally well-maintained modern road serving the regional administration and the House of Soviets makes them look doubly overgrown and neglected. The House of Soviets, its car park full of official Volga cars, is a rare Constructivist edifice, not at all what you would expect within a kremlin, and mainly interesting today as a rational building starkly contrasting with Stalin's aggrandizing fantasies to come.

Locals – Nizhegorodtsy, to use the metrically enchanting Russian term – use the kremlin as a short cut or a pleasant place to stroll. There is a splendid river view from its plateau. Local youths meet friends, smoke, and exploit the contained wilderness. But it is a wilderness, fraught with the dangers of an urban park. At five in the afternoon, when all official places of work close and people hurry home, it seemed to me abandoned and made me quicken my step and glance around warily. I saw boys climbing up the kremlin wall with a ladder and guessed how the recent fire in the White Tower had started.

Outside the kremlin walls, through the gated redbrick Dmitrovskaya Tower, begins Nizhny's best-known street of the upper town, the Bolshaya Pokrovka. On the sunny day we explored it from the *Chernyshevsky* the umbrella-ed tables outside the street cafés, the exhibitions of art for sale, even the bookstalls and tables of groceries set up by private traders for a small licence fee in these early days of post-Soviet capitalism, all looked very inviting, though we paid dearly for foreign beer and no coffee. Still, Nizhny was alive along the Pokrovka, and almost all its buildings attractive. This was the street housing the theatre, many shops, a market and a rather grand, perfectly restored bank in the Eclectic style of the early

1900s. It recalled for me pedestrian precincts in Vienna and Pula and gave off richly the feeling of central Europe.

The Bolshaya Pokrovka represents only a stage in Nizhny's long and complex life. Generally, and especially close to the water, and on the Strelka side, and around the Fair, Nizhny is a profoundly Russian town. I feel this because, for instance, just a small distance from the Pokrovka, across one of the steep, cobbled ravines that divide the town vertically, Maxim Gorky lived as a child with his grandparents. The tortured life he described in *Childhood* happened here. The great wooden cross which symbolized an uncle's guilt for his wife's death and which crushed the boy's adult friend Tsiganok still lies in the yard. The museum staff recite long passages from *Childhood* as they take visitors from one dark, low-ceilinged room in the wooden house to the next. Gorky's grandfather was a dyer, who had once worked on the Volga as a barge-hauler. His grandmother was a saintly figure, ignorant but devoted to the Scriptures. Family tensions and temperaments led to terrible violence. Grandfather compulsively hid all that was his in a trunk. You can still see this chest, which stopped his personality disintegrating with every domestic crisis. The young Gorky, born Alexei Peshkov, was beaten mercilessly. He saw his unhappy, early-widowed mother brutally treated by her second husband and witnessed the instant she went pale after beating her son with a hairbrush. She died the next moment, sitting in her best dress. He saw his grandmother forced out to beg and was himself thrown out at the age of eight to earn his living.

Gorky tasted Nizhny low life. At school he was laughed at for his poor clothes. Another writer, Anatoly Mariengof, born almost forty years later in 1897, was privileged to take a gentler view of the town from his family's house on the Bolshaya Pokrovka. His father was an educated man who represented Singer sewing machines in Russia, and saw to it that Tolya attended a grammar school. His mother died early. The son saw things thus fifty years later:

> My town is dear to me, sweet and lovable the way I left it almost half a century ago: the river banks with their tall grass, the wooden bridge across the Volga, the steep cobbled streets where streams of foamy water ran down either side in spring and autumn

[. . . .] Nizhny! The long mouse-coloured fences, the oil lamps, the convoys of sewage barrels and the atmosphere of wild abandon and the greed for money at the All-Russian Fair. The monasteries, the wealthy merchants' mansions, the prison in the middle of town, and across the [Oka] river the Sormovo factories, which even then were already Red. The ringing churches, the little chapels with their miracle-working icons dressed in ruby necklaces and the flickering flames of one-kopeck candles beneath them, lighting up the faces of the miracle-workers painted on cypress. And one house away drunken vodka merchants behind green curtains [. . . .] I should like my native town, my Nizhny, to remain like this in my memory for a long time.

Mariengof mentioned the shipyards of Sormovo on the Strelka, which reached their height in his day and helped bring Nizhny its prosperity – also its first taste of proletarian revolution. These were the same shipyards where Gorky as a young boy hung about the stevedores and at twelve got a job washing up on a steamer. The shipping industry had its beginnings in the fourteenth century in response to trade opportunities in the Near East, and owed much to an Englishman, Antony Jenkinson, who in 1558 won permission from the tsar to build galleons. Jenkinson, a pioneering Volga trader, Muscovy company agent and Queen Elizabeth's ambassador to Russia, later perished in a shipwreck in the Caspian. There is a whole, little-publicized museum here in Nizhny dedicated to the history of Volga shipping.

Nizhny Novgorod is in other moods again along its Volga embankments. The Lower Embankment along Mayakovsky Street used to be known by its Stroganov church, a rare example of Russian Baroque, decorated everywhere externally with a kind of stone lace. At the height of Nizhny's pre-Revolutionary identity as a mercantile centre this street contained nine out of the city's ten banks in neo-classical and *style moderne* buildings. You can still see the Volga Steamship Company with its ornate façade of decorative arches at number 23. On either side of this street with its roots in the seventeenth and eighteenth centuries nothing rises higher than three storeys. Today it is broken down and atmospheric, with a glittering, meaninglessly named Liberty Liberty shop alongside a decrepit *pelmeni* bar. I peered in but this sad saloon, allegedly selling Siberian pasta, in reality served only beer. Nearby seamstresses worked heads down in a below-pavement factory, like a scene out of pre-war industry. The Volga restaurant advertised itself with a façade carved out of wood like a steamer. The word 'Volga' was written so that the letter 'l' resembled a rolling wave. The Mayakovsky cinema, in another *moderne* building whose origins seemed to coincide with pioneer moviegoing, was showing *The Woman with the Million Dollar Legs*; given the economic and ideological crisis in its own industry, Russia has gone over almost entirely to dubbed American films. Mayakovsky Street continued into the smaller Kozhevennaya, 'Leather Street', where in 1901 Gorky organized a club for the poor. Here is where, if I were a speculator, I should buy the whole terrace and convert it into residential waterside mews. Men with a van and an eye for today's chances were unloading Western cigarettes and alcohol into a row of warehouses.

The lower town is exhilarating, but in my few days in Nizhny I would climb up to the Otkos whenever I wanted peace, and to indulge my mixed feelings about Russia. Stretching from the kremlin almost to the Pechersky monastery five kilometres downstream, this was the place to stroll, to gaze at the river, even to drink coffee and something at least labelled wine in that free-thinking summer of 1993. It was the chicest part of town, lined by the stately old university buildings and grand mansions of the age of Alexander I.

A staircase links this Upper Embankment to the lower one, these days a broad traffic freeway in front of Mayakovsky Street. The staircase is so fantastic that it must be seen from the water. It lies engraved in yellow and white stone on the green hillside, and from the Volga it appears like a giant keyhole clumsily outlined in white icing. At the top stands an heroic statue of the pioneer aviator Chkalov, the man who also gave his name to that headquarters of shipping repairs, Chkalovsk. At the bottom, across the highway, the great Nizhny staircase leads to the small river boat *Hero*, which battled the White Guard fleet in the Civil War and Nazi Germany at Stalingrad. It is the kind of flight you would expect to see in a staging of *Cinderella*, paving the heroine's way majestically down to the ballroom. Except that here the ballroom is the Volga itself. This view of Nizhny's greatness was thrown up by Stalin's age: a naturally dramatic site where happy Russians could process down to their sacred river and celebrate life on its banks. Until a recent fire there were indeed free and very popular open-air concerts in a wooden shell close to the *Hero*, on the riverbank.

Look at the excesses of Stalin's architecture and you will see that it has something fundamental in common with a Hollywood set. In the West totalitarian politics came of age in an entertainment world of Brylcreem and tapdance shoes and million dollar legs. The age of mass murder was also the age of musical comedy. As it happened, Stalin's favourite film was a musical comedy set on the river, *Volga Volga*. It appeared in 1938, when the Purges reached their height.

The two hundred and fifty-seven Chkalov steps, which I climbed myself to count, were built with imprisoned German labour during the war, and were crumbling and cracking by 1993. A large notice at the top warned against too many people occupying the staircase at any one time, though that was too late for me, who had climbed from below. Anyway I was watching the function that this abandoned Communist monument had now, as if it were an item in a fairground. Some young girls stood at the top, throwing out a challenge. The boys had to run down the steep arms of the staircase, collect an empty Spanish champagne bottle at the bottom and return with it, while the girls cheered the winner and jeered the losers.

The area around the Chkalov monument at the top of the steps has become a meeting place for friends and lovers. The stupendous view over the broad Volga, reed-fringed on its far bank and with barges and passenger ships and local motor launches to-ing and fro-ing, keeps this spot from post-Communist decadence. Voices carry unnervingly on the wind. The water itself is noticeably shallow. You can see those bushy outcrops and sandbanks which before the mid-century made navigation so difficult; the tall cranes of the Strelka; and in the downstream distance the industrial town of Bor with its big pink and pale green factories like a toytown.

Out of sight beyond the Strelka lies the giant Gorky automobile factory.

This city speaks to me so much that I wonder what made it. Communism, which closed it to the outside world after a hundred and ten years of the international Fair, certainly did not. Communism only gave it dubious fame as the place where the leading human rights campaigner of the Cold War, nuclear physicist Andrei Sakharov, was brutally exiled from Moscow in 1980 for six years. I blush to remember the desolate backwater the name Gorky conjured up in those dark days when pictures of an ill Sakharov slumped on a park bench appeared on the front of *Bildzeitung*, accompanying news that he was on a hunger strike. I had no idea this cosmopolitan city existed, the creation of nineteenth-century free trade, for which it was made to pay so dearly under Communism.

It's back now as what one Russian described to me as the cradle of the new capitalism. The Fair has been reinstated after a gap of sixty-two years. The only question on everyone's lips is: can Russia, can Nizhny live with the truth of social division which the return to capitalism must bring? The city may rediscover its old complex self, or there may be conflict in the streets.

In his first novel, *Foma Gordyeyev*, Gorky told the story of a merchant's son who threw himself into debauchery and became a wandering pseudo-mystic because he could not accept the greedy, limited, harsh merchant's life. Later he created the thrilling *Artymonov Business*, which chronicled the downfall of a trading family. Orphaned and subjected to a rough working life far too young, Gorky was fascinated by the savage strength of merchant life and by its outcasts and rebels. Assuming a pen-name which means 'bitter', he was able to write about those suffering outsiders with a flair he could never bring to the Communist dream. He knew Nizhny life as conflict. The thriving international business city teemed with Russian disciples of Samuel Smiles while at the same time, in the forests along the left bank of the Volga, lived and prayed ferocious schismatics from the Orthodox Church. Nizhny housed side by side frantic men of action and those who, as one Russian author put it more broadly, 'could not come to terms with the prevailing conditions of society'. The conflict can be seen revived today in scores of ugly Portakabin kiosks about the city selling imported food and wine and spirits and other goods at prices shocking to the middle-aged and unpayable by the old. Everywhere are people who cannot afford to live and brawling drunks who appear not to want to. The one consolation is the city's active young leader, Boris Nemtsov, a physicist converted to the human rights cause by Sakharov and a conscientious man in whom people appear to believe.

In the Stroganov church and in the Church at large, so self-important in the new Russia that I must single it out for questioning, it is hard to say which culture predominates. Against the background of an iconostasis drenching the wall behind the altar with dripping silver and gold, clean-faced young men, as they do in Plyos, sing for money to unwitting tourists bussed there. What can a Westerner make of this too sudden brave new world which puts the flat where Sakharov was force-fed on the tourist itinerary and names the summer concert season after him? Life everywhere here seems desperately short of authenticity.

This social conflict, though, is Nizhny, along with the beauty of nature and the charm of individual Nizhegorodtsy. No wonder it is a strong city, a city which even in Soviet times the central authorities feared enough virtually to starve it into submission by diverting much of its food to Moscow.

In Nizhny's central Minin Square I met the man who was to be my companion for the next three weeks. I didn't need organization nor even a translator, but I wanted a human being to fall back on and Alyosha was certainly that. He held out his hand and we plunged into a conversation that was to last twenty days.

'I need to walk. I have been sitting for two days in a train and now on the boat.'

'Fine by me. I love walking.'

We walked the length of the Pokrovka and went left at the statue of Chernyshevsky. Yesterday's man was rapidly becoming the *éminence grise* of my journey. The whole urban ramble took an hour and a half. We talked so much we didn't notice. It was an oddly honest conversation from the start.

'I thought you wouldn't find the square.'

'Well, I did.'

'I would like to buy you an ice cream.'

'That would be nice.'

We licked these tasteless pink wafers, which at least were large. I'm always hungry in Russia.

'This ice cream has no taste.'

'You are wrong. The ice cream is very, very subtle. It is very subtle, like Russia.'

I felt a thick coat of fat on my tongue and countered that frying ice cream was a Russian custom new to me. By now we were laughing so much an enterprising photographic agency snapped us: a couple enjoying being together, having a friendly dispute. I asked for a bodyguard and got a man I could talk to and an extraordinary writer. A few hours later, knowing our Russianness and Englishness mattered less than the thoughts and experiences we were about to share, we boarded our new boat, the *Komarno*.

In the hour of our departure, around 2pm on Saturday, 14 August, a journalist from the Nizhny sailors' newspaper, *Bolshaya (Great) Volga*, knocked at Alyosha's cabin. From a basket, like some goddess of safe journeys (she had divine looks too), she produced a home-made bilberry tart and a bottle of Russian Golden, a new apple 'champagne' on the post-Communist market.

'This is Lena. She got the tickets for us.'

Books and pamphlets emerged and the inevitable lapel badges, which Russians covet. I hate badges but it seemed only right to pin this one saying *Rechflot* to my T-shirt and beam gratitude at Lena.

Alyosha didn't drink alcohol, not a drop ever, but we girls quickly found the tooth glasses, and all of us tucked into the glistening, moist, nearly black pie on a pink plate. Lena's help was curious. One day Alyosha, who works for the literary journal

Volga, rang her up at the *Bolshaya Volga* (the two being about as closely related as the *Times Literary Supplement* and *Lloyd's List*) and asked for assistance. No other way could a citizen of Saratov, twenty-four hours away by train, have bought boat tickets departing from Nizhny. Service bureaux do not exist in this deliberately inconvenient country. What replaces them is the guild mentality. There was that kind of bond between Mikhail on the *Chernyshevsky* and his fellow First Mates all down the river. People help those in the same line of work, for somehow something must get bought, arranged, achieved, acquired or the place would stand still. (Curiously, since the time of Catherine the Great official Russia has denounced the Masonic network. I see why now: it's its nearest rival.) Still, it's an odd system, probably less a hangover from Communism than a perennial feature of Russian life. Moreover, I do believe Lena, who had a secret electronics job before the Soviet collapse and told us how she was briefed to lie about her employment, expected me to write the correct thing, whatever that was, in exchange for her services.

'Write something about the Volga and we'll photograph it for our newspaper!' she would ask on my return.

When I did, under pressure, express some thoughts about the sluggishness of the river Volga and the Russian people her brow clouded like Jove's. Still, our conflict was in the future, and meanwhile she gave me a map, which I hadn't been able to buy in London or Moscow. I saw that the Volga could be the outline of North and East Africa, with Samara in the Horn, except that in the far south, from Volgograd to Astrakhan, the toe kicked back instead of forward. The profile was exciting.

Lena, another woman in a stiff white cotton dress, waved from the quay. 'This is a happy woman!' commented Alyosha admiringly. I decided I had no clues to her nature, though I could see her success. We adjourned to enjoy our departure.

On deck not even intoxication diminished the quality of the view out of Nizhny. There is one tall *style moderne* building on the waterfront, with sharply pointed gables, which instantly conveys one of Nizhny's identities as a north European city. Built by the Rukavishnikov merchant family in 1911 as part of a large complex which also included a bank, it still functions as a garment factory and is at its best viewed from a short distance across the water. Later the son of Rukavishnikov rejected everything to do with 'capitalist' achievements, writing a book called *I Curse My Line of Descent*.

We passed the Strelka and the cranes, and the Alexander Nevsky Cathedral. I thought of Gorky as the distance grew from the town, another writer who experienced the Russian pursuit of wealth as devilishly grim. I know Russia today is crowded with its new rich, but equally it is busy with a national antipathy to money-making. The conflicts embedded in Nizhny history still stir fierce emotions. Nizhny low life drove Gorky out to the Volga both literally as a boy and years later in his writing. He fled from a life 'unfolding itself before me as an endless chain of hostility and cruelty, as an incessant, obscene struggle to possess what was worthless' and found work on that steamship which fortuitously possessed a magical name: *The Good One*. The Volga with its beauty and calm gave Gorky a unique experience of purity.

Many Russians still seek that 'purity'. Perhaps they would have experienced it had the *Komarno* on its departure played 'The Slav Woman's Farewell'. Instead came a blast of pop music, a sign of the times, but a jarring discord in a ceremonious country with its own musical and celebratory traditions. Older people are bound to have aesthetic objections to the new Westernized Russia. As an old visitor I almost count myself among them. Yet if that is the price of freedom, what can one say?

Only this, I think. When I come to Russia, I know I believe in something called progress for this country, and also that it does not equal imitation of the West. Russia has never been able to find the right progressive path, and in that, because so much imitation and loss of face is involved, have lain centuries of shame and sadness. The West should never feel flattered. It is the worst things that end up being transferred.

7

Of Paddle-steamers
and Liners
and the Russian People

THE *Komarno* was a passenger cruise ship, whereas the *Chernyshevsky* had been a holiday liner. The reception area was darker and no desk existed – only the purser's office in one corner. There was information about the crew, and a very detailed timetable on a side wall, but no photocopies or translations. A high-relief map sketched our course down the Volga, with distances in kilometres from Moscow. Some of those distances and the timetable I copied into my notebook, a sight which caused every passing Russian to stop and check whether he or she had missed something. Outside the system, I was behaving oddly.

Beside the timetable was a clogged trough for washing fruit. A big notice said: 'No Washing-up'. I wondered if the ship was mainly self-catering. In early steamer days – when incidentally there were no cabins, only single-sex dormitories – all passengers had to bring their own food, with only that samovar of hot water for drinks supplied. On the *Komarno* it turned out that there was a kiosk for those who wanted to bypass the restaurant. It sold sausage (which no self-respecting Russian eats these days for fear of what it comprises), hard-boiled eggs, bread, biscuits, beer, and some sweet alcohol and chocolates. The lady who served there was big and jolly and wore a white overall, the way Westerners once imagined all Russian women were.

I wandered about, looking at everything. As I say, Russians don't

51

like this sort of behaviour – they've long since learnt not to be curious – and though some passengers were instantly friendly, many were cautious. One dowager critic of my oddness turned away when I greeted her without an introduction. The crew looked shabbier and physically less healthy than on the *Chernyshevsky*. And we only had three and a half decks, including the third-class accommodation in the hold.

Still, my happiness was great. The *Komarno* meant I would get to Astrakhan in ten days' time. Meanwhile the top deck at least was light and my cabin promised to function. The washbasin provided hot and cold water. There was a radio again, a bed with clean linen stored overhead, a table with a lamp and a pretty yellow-checked curtained window with a wooden shutter. On the bed an ingenious crimson velvet armrest opened out to make a pillow-cum-headrest at night and buffer collisions with the windowsill. A blue light, the colour of a police alarm and meant as a beacon in the dark, could be illuminated over the washbasin.

Alyosha and I sorted out our money matters after Lena went. I paid him for his company and reimbursed him for my tickets. He had paid a little less than 55,000 roubles (55 US dollars) each for us, the total cost of the round trip Moscow–Astrakhan–Moscow. Third-class passage would have cost only 10,000 roubles, that is, 10 US dollars, or ten litre bottles of genuine Coca-Cola. I wasn't complaining about the price, nor normally would Russians. But inflation had made Volga cruises expensive this year.

The *Komarno* had only communal showers and lavatories. That was a shock after the *Chernyshevsky*. I bypassed the shower problem (and the need to search for the lady with the key) with basin and flannel, which evoked itchy memories of childhood, though at least the weather wasn't cold. But there was no way of avoiding the lavatory. From revulsion I felt my fingernails retracting into my fingers, and my fingers into my hands. In first-class the lavatories were cleaned more often than lower down the ship. There is always a sense of hierarchy in Russia, the net result of which is that if you have money or are foreign you are entitled to more hygiene. But still the cleaning was ineffective. Perhaps the chemicals cost too much. In consolation I presumed the past was worse. When Chekhov traversed the Upper Volga he was so intrigued by the innovatory white throne on board that he wrote home about it.

I wandered off again. The snacks kiosk had some nice postcards of other aspects of life with *Rechflot*, but it didn't sell lavatory paper. That was another problem. Really I should have remembered that nothing is supplied in non-Westerners' Russia. Alyosha had been asleep, and his lips were still blue from the bilberry pie as he handed over half his private supply. 'You asked for a passenger ship, not a tourist one. Of course they're not so luxurious,' he observed soberly.

Barely an hour out of Nizhny we suddenly stopped at an anchorage apparently in mid-countryside, a place of flat green fields and sandy banks, with motor boats zipping about the water, despite the cost of petrol. People streamed from the *Komarno*, as always with shopping bags. Others slipped into swimming costumes on the shore and bathed.

Next minute I was swimming in the Volga too, never too far from the towering ship's stern, but as hard as I could go, without dipping my head under. It looked murky but I had to test it. Actually it seemed like the eighth wonder of the world. The water was warm, at least 21°C, and perhaps it was only muddy from sand. Russians, careless about themselves, swim in it anyway. Floating on my back, I studied the group of people who had come on foot, on bicycles and in motorcycle sidecars to meet the boat. A man in a blue shirt and a white cap, and a slender, wiry, middle-aged woman in a cobalt dress with black socks and shoes, were selling bilberries on the quay. Young girls were touting huge plastic bowls of ripe cherries, a speciality of the Nizhny area according to the 1856 English traveller William Spottiswoode.

'Is it safe to swim here?' I called to a man who had blood pouring down his white shin. Of course, he said. I kept one eye on the stony shore, no doubt the reason for the cut leg. Suddenly the large mound of hay under which I had left my shoes and my watch and cabin key began to move. Young men had arrived to hitch the hay trailer to a tractor. And they say nothing ever gets done in this country.

'Hold on!' I rushed out of the water, scrambling over the painful stones. 'Don't move it yet! There's my watch.'

'Where do you come from?' said one, seizing suspiciously on my accent, sometimes identified as 'Baltic'.

'London,' I said.

They tried not to blink. They probably couldn't remember the last time they had seen a person from England, if ever. But they weren't fazed. They had nature on their side. 'The Volga is the best place in the world to bathe. Go on, say it! You can't disagree.'

'Oh, yes! The best place I've ever been. I like it here.' But what I wanted to know was: where is here?

'The Anchorage Memorial of the *Paris Commune*.'

'What?'

'It's where the crew come from.'

Ah, so we had stopped for them to collect cherries from their sisters. How charming.

Actually when you finally work out Soviet nomenclature it is as satisfying an exercise as a crossword. Everything fits. You just have to understand the clues towards the revelation of an impressively self-contained interlocking system. Self-contained was how Soviet culture was meant to be, uncontaminated by other cultures, and wholly new and special. And by renaming places after heroes and historical events, the same principle of repetition as naming ships after key cultural figures, some of the message would get through to everyone. Soviet culture, a nineteenth-century philosophical answer to nineteenth-century problems, was like nineteenth-century rote schoolteaching.

The *Paris Commune* was a cutter based here, like the *Komarno*, for repairs. It became famous when it managed to deliver some supplies to Stalingrad, in the early stages of Russia's greatest Second World War battle against the Germans. Its name came from that event of 1871 in Paris which was interpreted by the Communists as a foretaste of the Socialist Order which would sweep the world. Lenin in particular devoted hours to analysing why the cause of the Paris Commune was lost. The positive hero of possibly the most famous book in Soviet socialist realist literature, Nikolai Ostrovsky's *How the Steel Was Tempered*, retired from the battlefield to write an essay on the same subject. So that's where we were now, moored at the juncture of half a dozen essential Soviet causes. In a single name was contained all the ideological and national pride required to keep Russia Soviet for seventy-four years. Reflecting on all this I had to run back to the boat still in my costume, not to miss the departure. The dowager gave me a scathing look.

With the Anchorage we had entered a celebrated stretch of the Volga, extending from the mouth of the Oka. The banks are sandy, the beaches are neat with pretty wooden windbreaks, and, from this point properly called the Central Volga, the river grows ever wider. It was now perhaps 15km (10 miles) across, allowing the liners to plough their furrows through a vast open space.

Alyosha woke up and came to find me at the rail. Revitalized by my Volga baptism, I wanted to talk river words, having toured the museum of the history of shipping in Nizhny the day before. He, my guardian and companion, was still groggy, so I talked and he watched. Most of the river words seemed to be German, like *farvater*, *spil* (capstan) and *vint* (windlass), or English like *kabestan* (capstan again) and *flag*. German experts who helped modernize Russia from the seventeenth century introduced many technical words into the modern language. The British with Antony Jenkinson and the Russia Company on the Volga had made their contribution even earlier.

Russian sailors go on *vakht*, from the German for watch-duty; *sturmany*, like the mother of Mikhail on the *Chernyshevsky*, take the helm. I began, moving into the prow of the ship, to sing that wave-pounding chorus from *The Flying Dutchman*: 'Steuermann, lass die Wacht!' that is, 'sturman, ostav' tvoi vakht!'

'You sing,' observed Alyosha. 'That's good. I too love music.'

I liked his dry style. It was the opposite of mine.

After a pre-history of hollowed out tree-trunks, the first real Volga ships by barrel construction were galleons, such as Jenkinson and other Western seamen introduced in the sixteenth century. In 1733 Adam Olearius, the noted German traveller and scholar, sailed in on the first warship, Dutch-built, that the Volga had ever seen. The river, meanwhile, developed its own picturesque sailing barges. The next major step forward was the steamship, but the Volga steamship industry took half a century longer than that of Western Europe to become efficient. Some twenty-five years after the first, again Dutch, steamship crossed the Atlantic Oliphant wrote in 1853: 'It is difficult to conceive that so magnificent a river as the Volga shuld be so desecrated, or so noble a power as steam so abused, as by the astounding contrivance which passed in the day before we arrived at Saratov.' What Oliphant saw was a horse-powered contraption, first introduced on the Volga in 1813 to replace the combination of sail-power, oarsmanship and human-hauling which had maintained Russian shipping for the previous two and half centuries. The peculiar problems of the Volga – the calmness, the shallowness and the struggle against the current while moving upstream – all contributed to nautical eccentricity.

The broad, flat-bottomed, horse-powered boat, of barrel con-struction, with a maximum load of 50 tonnes, required a crew of up to seventy and between eighty and two hundred horses to ensure its progress at 10–15km (16–25 miles) per day. Slow as it was, this equipotent machine was considered the best means of transporting salt and grain by river for the next fifty years. In 1816 there were thirty-six such ships; by 1846 their number had risen to two hundred. Blame for this classic Russian marriage to awkwardness could be directed at a foreigner called de Barda, whom in 1819 the Russian government invited to develop his invention. But mostly the Russians have preferred to claim the achievement for themselves, citing a brilliant young serf from the Volga village of Kadnitsa named Mikhail Sutyrin. Sutyrin adapted de Barda's idea for use on existing ships and made its implementation ten times cheaper. De Barda had the horses activate a pulley by walking a circle, but Sutyrin's device allowed them to do the same work standing still, the moving platform on which they stood being connected to a vertical shaft. Thus the beasts gave as much energy while using less, and were able to feed simultaneously. Still, you may ask, what did the pulley on the horse-powered boat pull? Answer: a cable, attached to an anchor planted ahead and dug into the river bed. The boat was hauled level by horse-power and the whole process began again.

The system seemed just as Byzantine when horses were not involved, and all because the Volga was shallow and wide and because available steampower was unable to defeat its currents when hauling a load upstream. A vessel known as a *kabestan* progressed towards a forward-cast anchor by means of a steam-powered capstan (hence the Russian name) winding in the cable. A small steamboat carried the anchor forward. And still every kind of vessel became lodged on the sandbanks, together with any extra barges it might have in tow.

The laborious absurdity of all this belongs to the Volga. So too does another cruel system based on animal energy, this time human, which took until the end of the nineteenth century to die out completely. It is one of those ironies of economic history that when the first self-powered boats appeared the human beings they threatened to displace, the barge-haulers or *burlaki*, were incensed. It is also ironic that they dragged the most beautiful boats the Volga has ever seen, to wit tall wood-carved sailing barges with white sails and the owner's name engraved on the stern. From the mast flew a pennant depicting St George. These were the Volga *rasshivy*, named after the ancient business of sewing together the boards to build a boat. Some of them looked like a child's drawings of a floating medieval castle or tent. A kind of upraised curtained wooden room served as the captain's bridge and quarters. Gautier compared the craft he saw in 1861 to 'great wooden trains on the Rhine which carried villages of shacks and provisions for the table of Gargantua'. In 1926 Cecil B. de Mille made a silent film about the *burlaki*, a fine testament to their misery and their beautiful ships, called *The Volga Boatman*.

Modernization did eventually come to the Volga, despite fears, expressed to Gautier, that Holy Russia would freeze to death if all its wood was burnt to power ships. That same year as Oliphant made his dismaying journey south the steamship company Caucasus and Mercury came into being. Both it and its rival firm Along the Volga were encouraged by the successful performance on their river of steamships built in Rotterdam. Barges were constructed on the new model to carry freight, and then passenger paddle-steamers on the American pattern made their debut, at first with a rear wheel, then with a side wheel. First-class passengers had cabins, second-class covered accommodation, while third-class and steerage lived on deck. A company called Samolet, literally 'self-flying', owned these steamers, which is confusing, because in the twentieth century the name became the generic Russian word for 'aeroplane'.

A trip on a steamer was erotic, suggests Russian literature from Chekhov to Bunin and Gorky. It was a mirror to that human self-deception called romance – tinselly and tawdry and sad and also enchanting. The boxy two-tiered wooden Volga steamer, decorated with awnings and punctuated with lifebelts and a pair of cheery heroic funnels, looked both functional and seductive, with its implicit suggestion of sweet sorrowful partings and new adventures and beginnings. It played a vital role in Ostrovsky's play *Woman Without a Dowry*, much as the train did in Chekhov and Tolstoy.

While love went on, though mostly cruelly, so did business. Very quickly Volga shipping was revolutionized by oil: by the need to transport oil efficiently from the Caspian and by the oil-fired engine, invented under the pressure of economic competition. From the shipyard at Sormovo the Volga-based firm of the Swedish Nobel brothers, who made their greater fortune in Caspian oil, built the first oil tanker, the *Zoroaster*, and in 1903 the first diesel oil tanker in the world, the *Vandal*. The Rothschilds competed as shippers. Meanwhile all the steamship companies with names like Along the Volga, the Eastern Steamship Company and the Caucasus and Mercury went over to oil. They built oil-fired freighters and also liners (the English word was used in Russian), thus extending the benefits of improved business to leisure. Some of the first two-deck motor ships to cruise the Volga, turned out by Sormovo in 1914, were said to be still in use a decade ago. That year also saw the opening of the vital passenger-goods cruise line from Nizhny Novgorod to Astrakhan, which we were now riding.

Volga shipping was thus essentially modern by the time of the 1917 Revolution. Afterwards the only immediate necessity was to change the names of boats with dynastic Romanov names into those politically more appropriate. Thus *Princess Tatyana Nikolaevna* became *Spartak* and *Princess Olga Nikolaevna* was renamed *Volodarsky*. In reality, of course, the princesses were more than renamed by the Bolsheviks: together with their mother and father, sisters and royal household staff, they were murdered. Meanwhile the ships sailed on and the mighty capitalist heritage which had at last modernized the Volga was repudiated and discarded.

There have been developments since. Soviet Sormovo pioneered the building of world-class ships which could not only sail the Great

Volga, but glide along the canals and tackle the seas beyond. Shunters were also developed to push, not tug, barges, which made for much more streamlined movement. Meanwhile the liners have grown bigger and more luxurious, though many of them appear to have been built by the Soviet Union's old Comecon partners, East Germany and Czechoslovakia. The *Komarno* is named after the Czech yard where it entered service in 1959.

I emerged from my shipping survey not doubting that the Volga possessed a grand merchant fleet as little as five years ago; and personally feeling the pity that nearly half of it lay idle. Incidentally the curator of the shipping museum, an old merchant sailor, asked me to guess his age.

'Seventy?' I suggested gallantly.

'Eighty-four!' he announced, thrusting a copy of his *History of Volga Shipping* inside my jacket. It contained a picture of him looking younger and wearing several rows of medals; also reams of information. 'Don't show my colleague the book. I'm afraid she'll get cross.'

I had hardly wiped the smile of complicity off my face when she appeared. 'Sergei Grigorievich, you won't forget to give the lady from London a copy of your book?'

'Ah, Sergei Grigorievich,' I whispered as I left. 'It's true, then, that all Russian men are afraid of Russian women.'

He nodded and looked rather shy for a man of eighty-four. Such is the erotic profile of the nation.

G etting ready for dinner, I found that green Volga weed from the Anchorage Memorial to the *Paris Commune* had stuck to my ribs and dried there, so that I resembled the side of a lock. The radio in the cabin could be lowered but never entirely switched off, because it was used for announcements. I was keen to tune into the new Russia, so I left it audible most of the time. Now it was playing 'O sole mio!' whereas I would have welcomed more Wagner. I sprayed on the perfume which I carried with me like an eighteenth-century lady with her smelling salts, and opened the cabin door.

'Beautiful!' Alyosha cried, spruce and glowing in a clean shirt. 'I have never smelt such perfume in my life.'

We wolfed our first two courses. There was tomato and cucumber salad and non-Volga fish and mashed potato and tea. It wasn't enough. We shared our table with a family of three, mother, father and teenage son, who refused to practise the art of conversation. We too, dedicated to our hunger, had not been devoting much time to talking, but at last we looked up.

'I'd like to be an Englishwoman exploring the Volga,' Alyosha said.

I said it was liberating to travel anywhere, but Russia was peculiar. It seemed so precariously perched on the edge of the West that I always revised my idea of life when I came here. As for the Volga, it would give me my first real taste of Russian provincial life and its history. My previous experience had been mainly of Moscow.

'Tell me more about wanting to be someone else!' I said when it was my turn to ask a question. He had already told me he had written a novel about assuming other identities, a project which capitalized upon necessity here.

'It's to do with not being able to appear yourself. In the past literally you could never get shoes or a jacket which fitted you or only by chance. My idea is that people's lives don't fit them either. So they have to will themselves to be someone else. One of my characters becomes a chicken, briefly.' He laughed. 'Everything here is both funny and terrible. Well, you know that.'

Yes, I do, but every time I am reminded of it it seems like a fresh revelation of living absurdity. How can life be so funny and so terrible, as we will experience it all down the Volga? Russia is funny like *Waiting for Godot* is funny, Alyosha replied.

After dinner we wandered into the TV room, but the TV was broken. The piano room had dust covers over the upholstery as if the furniture were in transit, and low-watt bulbs which made the skin of the few people ensconced there look yellow. A man in a tracksuit stopped playing when we came in. He played well, but the instrument was out of tune. These boats are laid out just as they were a hundred years ago. I have read other travellers' accounts of the music room and who was playing; Maurice Baring encountered a near-genius. But some things are new. Outside under the stars the crew had improvised a discotheque with a ghetto-blaster and a circuit of flashing blue lights, but only children were dancing to the anonymous beat.

In Alyosha's tidy cabin (mine was already disorderly), behind the drawn wooden blind, we made black coffee with water from the cauldron and his jar of coffee powder. Since perestroika this nation of tea drinkers has acquired an expensive passion for imported instant coffee. The result tasted of liquorice, but as we sat, he at the cabin desk, me on the couch, at right angles to each other, we compensated with talk, lovely incessant curious talk which would last twenty days.

My suspected feminism briefly derailed us. 'I won't let you patronize me, that's all.' Russian men are irritatingly old-fashioned, but I wasn't going to make a lot of it. Alyosha's patriotism was far more interesting. It involved the Russian common people – the *narod* – of whom I had always been wary.

'I am a patriot. I am sorry my country is so backward, so run down.'

'I understand that. I haven't come to criticize. I just want to see.'

'I am a patriot and I am of the people. I love my country and, well, I must love the people since I am one of them.'

'You're an individual. Individuals are what matters.'

'You can't say that in Russian. Individual people. You sound like a literary caricature from the 1920s.'

'Goodness! All right – let me say something else. I don't think you, Alyosha, are ordinary. You have made yourself quite distinctive. You think about what you do. You write about it. You've found a way of surviving in this country and still loving it. That's special.'

'All that may be true. But I still belong to the people.'

By patriotism, Russians mean feeling the whole burden of Russia more keenly than their individual fates as protesters, politicians and KGB spies. Alyosha writes for this whole Russia as Vysotsky, Misha's and now Alyosha's hero too sang for it. It's something we in the West can only look upon from the sidelines, that indelible link between individual, history and nation that we still observe in Russian literature and can no longer find in our own. I remembered the sadness of Misha, still singing Vysotsky songs but wanting desperately to emigrate, and 'the people' whom Boris Godunov betrayed. Art intuits the perfect relationship of individual to 'people', but how hard that relationship is to find in practice! This is the perfection that Russia has sought in its writing and thinking. It has pursued community, not individual truth, which shows how different it is from the West.

'You drink the whisky.' I had brought along a couple of duty-free bottles to soften our long Volga evenings. 'You drink and I will get, how do you say – high? – watching you.'

I drank a couple of mouthfuls out of the toothmug.

'So now I will tell you why I don't drink. I used to drink a great deal. I liked it. I was happy. I was a lively person. People liked to be with me. I told my wife before we married I couldn't change. Often I would drink in bouts. Then once at the end of a fourteen-day bout my heart stopped. My wife found me. Fortunately she had contacts at the emergency services so they came quickly.'

I leaped up at the idea that they might have come slowly, but he just grinned. Russia is such a parody of the West.

'My heart has never been the same. That's why I must sleep every day. And not drink! When I drink again I will drink like you, just a little.' His lips curled, anticipating the satisfaction. 'Incidentally, the way I was, drinking in hard bouts, that was what killed Vysotsky too. He was also a great patriot.'

8

Kazan and
Pugachevshchina

THE DISTANCE from Nizhny to Kazan is roughly 400km (250 miles). Yesterday afternoon and evening we completed the stretch of the forested Transvolga still considered inhabited by Old Believers, along the left bank past the monastery at Makarievo and the confluences with the rivers Kerzhenets and Vetluga. After enforced atheism and Sovietization few remain, but Spottiswoode met many Old Believers on his boat from Nizhny to Kazan one hundred and forty years ago. Adherents to the letter of the Bible, they opposed modernization in national ideas, customs and dress and helped keep Peter the Great's window on the West half-closed. Just beyond Nizhny on the Volga right bank lies Vasilsursk, where Gorky wrote that novel which contained so much about Transvolga dissent, *Foma Gordyeyev*, in the summer of 1899.

From this profoundly Russian heartland the Volga then quickly moves into an area of great ethnic variety. Just south of Vasilsursk, extending east across the Volga, begins the Mari Autonomous Republic of the Mari or Cheremis people, including the river town of Kozmodemyansk. Adjacent lies the Chuvash Republic, with its capital on the river, Cheboksary. The Chuvashes have Mordovians or Mordvinians as their neighbours. Their Autonomous Republic lies west of the Volga as the river strikes out east to Kazan, the Tartar capital. Udmurts, Komis and Komi-Permyaks are officially at home to the northeast. Further southeast lies the former Soviet Autonomous Republic of Bashkiria. There are also in all these regions Kalmyks, who, at home in the semi-desert between Volgo-

63

grad and Astrakhan, have drifted northwards. In sum, a wider mixture of ethnic groups exists hardly anywhere else in Russia.

The Finnic peoples in the eighth century were the earliest arrivals. Next came the Hunnic Bolgars, who established their capital near Kazan. The Bolgars absorbed local Finnic peoples and Turkic nomads and migrant Slavs until in turn they were conquered by the Mongol Tartars under Tamburlaine. Marlowe's play has lines spoken by that leader with his Egyptian love in mind:

> My martial prizes with five hundred men
> Won on the fifty-headed Volga's waves,
> Shall all we offer to Zenocrate.

Thereafter the descendants of Genghis Khan ruled the Central Volga for two centuries.

In Spottiswoode's day the ethnic variety was still apparent. Russians bought postcards of their exotic neighbours in national costume. Today that variety is discontinued in the existence of peoples with paper states and much undermined or scarcely developed independent cultures.

The Volga languages are dying. The Bashkirs speak a Turkic language related to Tartar and Kazakh. Kalmyk is a Mongolian language. The Chuvashes speak a unique language related to the Turkic family, while the Mordovians use a Finno-Ugric language. Mari or Cheremis is also a Finno-Ugric language. Some of these tongues are Uralic and some Altaic, the first group related to Finnish and Hungarian, the second to Japanese and Korean and Paleosiberian. The Tartar language is the most widely used.

We glided under the huge iron-girdered road and rail bridge 40km (25 miles) outside Kazan just as a train crossed it above our heads. 'The second shift is invited to the restaurant,' announced the radio, which was a relief, because we had woken up hungry. Yesterday we had ticked boxes on a tiny detailed sheet, like a football pool coupon, to indicate twenty-four hours in advance what we wanted: rice kasha, black bread, tea. There was no jam, but we could have ordered cheese and/or a hot meat dish. Neither of us wanted meat the three times daily it was offered – personal ecology,

I suppose. So we stayed hungry, resolving to order two bowls apiece of whatever kasha was on offer in future.

During breakfast Svyazhsk passed on the right bank. This was the launch-point for Ivan the Terrible's historic conquest of the Tartars at Kazan, the event which changed the Central Volga and marked the beginning of the Volga's real history as a Russian river. At the confluence of the Volga and its tributary the Svyaga, in the winter of 1550–1 Ivan ordered a wooden fortress to be erected on the territory of the enemy Tartars, whose rule of the Volga was badly obstructing the trade of the expanding Russian state. It was a classic military plan of the same stealthy order as the Greeks' wooden horse at Troy. An entire wooden kremlin, fortress and village, was secretly built in the woods around Uglich. Come spring it was floated down the Volga on barges and erected on a wooded hill. After defeats the previous year the Russians appreciated the strategic value of the only piece of high ground for miles. Transporting the flat-pack kremlin took thirty days. Trees were cut down on the hilltop to clear the Svyazhsk site, but enough were left to form a screen. By the time the Tsar arrived he could be welcomed by a thriving colony of compatriots at one of the largest fortresses in Russia. The following year, 1552, with an army of one hundred and fifty thousand launched by barge from here, the Russians took Kazan.

Today there is only a small island to see, all the lower-lying land having been flooded to make the Great Volga. Yet the picture is not false because by nature every spring Svyazhsk looked like this, ringed with water. The town retains several churches, built after the Russian victory, and a ruined monastery. Its shield shows the kremlin arriving by ship, escorted by five fish. Russian guides compare Svyazhsk with the invented island of Buyan in Pushkin's fairy-tale *Tsar and Sultan*.

Kazan came into view on the opposite left bank. Where was the once vaunted skyline of Byzantine bulb domes and soaring minarets? Often in Russia one feels greedy for the vanished past. Trying to understand the present through the past creates a sense of emptiness.

Alyosha found the captain, who advised us to protect our cabins against shoreside robbers by wedging a pen or spoon or some other metal object between one of the lower wooden blind slats and the bottom of the window frame. That way the blind couldn't be forced down. What I feared most about Russia was being robbed. Because of the absence of banks and the widespread justified distrust of them, everything had to be paid for in hard currency cash; so I had to carry on my person a small fortune in a land where fifty dollars was the captain's monthly salary.

The Kazan river station lay some way out of the city. The site was old, but the plate glass and concrete building new. We had almost reached it, with the *Komarno* flying the *Rechflot*'s red pennant with a yellow star, when two young men raced up in a speedboat, loudhailing encouragements to passengers to have themselves photographed. There were not many takers, because no one had any spare money. Indeed, when we disembarked we found that the city tours previously organized for ship visitors had been discontinued. We caught a local bus into the old centre.

'It's the capital of the Republic of Tartarstan, but it's a Russian city,' announced Alyosha.

I could hear from the name that it was Tartar, and see from today's reality that this city of around one million people was Russian. One task was to make sense of Russian attitudes to Tartars, the people from the outback, the 'Wild East', the nearest equivalent to America's indigenous Indians. The Volga here marked the limits of the old Russian Empire, before the ventures into Central Asia and the opening up of Siberia. The second task was to know who were the Tartars.

Gorky's work is full of disparaging references to Tartars speaking heavily accented Russian and behaving in a sub-Russian way. When he was a child his grandfather lambasted Tartars, Bashkirs and Kalmyks. It was the sort of antagonism which for centuries has roughened the surface of relations between the English and their neighbours. Yet Gorky described himself as Mordvin and his grandmother was Tartar or Chuvash, depending on how her husband wanted to curse her. Gorky had a strong Volga accent (a lot of stressed 'o's from Nizhny, unlike the slurred sound characteristic of Moscow and Petersburg). The mirror told him that with his high cheekbones and dark complexion he also looked exotic. That worried him as a young man but later he preferred his looks to Lenin's, who physically took after his Kalmyk grandmother.

Differences can't be taken too seriously when many people's blood is mixed. Or they ought not to be. In Russia before the Revolution many noble families were of Tartar origin. They moved to Tartary at Ivan the Terrible's encouragement after the conquest of Kazan, and later generations interbred with local inhabitants. The eighteenth-century poet Derzhavin, the nineteenth-century satirist Mikhail Saltykov-Shchedrin and some of the Turgenevs, including the famous novelist, descended from such mixed stock. Nor in those happier days did difference imply superiority. Gorky incorporated in his books racial remarks which were not racist in intention. He could write of the wind breathing over the Volga like an angry Tartar. As a schoolboy he used Tartar and Mordvin as nicknames. He feuded with Tartar lads, and also admired their strength and kindness. He still found 'half-Tartar' Kazan strange when he arrived as a would-be student. 'They spoke a very funny kind of broken Russian. In the evening I could hear the strange voices of the muezzins calling from the high minarets and I thought that their lives were ordered in a way different from mine, that they were strange, quite unlike anything I knew and this brought me little joy.' On the other hand he was drawn to the Tartar quarter 'where good-hearted friendly people lived their own pure and clean lives'.

More sinister attitudes to Tartars, though, did exist. That Boris Godunov was of Tartar origin added fuel to the boyar conspiracy led by Shuisky against him. That point was picked up by Pushkin in his tragedy, and the poet had Boris express the sentiment that mind was more important than breeding in ruling Russia. Tolstoy's story *After the Ball* exposed the careless inhumanity of the Russian ruling class: the soldier being tortured was a Tartar. So there was mental discrimination and fear in the deepest recesses of the Russian mind. To Russia the Tartars were the people who had cut them off from Byzantium, who had imposed servitude. Latterly they were perceived as waiters or cab drivers, and the word 'Tartar' covered all the minority, non-Russian peoples. To this day the Tartars counter that they are not the barbarians. They point out fairly that their medieval empire was civilized, literate and tolerant.

The ancient rivalry between Russians and Tartars for the status of civilization has resulted in a Pyrrhic victory for Tartarstan today. For more than two centuries tsarist and Soviet Russia encouraged the Central Volga to retain its ethnic diversity, to prevent any one culture becoming dominant. They most feared an Islamic Central Volga state, such as Tartar and Bashkir intellectuals pushed for during the Bolshevik Revolution. That projected state, Idel Ural, a name linking the Tartar word for the Volga with the mountains to the east, would have included all the small peoples in between. What were created instead, as a preventative measure disguised as a generous one, were the Autonomous Soviet Socialist Republics of Bashkiria (1919), Tartaria (1920), Mordovia or Mordvinia (1934) and Mari (1936). Similar republic status was granted to the even fewer Urdmuts and Komis.

The populations of these nations without states are thoroughly mixed with Russians and each other. Their lands are rich, with oil wells in Tartarstan and minerals and forest everywhere in the north and in the west, where there is also dairy farming. The Bashkir steppe has oil, natural gas and grain. But they remain dependent for trade on Russia, so even now can only sever links in name. That is their economic and political condition. As for their nationalism, in the late twentieth century, with racist violence increasing in Western cities, and ethnic ghettoes predominating over integration everywhere, and a lacerating, dispiriting war having destroyed the unity and humanity of former Yugoslavia, one comes to expect ethnic friction. But apart from one piece of graffiti, saying 'WE WANT TO BE BULGARIANS!' – meaning, I suppose, Bolgars, and probably written by Chuvashes to annoy their Tartar friends – there was none in Kazan that I could see or feel, nor any obvious conflict in any of the neighbouring autonomies. Later, in London, Dr Shirin Akiner of the School of Oriental and African Studies confirmed the unnewsworthy peacefulness of the Middle Volga.

The bus stop we wanted in the centre of Kazan was Freedom Square, all wide open spaces, vast concrete bureaucratic edifices from the 1950s, formal gardens, toytown black lamp-posts with frosted white globes, and a huge cult statue of Lenin. As usual the civic centre reflected some absurdly misguided dream of what it takes to make people happy. 'All Russian towns are the same,' added Alyosha. 'You shouldn't expect them to be different.' In Freedom Square there was a poster in Tartar commemorating seven hundred and fifty years of Islam, but no sign of Moslem life. This is the biggest change in civic atmosphere since Gorky's day: Soviet rule imposed a massive process of secularization.

On the corner of the square and the main street leading to the Kazan kremlin we bought a newspaper. Another vendor offered us a Tartar holiday sweetmeat called Chak Chak – a mass of tiny balls of fried dough, like chick peas moulded together in a sticky syrup; but apples and sour grapes were easier to carry. In their dusty, makeshift regularity and uniformity these streets had something in common with the West that the Americans settled. But if anything was happening, we couldn't see it.

We turned to the newspaper for details of local crimes. The most common were robberies and muggings and street piracy, with pirates emboldened by bottles of popular liqueur like the fake Amaretto that Russia lapped up in 1993. (The makers of the real Amaretto would threaten before the year's end to take the country to court.) On violence in Kazan, I had read of teenage gang terrorism here in the 1980s and a fierce criminal protection racket. In his book *Red Odyssey* (1991) Marat Akchurin told how he called here on a nightmare car journey from Moscow to Central Asia in 1989.

'From what I've heard,' Alyosha replied, 'things are better in Kazan since the Mafia have taken control. The Mafia need order if they are to work. So they pay the young thugs not to make trouble.'

The new Mafia: all the violent, negative elements which used to be harnessed to the Soviet state are now out in the open and fending for themselves. They have souped-up cars, either Volgas or BMWs or, best of all, Mercedes, and wear leather jackets. There is an offensive sharpness and speed about their manners which is not the natural Russian way to insult one's neighbour. The only difficulty comes in distinguishing *mafiosi* from businessmen. The new *mafiosi* also call themselves *kommerzanty* and go into *offisy* and send *faksy*. Their spooks sit in so-called private and commercial shops lodged with menacing impermanence in dark damp basements, asking high prices for imported chocolate and coffee and orange juice. So where are the honest Russian businessmen today? Gangsterism has mushroomed with this country's manic, instant capitalism. This morning the top item on the radio news, linked to a visit by Prime Minister Viktor Chernomyrdin to Washington, concerned the gun law in America. Indirectly, as was always the Soviet habit with current affairs, Russia was wondering whether it should limit guns or follow the American example and plead the need for self-defence.

We passed a couple of these commercial shops, then a tea and neighbouring coffee house with typical Tartar wooden latticework and arabesques on their façades. On closer inspection, however, both proved to have been Sovietized, for both lacked tea and coffee, and with their Western pop music they could have been anywhere undesirable in the world.

Kazan struck me as a confused place, which, stricken by inflation, had lost its priorities. All the trains to Moscow were oversubscribed by locals seeking a market for their first- and second-hand goods. In the newspaper some people argued that the money Kazan once spent on civic pride – on fountains and flower-beds – should now feed the town's many stray dogs. I doubted that funds would run to Yelena and Mario's petfood.

We set off up Bauman Street, the main business thoroughfare, preternaturally quiet on a Sunday and still named after a Bolshevik activist assassinated before the Revolution. Further in the direction of the kremlin, our ultimate goal, lay the ornate Petropavlovsky church, humming, glittering, all gold and sky blue inside, with all its precious icons under glass. There is a famous Orthodox icon, Our Lady of Kazan, which blessed the Russian victory led by Minin and Pozharsky against the Poles. To this saint with a round face Gorky's grandmother used to pray. The original was taken to St Petersburg by that city's founding Tsar, for his Kazan church, but copies abound.

Mohammedanism might have been destroyed in Kazan, but Russian Orthodoxy was thriving. A crowd of all ages bustled and worshipped in the light, dazzling interior with the saturated gold iconostasis. Elderly women collected their grey books of the dead, resembling the family allowance book my mother took to the post office in the 1950s, and queued with them to have the white-robed priest say prayers for their deceased. Costly restoration work had been carried out with impressive speed, and smelt of money. Money and the Church again: the Petropavlovsky Sobor, or Peter and Paul Cathedral, another example of Russian Baroque, was built by an eighteenth-century merchant to thank Peter the Great for permission to run a state factory in Kazan. Resurrected commercial Russia and the liberated Church run parallel these days like a pair of trotters. I keep returning to my dislike of the Church because it strikes me as an unpromising escape from reality. Russia is so ready to pour all this quick-setting spiritual concrete, such as was shovelled out on the radio earlier today, into the cracks of a life ruined by ideology. But why replace one ideology with another? And anyway the Soviet ruin was far more profound than any return to the faith could alleviate.

Yet the desire to return to religion must be strong, just because it was banned for so long. Under Communism official religious life in Kazan was badly hit. In 1960 only two churches were open for worship. 'Besides, all this religious mania will pass,' says Alyosha. 'People don't really believe. We Russians are truly, without coercion, a nation of atheists and pagans.' I'm not sure. Communism was a religion.

Now we had reached the silent white kremlin. It was built after Ivan's conquest in 1552 on the site of the Tartar Khan's palace, and its Blagoveshchensky church celebrates the Russian victory just as does St Basil's on Red Square in Moscow. The external result today is fabulous blue domes blazing with gold stars under an Asian sun. Inside is a Tartar government archive. There is little the autonomous Tartars can do politically, but at least they are back on the hilltop, and their government headquarters stretch over the backbone of the hill. They have little visible past of their own, because the Russian Empire built Orthodox churches on every Islamic site.

To a rare Russian warrior, Prince Andrei Kurbsky, hero of the 1552 battle but also a thinking man who cared as much to record what he found as to subdue it, we owe our picture of the Tartar Kazan that the Russians absorbed. High above the Kazanka river the Khan's palace exulted on the hilltop and five minarets aspired to infinity. The oldest mosque today is the Mardzhani, built in pink stone in 1766. More were built in the eighteenth and nineteenth centuries, and before the Revolution there were about fifteen of them. Now only the nineteenth-century Azimov mosque keeps the Mardzhani company.

The deserted monumental kremlin that we strolled through was quiet, but we had to imagine Kazan as it once was, a dirty, rough place, used to calamity, with a history in the sixteenth and seventeenth centuries of fires, robbers, murderers, violent packs of dogs and moral debauchery. Here inside the kremlin people lived unbearably close and prayed to God to get from one street corner to the next.

The seventeenth-century redbrick Syuyumbeki Tower contrasts starkly with the blinding white Russian parapets. Syuyumbeki is not quite a minaret, nor is it a mausoleum, though legend links it with the last Khan's wife and also with the faith. Its topmost gold sphere, surmounted by the Islamic crescent, was opened in 1830 to scotch the rumour that it contained precious Islamic documents. Sixty years earlier it was from the Syuyumbeki Tower that Kazan watched Pugachev approach.

Now this was a great graphic event in Kazan's history, the one to make a film about, the one to adorn postcards, the centre of any putative *son et lumière* show up here on the hill, though all those vulgarizations will have to wait until Russia – and Tartarstan – acquire a tourist industry. The tale itself must suffice. It's certainly good enough, and was told by Pushkin with Shakespearean relish.

In 1773 Emilian Pugachev, a Cossack from the Yaik river area between the southeast Volga and the Urals, began a crusade against the miserable condition of a Russia ruled by the landowners. His army attracted criminals and outcasts but his cause also harnessed real discontents, particularly among the Bashkirs, Tartars and Kalmyks from the south Volga, and the Russian peasantry. The size of the army quickly grew to thirty thousand, causing the greatest threat to domestic stability in Catherine the Great's reign. Pugachev claimed, to add to his credibility, that he was Catherine's murdered husband Peter III. There wasn't much logic in that. But the pretence played effectively on Russian superstitiousness (the kind that in Pushkin's play made Boris Godunov wonder if the young Dmitri had been resurrected or not quite finished off). On a summer evening at the end of June 1774 Pugachev crossed the Kama and came to look around Kazan. The Russian army lay routed ten miles behind him. Further back he had left a swathe of brutal hangings and tortured landowners. Before his cause took wing he had once been imprisoned in Kazan and escaped, so perhaps he bore a special grudge. In any case, how Kazan, watching from the Syuyumbeki Tower, must have feared his approach! At the mention of his name, already officially banned, people fled from their towns and country peasants rose up against their masters. Even as far away as Siberia Russia quivered with insurrectionary fervour at Pugachev's name. Kazan would not be spared. Next day Pugachev and his men returned to the city dressed as women and monks and set fire to the kremlin. Kazan was virtually burnt to the ground, losing two thousand houses. Priests were slaughtered in their churches.

Pugachev's way then led for the first time across the Volga to the right bank. The western shore rose up in his support, peasants against masters, Old Believers against new persuasion Orthodoxy. Eventually it seemed that he threatened Nizhny and even Moscow, but he went back south instead, where he was eventually captured, betrayed by fellow Cossacks. He was taken in a wooden cage to Samara and Simbirsk and thence to Moscow.

A partial ban on the Pugachev phenomenon, limiting access to sources, was still in force when Pushkin wrote his chronicle *The History of Pugachev* and a story, *The Captain's Daughter*. Against government pressure he preserved forever the extraordinary charisma of a popular hero. In *The Captain's Daughter* it seems only yesterday that, magnificent on a white charger, the red-bearded Cossack Pretender rode into fearful trapped Russian garrison towns. Pugachev was a loose-living Don Cossack, habitually in trouble, whose escapes from imprisonment were legion. Now he believed his own myth, now he did not. He had a wife, but he took another, younger and nearer-to-hand, whom he promised the title Empress and provided with ladies-in-waiting. The Russians, meanwhile, seized his original wife and family to prove his identity, should he be caught.

If it still existed, I would like to see the ornate pale green wooden galley on which Catherine sailed to Kazan to endorse a triumph which, Pushkin showed, cost many good Russian lives. It was the kind of ship already rare in the late nineteenth century when a Russian traveller admired it. I would also like to find or resurrect one of the government gallows ships that sailed the Volga, executing suspected rebels. Finally I would like to know Catherine's personal view of the man who, in pretending to be her husband, tested her possible involvement in his murder. After his execution in 1775 Pugachev became a legend like Napoleon. Russians spoke in whispers of *pugachevshchina* and used the name to torment their children. Catherine even changed the name of the Yaik river, where his exploits began, to 'Ural', in the hope that Russia would forget. Kazan did not. In front of the Spassky Gate of the kremlin there took place a ritual hanging and burning of his effigy, an event still recalled over a hundred years later.

Today's sun-drenched, quiet Kazan seems uncanny because of all this violence in its past. The view from the far end of the kremlin over the confluence of the Volga and the local river Kazanka is of inscrutable forested lowlands, bungalow houses nestling in the trees below, and not a minaret in sight. The kremlin 'gardens' were overgrown and unkempt to me, though to Alyosha they appeared quite normal. The most picturesque view of the kremlin was once to be had here in the reverse direction, looking up from the Kazanka, with a sprawl of wood piles and shacks in the foreground where also lay the often flooded Tartar quarter. In old photographs this arrangement had the effect of showing heaven-inspired despotic power towering over hard work and humility, and Russians over Tartars.

Now that the Volga runs higher the mouth of the Kazanka is broader and its banks beneath the kremlin wall are concrete. In the water sits a famous early nineteenth-century monument to the fallen at the 1552 conquest of Kazan, a fanciful quasi-Egyptian flattened pyramid with a dark vault of bones, entered through Empire-style doorways. It rises up like a fabulous stone bell-wether, as if it were the only still visible sign of a submerged civilization.

Beside the kremlin's Spassky Tower we hovered with the newly-weds who had come for the traditional photograph. This perfect white wedding cake, with a green and gold clock, belfry, pencil point and crowning gold star, formed a too perfect backdrop to the monumental statue of the Tartar poet Mussa Dzhalil, the young victim of a wartime German prison camp. It is hard to believe that less than a hundred years ago this cobbled, steeply sloping square was the vital centre of Kazan, with all its thriving commerce concentrated in the *gostinny dvor*, which was the permanent market, and with religion represented by the Bogoroditsky monastery.

9

River of Boredom, River of Justice . . . Whose River Is the Central Volga Now?

FROM THE Spassky Tower runs a broad road, still called Lenin Street, lined with tall, solid administrative buildings, parallel to Bauman Street but steeply higher. It leads to the main neo-classical building of the university. The setting for Russian imperial education here is one of the few neat and pretty sights in Kazan. The university has gardens and an observatory; it is surrounded by wooden houses in a state of good outward repair, ranged along a steep cobbled hill that eventually leads back to Freedom Square.

Catherine's erstwhile lover Prince Potemkin left all his books to the Kazan library, which provided a foundation for the university; but learned reactionaries, in whom Russia was rich, kept finding political objections. A typical illiberal was the first rector of Kazan, Magnitsky. Nicknamed Mr Loathsome, he got his come-uppance when he was sacked for embezzlement in 1827.

Kazan was one of seven Imperial universities (Moscow, St Petersburg, Kiev, Vilnius, Dorpat and Warsaw) and, unlike most of those which were fraught with nationalist dissent, it was politically quiet until the 1890s. German professors dominated the scene, as they did everywhere in Russia. Ethnographers took a mainly passive interest in the Central Volga region and its native peoples.

76

Exceptionally, Professor Karl Fuchs carried out personal experiments with Tartar women. He liked to make them fall in love with him, and then, when he withdrew his affection, to study the cultural qualities of their declarations of devotion and unhappiness. How could it be that these women were so profound and eloquent when they were Tartars? he asked himself. There must be some quality in Tartar culture after all. His case recalls the real-life prototypes for Professor Higgins and Eliza Doolittle.

Otherwise the Kazan professors kept themselves to themselves and got on with their work. Science and mathematics boomed. Kazan was where Nikolai Lobachevsky, to whom the city has a statue, pioneered non-Euclidean geometry. Gorky once shared a ramshackle Kazan tenement with a mathematician who would shout out: 'Geometry's a cage, yes! A mousetrap! A prison!' which represented one extreme of the scholarly atmosphere of the city. A more sober Kazan mathematician was Lenin's father, Ilya Ulyanov, who studied under Lobachevsky and became a teacher in Astrakhan. Today, as if to continue Kazan's link with revolutionary curved space, the latest physics block of the university has emblazoned upon it Einstein's relativity equation: $E = mc^2$. Through Lobachevsky and Einstein led the path into nuclear physics. Such wondrous science gave the Soviet superpower its basis.

Some Kazan students became famous, though none of them directly thanks to the university. In autumn 1844 the sixteen-year-old Leo Tolstoy, having lived with his brothers and relatives in the city, enrolled as a student of Oriental languages. Within a year he had flunked his exams, lost his virginity to a prostitute and switched to law. Never good at passing exams, he struggled on for the next two years until illness suddenly revealed the sheer happiness and benefit of working alone. He packed up his books and returned west to Yasnaya Polyana, near Tula. Only when he realized that the formality of Kazan or any university was intolerable to his budding talent, and that his real masters were not textbooks but great writers, did Kazan become significant. He now devised an ambitious plan of private study, which, coupled with the self-improvement programmes which were already a compulsive habit, made him invincibly eccentric as well as a writer of genius.

Lenin arrived forty years after Tolstoy. Volodya still faces the

Ionic pillars of academic Kazan, but the unique statue is not truthful, because the relationship between these powers was one of confrontation, not belonging. The university expelled the future activist in 1887 after only four months of studying law. He was alleged, probably unfairly, to have taken part in a demonstration. What did him more harm was the execution three months earlier of his elder brother Alexander for a bungled attempt on the life of Tsar Alexander III. Like Tolstoy, without the support of an institution Ulyanov withdrew to work alone and become himself. He lived near Kazan at the new family home his mother made after their double bereavement, his father having died only months before his brother.

The third would-be famous Kazan student, Gorky, never managed to enrol at the university at all. He arrived in 1884, wanting to change his life, but found his way barred by lack of formal qualifications. His situation, that of a young man who had educated himself out of his class, plagued him, the more so because he didn't feel at home with intellectuals either. A teenager adrift, he ended up working in a Kazan bakery, where conditions were so wretched that he raised them to the status of myth in his later story *Twenty-six Men and a Girl*. The idealism of the bakers in that story represented his own misguided hopes *vis-à-vis* the brutality of Russian life. In reality his hopes added to his isolation. Since early childhood all that he had involuntarily witnessed of relations between men and women had frozen his sexuality. At nineteen he had no intimates, neither physical nor of the heart. He decided on suicide. Beneath the kremlin wall, on the banks of the Kazanka, he shot himself, aiming for the heart and permanently damaging his lungs. He tried again in hospital, by drinking acid. Later his parting note was handed over to the Blagoveshchensky church. He was called before the ecclesiastical authorities, to whom he rejoined, impenitent and never a believer: 'Next time I'll hang myself from your gates.'

It seems a peculiar conceit of our age of meritocracy, shared by Soviet idealists, to believe that universities make men and women. What universities determine are the attitudes of their students to the uses of learning. They show what it is possible to do with knowledge: pursue power, foment revolution, make a fortune, build a secure nest, discover and improve oneself. Tolstoy envisaged through his acquisition of knowledge a better humanity. Gorky envisioned a more humane world. Ulyanov senior pursued decency and security, while his son became devoted to their overthrow.

One use of learning is to show ways of overcoming boredom. Volga boredom in our case. Kazan so bored Gorky that he learned to play the violin. Lenin for the same explicit reason devoted himself to chess. At the same time both Gorky and Lenin became embroiled in the political circles of the day, always a highly characteristic way for Russian intellectuals to pass the time. Gorky briefly succumbed to the mystery and intrigue of Kazan's pre-revolutionary Fedoseyev Circles. Young men, mostly students, endlessly reviewed Russia's possible ways forward beyond the despotic power of the tsar. Every dream of getting something done, including terrorism, appeared more attractive than the boredom of the status quo. But soon Gorky abandoned the Circles. He felt he had met in life, in the odd personalities he respected – a doctor, a vet, an ex-prisoner from Siberia – more than ideas labelled 'populism' and 'social democracy' could ever offer. He was always an artist, against whose breadth it is useful to measure Lenin's far narrower, more theoretical and cautious life.

Boredom, though. Does Russia not induce political upheavals as a form of entertainment, as the ultimate antidote to provincial boredom? It is so difficult in this country to separate the pursuit of truth from entertainment. In autumn 1993 thousands of Muscovites came out to watch President Yeltsin's troops bombard rebel parliamentary deputies occupying the White House. Women with shopping bags sat amid police cordons and TV crews and scuffling crowds, as if at last something were worth watching on the Life channel. Gorky wrote in *Childhood* almost ninety years ago: 'To Russians through the poverty and squalor of their lives, suffering comes as a diversion, is turned into a game and they play it like children and rarely feel ashamed of their misfortune. In the monotony of everyday existence grief comes as a holiday and a fire is an entertainment. A scratch embellishes an empty face.'

Yet Trotsky contended that Lenin was formed as much by the whole Central Volga as by Kazan, and certainly not by boredom alone. He began his book *The Young Lenin*:

Whoever is born on the Volga carries her image through life. The uniqueness and beauty of the river lie in the contrast of its shores; the right a high, mountainous barrier against Asia, the left a level plain sloping away to the endless east [. . . .] The two Volga rebellions constitute the authentic peasant-revolutionary tradition of old Russia. In spite of their portentous scope, however, they brought no relief to the people [. . . .] The old Russian cities, mere accumulation, of the nobility, the bureaucrats, and their retainers, contained no progressive forces of any kind. That is why, after each of these grandiose movements of the seventeenth and eighteenth centuries, the Volga washed the bloodstains into the Caspian Sea, and the tsar's and the landlords' oppressions weighed heavier than ever.

For Trotsky's Lenin the Volga was the history of oppression, a river of blood. As important as any one town he might live in, or book he might read, the Volga compounded Lenin's loathing of existing Russian society.

Throat-drying sun and dust hampered our return along the now busier main road over the Kazanka river. In the crowded, swaying bus back to the port a swarthy, bright-eyed Tartar in an Air Force green shirt and his Russian friend kept me upright. To the Tartar, who had the unofficial job of cancelling everyone's tickets, I chatted about his language. Tartar was reserved for important and intimate things, Russian was for work and public life. My friend had no animus against using both tongues. Yet he was pleased that post-Soviet autonomy meant that all lessons in schools would now be taught in Tartar. I wasn't sure I agreed. I mean, how would it be these days if Welsh children were only educated in Welsh? In a reshuffle of bodies after a stop he offered me more space. I accused him of trying to pass on the burden of ticket-punching. We laughed our way back to the river station, and I felt sorry to be leaving

Kazan so soon. For one thing, I liked talking to this man; for another, I had no idea about Tartar life and the Tartar Volga.

In fact Tartar life and the Tartar Volga are enormously far from our grasp today, as far removed as the days when the Volga was the Ra or the Atil, and further than they were even five years ago, when Tartar literature was automatically translated into Russian, with the benefits of Empire.

The Ra was how the Alexandrian geographer Ptolemy knew this river in the eleventh century. To the Tartars it has always been the Itil; to the Arabs of old it was the Etel or Atil. Defining these unknowable Volgas helped me realize that the Volga only became entirely Russian when Ivan the Terrible took Kazan. Philologists have never determined where that name came from, but suddenly there it was, deeply Russian.

Thus it was remembered by Ivan Bunin, the first Russian writer to win the Nobel Prize for Literature. At seventy-three, he was an old man in exile in the south of France, with the Second World War snatching at his tenuous well-being and his early friendship with Gorky long past. The distance vanished in the vivid prose of his short story *The Riverside Tavern*:

> The Russian provinces are pretty much the same everywhere. There's only one thing in them that's quite unique, and that's the Volga itself. From early spring right up to winter it is always and everywhere extraordinary, in all weathers and whether it's day or night. At night you can sit, for instance, in a tavern like that one and look out of the windows which form three of its walls, and when they are all open to the air on a summer night you look straight into the darkness, into the blackness of the night, and somehow you sense especially keenly all the wild magnificence of the watery wastes outside; you see thousands of bright-coloured lights, you hear the splash of passing rafts and the voices of the peasants on the rafts and the barges and the wherries, shouting warnings to each other; you hear the varied music of the steamers' sirens, first booming then low and, merging with that, the notes of the fast-running river boats; you recall all those brigand and Tartar names – Balakhna, Vasilsursk, Cheboksary, Zhiguli, Batraki, Khvalynsk – and the great hordes of dockers on their

jetties, then all the incomparable beauty of the ancient Volga churches . . . and all you can do is shake your head. Indeed is there anything to compare with this Old Russia of ours? But then you look round and ask what, if we're honest about it, is this tavern? A structure on wooden piles, a log barn with windows in crude frames, packed with tables hidden under grubby white tablecloths, with cheap heavy cutlery, where the salt in the salt-cellars is mixed with pepper and the napkins smell of cheap soap; you see a platform of planks, a farcical stage for balalaika players, accordionists and lady harpists, illuminated along its back wall by kerosene lamps with their blinding tin reflectors; you see yellow-haired waiters, a landlord of peasant stock with thick hair and little bear-like eyes – and how can you reconcile all this with the fact that again and again a thousand roubles' worth of Mumm and Roederer is drunk in one night! All that is Old Russia too. . . .

The Central Volga, a concentration of the whole river, was removed from those quarrels between Slavophiles and Westernizers which polarized life in Moscow and St Petersburg into Russian-Asian and Russian-European. It throve, amid intellectual and artistic mediocrity and quaintness, on the drive of trade and money and that attraction of good living not far removed from the land. Its material standards could be wealthy and decorative on the surface, crude, harsh and backward just beneath. This was the real Russian tradition, only a breath away from the steppes of the East.

In this atmosphere of Old Russia Shalyapin was born in Kazan in 1873 and grew up with Volga music. Like Gorky, Shalyapin too wandered among the stevedores by the river, looking for work, drawing inspiration from the *burlaki* for the gestures and intonations which would one day make world-famous his interpretations of the great heroes of Russian opera, Boris Godunov and Prince Igor. Yury Protazanov's atmospheric film of Ostrovsky's play *The Woman Without a Dowry*, set in merchant circles on the Volga, would, if it were better known, also help to broadcast to a wider audience this cruel and beautiful world of material decrepitude, human meanness and occasional fantastic dreams.

The Volga entered early and effectively into Russian national self-awareness because of its fertility. It attracted such an influx of Russian settlers that what once was a wild province, second only to Siberia, became a familiar home. On the Volga banks Russian life and trade flowered. In its waters the melancholy Russian soul found new objective correlatives for its inner joys and disappointments, and the sybarite, be he merchant, lord or peasant, found satiety. The only region which could claim more economic migrants in the nineteenth century was Siberia. The Volga's lovers, meanwhile, turned river into art.

Now after four hundred and fifty years, whatever his character, whatever his intellectual persuasion, and partly because of that art, the Russian feels the Volga is the real Russia. I do not think there is a great difference between generations here, though the latest, exposed to modifying transatlantic influences for the first time in eighty years, may soon differ. The Russianness of the Volga was Tolstoy's sensation when, fifteen years after he had left Kazan University, he passed this way again by river. Before him Pushkin acknowledged the definitive, anchoring attraction of the Volga and its history. Ostrovsky, Nekrasov, Gorky, Bunin, Alexei Tolstoy and yes, even Lenin, all described Volga magic.

Geographically the Central Volga ends soon after Kazan at the mouth of the Kama, but the concept extends loosely to include Ulyanovsk (which used to be Simbirsk), Samara and Saratov. From here come classic fairy-tales and magic figures and settings, and the legends drawn from real life of the seventeenth-century pirate Stenka Razin and the renegade Pugachev. When Pushkin is declared the most Russian of writers, and the most loved, it is well to remember him as both a teller of fairy-stories and an historian, both genres connected with this region (for many of the fairy-stories are Eastern). You will not get this impression from dreary ex-Soviet museums up and down the river which have not yet had time to change their exhibits, but the Pugachev rebellion lodged in Russian consciousness like the Trojan War in the minds of the Romans. The early nineteenth-century chronicler Sergei Aksakov described how his immediate ancestors wandered half the Volga to avoid the robber scourge touching their otherwise happy family life. Pushkin is now the Virgil of Russian eighteenth-century history with his tale *The*

Captain's Daughter set in the decade of Pugachev, and now, for the devastating objective concision of his report on that wild and violent Pretender, and the tragic sacrifice of Russian soldiers, its Tacitus. I cannot think of a richer place to visit, for the sake of Russian literature, than the Central Volga, with its centre at Kazan.

10

Have You Come
to See the Bears
Waste Their Lives?

BACK ON THE BOAT lunch was announced, but it would not be until 3.30pm. Famished travellers peered in through the restaurant's net curtains, wondering how to fill the time of hunger pangs. Customer service as a concept has not existed in Russia since about 1928 (though it took until after the war to die, and has never been as bad as it is today).

Alyosha slept. I broke a nail on the intractable wooden blind (having just remembered to rescue the tin spoon), twice changed my mind about whether to stay in the cabin, tripped over a permanent ruck in the carpet outside and finally sank into an armchair in the little reading room on the first deck, in the prow. So where are the drinks, then? *Seichas pryamo!* Alyosha has taught me this phrase in response to my constant unwitting expectations. You must be joking! Civilized life elsewhere in the world consists in making long days delightful, not gruelling, but in Russia there is never any relief. Everything is arduous, therefore in the end everything becomes boring because one has no energy. But suddenly beneath the gloom of these thoughts, and the feeling that I had made nothing of Kazan, came the pleasantest surprise. The radio was playing some pop music from my childhood, a tame and nostalgic experience. The Beatles' 'From Me to You', followed by Freddie and the Dreamers' 'I'm telling you now. I'm in love with you now'. A little man with a pug face in a nylon tracksuit suddenly entered and turned the radio off. I watched him flick through the channels on the huge, alas entirely functioning, TV. He was built like a single column of flesh. Bastard. I bet you can't understand that baseball commentary in English.

'Excuse me, I was listening to the radio.'

'Well, I want to watch TV.'

'But I was here first!'

'Too bad.'

Short of smashing the television set, I didn't see what I could do. I stalked off, furious, and picked up the remnants of the life-saving programme in my cabin. What was so bad about that, in the end? Not much, but I wanted to be in society and there wasn't any, just as there is no civility in the dining room. I decided all public life in Russia was appalling.

Lunch when it finally came didn't change my view. It included more rice in the form of a sweetened milk soup before the main course, plus some eggs stuffed with sardine paste before it and meat rissoles afterwards. I call them courses out of habit, and the food was good enough, but they were all brought at the same time, or whenever it suited the kitchen, plus the tea we would drink last, plus our neighbours' food. Very soon the table was piled so high with dishes lying edge to edge, some as yet untouched and rapidly cooling, and some dirty, that there was no room to wield a knife and fork. To enjoy the meal we so badly needed under these wretched circumstances was impossible. A faintly hysterical tone entered my voice as I declared the situation unbearable. I removed the dirty dishes to the floor, crying: 'How can it be that they serve the table on this bloody ship, and not the people sitting around it, eh, Alyosha? Is it an unforgivable cult of personality directly to hand a customer the dish he ordered and paid for, when he wants it? For God's sake! What a bloody awful country this is!'

'Putting the dishes on the floor won't get you anywhere,' Alyosha said calmly, 'though they'll put up with it because you're a foreigner. A Russian would be told to leave and not come back. He wouldn't get any food for the rest of the journey. Count yourself lucky.'

We sat quietly for a moment. Then he said: 'Still, you remind me of lots of things I've let slide, things I don't like about myself,' before plunging back into his food.

I slunk off to sunbathe.

Now our ship passed the mouth of the Kama. This river flowed in from its eastward source beyond Perm in the Ural mountains. The Volga, also vastly enlarged by the 650km (400 mile) long Kuibyshev reservoir, stretched 27km (17 miles) across, its broadest point altogether. We sailed for the rest of the day on a man-made sea.

For much of the nineteenth century the Kama, two-thirds the length of the Volga, was the penal route to Siberia. In Gorky, washing up aboard *The Good One*, its mouth evoked visions of incomprehensible human suffering. His story *The River Steamer* told of a tormented passenger acquitted of murder, but whose uncle and brother were among the convicts on the Siberia-bound barge in tow. The passenger exhibited the kind of metaphysical boredom more characteristic of Dostoevsky's novels, tinged with ghastly humour. He threw a mop overboard, set light to the underarm hair of a sleeping woman and eventually threw himself into the Volga.

Of his own direct experience Gorky wrote:

Our ship was towing a barge, which was painted dirty red as well, and it moved behind us at the end of a long cable. Its deck was covered by an iron cage full of convicts sentenced to penal colonies or hard labour. A sentry's bayonet shone on the bows like a candle, and the tiny stars in the blue sky glinted like candles as well. No noise came from the barge and it was brightly illuminated by the moon. Behind metal bars I could see dim, round grey figures – these were convicts looking at the Volga. The water sobbed and seemed to be crying, and then quietly laughing. Everything around me reminded me of a church; there was that same strong smell of burning oil.

Here was the non-believer so oppressed by human pain that he almost invented a church where he could pray arising out of the loved river. This passage from *My Apprenticeship* continued by linking the imagined church with his other sources of consolation: his mother's tenderness and his grandmother's compassion.

He saw Siberia-bound prisoners at the Kama–Volga junction 'cooped up like animals in that iron cage . . . the weight of their haversacks almost bent them double'. In 1847 Haxthausen put this human traffic at ten thousand a year. Only the Trans-Siberian Railway, built in stages between 1891 and 1903, banished the penal traffic on the river.

Chekhov passed this way on his pilgrimage to see where some of the prisoners ended up. Having come on the *Alexander Nevsky* from Yaroslavl to Nizhny, he took the service which ran, past Kazan, up the Kama to Perm. He was a quiet, amiable traveller, who tended to notice spelling mistakes on the menu more than to seek metaphysical answers in the depth of the water below. The weather was very cold on the Kama in May and it was impossible to remain on deck, though he got bored in his cabin. He slept to save money on food, but occasionally liked to gorge himself on beluga caviar. He noticed the taciturn merchants going to Perm to trade that beluga for Ural iron, and many Tartars, who came across as 'a polite and modest people'. There was a priest worth talking to, some assize court judges and a fake writer, boasting to the ladies that he had had a book published by Suvorin, Chekhov's own publisher. Thus Chekhov travelled on the river and amused himself, quite unlike the way Gorky worked and suffered, and each man found correlatives for his personality in the view from the river steamer. I admire Alyosha's amused stoicism. He admires my tenacity in the face of gloom.

At the southern tip of the mouth of the Kama, where the Volga resumes its natural narrower course, we sailed past the medieval Bolgar capital, Great Bolgar. This clever people of Turkic origin ruled here before the Mongol-Tartars descended from Central Asia and eventually overwhelmed and absorbed them over two centuries from 1223 to 1421. Until the eighth century they had lived, pagan and semi-nomadic, on the Lower Volga and the Don, wandering the steppe around the Black Sea. When the Khazars from Central Asia expelled them some resettled on the Danube in modern Bulgaria, and some sailed up the Volga until they found a suitable habitation just before modern Kazan. The Danube Bolgars became Christian, the Volga Bolgars Moslems. Builders and traders, the admirable Volga Bolgars bartered goods with arrivees by river from north and east and fished the Volga as far north as Nizhny. The Bolgars were not Slavs, though their name lives on in the modern world to describe a Slav people.

Today's remaining thirteenth- and fourteenth-century ruins lie outside a town called Spassk-Tartarsky but renamed in Soviet times Kuibyshev. The standing archaeological site, of small, practical, solid buildings with tapered towers and domes, centres on a minaret with an inscription from the Koran and a burial vault. Great Bolgar was begun in the tenth century when the Khazars of Baghdad sent thousands of craftsmen, architects and learned men to provide expertise and to help bring the two Islamic cultures closer. This form of annexation confirmed the Bolgars as Moslems. Traces of fortified ditches have been found, and weapons and jewellery. The Bolgars melted metal, wrote on birch bark, and were skilled in agriculture and military strategy. They looked at their image in bronze mirrors, made pottery on a wheel, piped water, forged iron, minted coins and cut keys. One of their learned men wrote a history of his people. A long poem called *Yusif and Zuleikha*, attributed to the poet Kul Gali in the thirteenth century, is considered the foundation of Tartar literature. The Bolgars' latest descendants, Soviet Russians, deprived of true history, built a landing strip so that they could fly in and study the relics of this distant, untouchable, cultivated people.

The Kuibyshev reservoir flowed on. After Kazan, steep limestone cliffs rose up on the right bank, with sharply hewn gullies exposing the preponderant red marl. Just south of Great Bolgar we passed a natural landmark on the opposite bank: the clifftop town of Tetyushi, founded during Ivan's Kazan campaign, with a monastery sacked by Volga bandits. Today the town processes food and timber. The timber industry, though, so lucrative for the Middle Volga, is mainly based on the left bank, where the steppe is solidly wooded from Nizhny to Kazan and intermittently down to Samara.

Across the reservoir a fierce, warm wind blew. I took the brunt of it, having escaped to the foredeck, away from the stern-faced matrons and their noisy children whose game with the shower was making the whole rear sundeck run with water. In Soviet days, at the beginning of every cruise, in addition to poetic jottings about river travel the radio operator used to play a good conduct tape, explaining where to empty rubbish and wash fruit, how the two sittings in the dining room worked, the need for lights out at 11pm and, finally, the requirement to keep children in order. If they still played the tape, parents and children were not listening now. It was another reason to mourn the Soviet passing. Beside me a pale podgy couple slid illegally under the metal barrier to lie out of reach of passing strollers, and two women stood.

The wide skirts of one woman blew over her face, leaving her standing in her knickers, tulip-shaped and faceless. When her face reappeared we both found the occasion funny, which was good for me, because I needed something to laugh at. Meanwhile into my mind leaped that musical comedy *Volga Volga*, which Stalin loved and which was in fact one of the finest Soviet films ever made. Grigory Alexandrov, who had worked with Eisenstein, directed. The story on the surface was simple and heroic. Provincial towns were invited to send teams to a musical Olympiad in Moscow. In Little Water the pretty and talented postmistress, though not selected, was determined to see her song win. She struggled with her rivals and the Volga elements. Finally a storm blew her song to Moscow. She was famous before she arrived.

In Russia *Volga Volga* is a piece of modern folklore passed down the generations on television. It was also much liked when it was released in the West in 1941, and only those who could read the Cyrillic letters on the side of the luxury Soviet liner which gloriously reunited the musical teams with their song could have recognized the source of salvation as Josef Stalin. For art triumphs here over propaganda. There are memorable shots of rural Volga life, stationary barges upturning, pigs swimming, people plunging in fully clothed and delightful song and dance routines. Alexandrov brings the theatrical anti-realism of Meyerhold to the screen.

But the film does have a message. The local mayor blocking the postgirl's ambition is a bureaucrat who stifled talent. The music of the film arose spontaneously out of the people's protest at being so undervalued. The winning song repeats over and over three linked ideas: the beautiful Volga, the life and talent of the people, and freedom. *Krasavitsa, narodnaya, svobodnaya moya. . . .* The beautiful river belongs to the people and promises them freedom to realize their gifts. This is *Volga Volga*: the 'Russian Hollywood' alternative to Stalinism; also the sad, painful Volga once more by art redeemed. But I begin to wonder if Russian art is not so strong because it is the only form of progress this suffering people have ever found.

'So you've come to see the bears,' said a nice man who pulled up a deckchair. He was Slava, a computer programmer whose work was secret until 1991, and the sort of man whose passport into the world is instant, successful humour, probably masking a rather melancholy character. Well, I needed that humour. He attributed his readiness to talk to a foreign stranger to being brought up in Lithuania, on the fringe of the old Empire. I attributed it to our liking each other. Out of embarrassment and liking I did a very Soviet dodging of the ursine question and muttered something about bears in Russian folklore. We grinned a bit at each other. He told me about his mother, who was put into a German concentration camp, then settled in Lithuania by the Russians who released her. Then, swallowing so many linking thoughts, he suddenly pronounced: 'Nostradamus predicted the Soviet Empire! Seventy two and a half years of misery.'

With that I was returned to gloom. I cast my sympathy back to Raisa in Plyos, and to Misha on the *Chernyshevsky*, who would go to France rather than let his talents be squandered. The wasting of human resources occurred throughout the Soviet century, when it was a travesty of the Communist ideal, and it happened under the tsars. In Russian literature the superfluous person is well known as one who might have given his country and his compatriots so much had he enjoyed the opportunity, or found his niche. From Pushkin's *Eugene Onegin* through Turgenev's *Hamlet of the Provinces* to Chekhov's *Three Sisters*, and from all the men and women and eternal students around these characters, emanates an energy which has never found a conduit. Slava said no one recognized talent in Russia, nor wanted it, until it was too late. Therefore people had to convince themselves – as in Chekhov, I thought – that they were working for the future. The thoughts of both of us went out to those who had been working for the Communist future. They included Slava himself.

We left the question of wasted lives hanging when Slava's businessman friend Valentin and a pale woman travelling alone – she was called Vera, but she might just as well have been Chekhov's Masha – joined us. Valentin, probably a businessman, not a *mafioso*, and Slava were travelling to Volgograd to stay with a friend, while Vera, a Marxist economist, had taken the trip as a cruise. Just as we were exchanging purposes Mr Homo Sovieticus in his tracksuit, plus Mrs, built like a Russian doll, waddled past hand in hand. Vera smiled at me. 'I was in the music room, you know. I saw him. He behaved terribly.' In my enthusiasm and rage I hadn't seen Vera. We had something to smile about.

'You look very nice,' said Slava, who was married and decent and decided after a while, perhaps after saying that, that he'd better go. He and Valentin were amongst the only Russians I have ever seen who after lunch had an unfinished bottle of liquor with them.

I asked Vera what she thought of the restaurant. Her objections weren't as fierce as mine but she found it expensive, and, like Chekhov, saved money by only eating once a day. Ideally, she said, she would have liked to sit with us. It was boring travelling alone. She had been forced to share a cabin with a woman who kept telling her what to do. I suppose we must have seemed potentially exciting, with my foreignness and our animation and chatter. A few years ago she wouldn't have dared sit with us, or talk to me.

And so the afternoon passed. About six, when the deck had cleared, Alyosha and I in our swimsuits did our keep fit exercises. There was still water either side of us, with only a sandy strip and a few trees visible on the left. He fixed a thick elastic strap to the rail and stretched and heaved against it. I kicked my legs and stretched my arms and touched my toes.

Dachas appeared on the Volga banks, splendid two-storey wooden affairs shaped like giant croquet hoops, with curved steep roofs for the winter snow to slide off and traditional wood carving decorating the exterior. Some were painted luscious pink and coral, and I spotted two swimming pools. About all this Alyosha, who had once spent a month in America, was determined to dampen my enthusiasm. The pools would belong to a trade union or some late official Soviet organization. They wouldn't be private yet. As for that coral paint, it was all the shop had, nothing in Russia expressed choice. OK, I said, but I would reserve judgement on that stifling aspect of the non-consumer society, because the striving for choice still existed, whatever its gratification. Not for nothing did Alyosha wear an immaculate green silk shirt on our best evenings. No doubt, had it been portable, he would also have brought house paint back from America.

The dacha culture has survived ninety years of puritanism, poverty and contempt for the joys of living. The idea is to get to the holiday home, humble or luxurious, as often as possible so as to draw strength from the fresh air and sunshine – and lay in berries and mushrooms and fruit – to face the winter. Samara, where we were headed, was always dusty and, as the town grew in the later nineteenth century, to have a dacha on the river became *de rigueur* among the merchant classes. Turn-of-the-century dacha culture reached one of its highest expressions on the Volga here, feeding the passion for private property and inviting architectural fantasy. There were dachas like medieval castles, some with crenellations and towers, others with chapels and extensive grounds and goldfish ponds. These have long since been cleared for firewood, but a rare villa in stone built by the flour-milling Sokolov family has just survived. The original had a terrace overlooking the river and the Zhiguli hills. Local historians, smitten by nostalgia today, seem to remember a time when the cream of Samara merchants sat there on cane chairs, listening to a string quartet or a gypsy choir and drinking tea. At sunset the Volga appeared to be a pink and blue road leading to an unearthly land. This spot was known as one of several Russian Switzerlands, and we would pass close to it tomorrow, reviewing thousands of new dachas along the way. Well, architecture is art too, and beautiful nature helps. I have to say that the sight of the dachas, and the hemp and buckwheat fields, and yellow sunflowers, made Russia seem at last habitable.

Roasted by the sun, my skin smelt of buckwheat. Reversing the miseries of the late lunch, the balance of the day seemed almost satisfying for the first time since leaving the *Chernyshevsky*.

I would eat dinner bare-shouldered tonight, I decided, and look, but only look, for Slava. Just before our sitting was called I caught Alyosha in his green silk shirt coming up the brass-railed stairs to our top deck with a bottle of Spanish wine. 'We're in luck! They had this one I know in the kiosk. It's not bad, I think. At least it won't make you ill like our Russian ones.' Reconciliation was in the air, gloom temporarily dispelled.

We ate slowly and I – no, sorry, he: I had to hand it to him because Russia is old-fashioned about the distribution of labour – opened the wine at the table with the corkscrew on my Swiss army knife. There was nowhere to chill it but it was quite bearable, with a taste like thin dry sherry. The grape was in there somewhere. Our waitress, who was actually rather friendly, with a smooth young round face, dimples and dark curly hair, provided a glass. I raised it to my companion and wished him a vicarious high. We tucked into soup and meat and pasta and a jar of sour cream with sugar for pudding. After dinner the same knife helped us hack out the bruises from the otherwise superbly flavoured little apples we had bought in Kazan.

11

Shape Life
or Lose It

'A RT AS A reflection of life? I don't think that's what Russians
need, do you? They've had enough of the real thing. They
don't want to read its imitation!'

We were seated at table and couch, in the yellow-gold of the
cotton curtain and the table lamp, with our liquorice coffee and
Alyosha with a pack of cigarettes. It was a warm night and behind
the curtain and wooden blind the window stood wide open. The
radio operator announced that the film *Robocop* would shortly be
shown in the music room; this was surely a pirate video.

Alyosha was rereading for the third time Gabriel Garcia Marques' *A Hundred Years of Solitude* and praising magic realism as
the way forward for Russian literature. I loved his preoccupation
with the artistic word, which kept him out of those traps looming
for passive Russian spirits, nostalgia and grumbling. Every day he
would say something like: 'I'm writing a dialogue.' 'What you said
yesterday about so-and-so gave me an idea. I'd like to write a
comedy about our Russian life.' 'It must be the Volga. I keep
writing songs!' These were not fantasies. At the end of our voyage
his theatrical producer and agent came to collect a stack of newly
typed work.

'Once you accept the need for art, whatever the form,' I finally
responded, 'that says a great deal about your attitude to life, surely?
The more you believe in art the more you believe life needs help,
interpretation, embellishment – otherwise how on earth do you live
it? I don't mean art as escapism but art as diverting interpretation,
art turning life into a constant fascinating engagement for the spirit

and the senses. From my point of view life needs art just like the Volga has been given art, to turn a vast unconscious existence into something humanly significant and loved.'

But Alyosha said that was enough cleverness, or words to that effect, and so I drank some more thin wine and we sat contentedly, hearing the before-bed strollers pass along the deck outside. Ulyanovsk, Lenin's birthplace, appeared out of the darkness, its nameplate above the river station blazing in red neon. It was 10.30pm and we were due to stop but not disembark. A very steep hill rose up dramatically from the right bank of the Volga. It twinkled with lights which suggested a deceptive prosperity and happiness. Yet Ulyanovsk seemed to have a rural character, with no visible industry and large expanses of emptiness. In fact the town was largely hidden from the river. The mystical philosopher Vasily Rozanov, on a Volga cruise in summer 1907, also found himself arriving here late at night, but while all the other passengers prepared for sleep he went ashore. This was where he went to school. As he wandered in darkness, he recognized the smell of the air. The experience overwhelmed him. Rozanov knew, I think, the same eroticomystical excitement to be found in Bunin's early stories and Rilke's poetry and many other writers' work. This faint apprehension of perfection, the sense of a possible fulfilment close by, the intuition that some people have of a supra-material reality of some kind, became the core of his work. Happily the Volga encouraged it.

Alyosha spoke tonight of reconciling his need for excitement with real life in Russia, and with the requirement to ensure that he and his loved ones survive. In him, of our evenings, I would come to hear the artist talking, the man who would always find extra excitement journeying in the life of his imagination, and the man who was not quite at home in any other life. I record here the story of one of his plays, in which two characters on neighbouring balconies discuss the moon. The one speaks of the moon's appearance during the day, the other denies this can be, until finally she agrees that life is other than she saw it. This play is life stripped down to a parable, and that parable coincidentally – it was not the author's intention – could describe the end of Communism, or a sea-change in any life, to do with acquiring faith or losing it, or falling in or out of love, or simply one day seeing that life can be quite, quite different from how it has always been before. That is the excitement at being alive which art has knocked into shape. Art is excitement knocked into shape. It's difficult to achieve, and much writing and painting and music is just a step along the way. But by this token life will never be dull.

I keep thinking: I have excitement about Russia, yet no faith that human life will ever become kinder, braver, more intelligible. Maybe it is enough. I know what Rozanov felt about the nearness of apparent perfection, which perhaps we feel most strongly because we are unsure of it. Alyosha said it was what he needed to stay alive, a little immediate disorder and uncertainty to make the sense of living palpable.

We turned in. A few events of the day re-presented themselves as I lay there under a single cover, experimenting with the blue light. Vera had asked to borrow a book and out of a small choice took the Bible, because she had heard it was worth reading. Alyosha said she wasn't really interested, just being polite. We live in interesting times when the West, the intellectual as well as the economic victor, has drawn up a Marshall Plan of the Mind to help Russian cultural life recover from the Cold War, the way the Allies helped Germany rebuild after 1945. What is one supposed to feel as a Westerner about this cultural rescue plan? Smug? I find it dizzying. On deck today I noticed a dark-haired man, who had the only well-behaved children in the dining room, reading a volume of the pre-revolutionary encyclopedia in a new binding. I wondered whether everything which counts for Western civilization, however battered in the West, was being learnt here again from scratch: history, literature, economics, public manners, the history of religion. I peered, trying to be discreet. The encyclopedia reader was consulting the volume for the letter 'Ya'. 'Ya' means 'I'. Perhaps he was reading about the good uses of egoism. If so, fine. There were five thousand words on the ego in the pre-revolutionary encyclopedia compared with fifty in the Great Soviet. I said to myself what I have already said out loud in this book: Please, Russia, love yourself a little more. But I wasn't being smug. I mean, are psychoanalysts, the role into which the traveller through Russia is cast, smug with their analysands?

The blue light was too bright and I extinguished it. Finally I closed my eyes, wondering whether Marques had ever invented a river like the Volga, and decided, yes, there were good enough rivers in his lands. His style is labelled magic, but why? All artistic imagination is magic, only perhaps there is not as much of it in our literature as we assume, for the age in Britain is dull, obsessed with social minutiae and ruled by the hollow combativeness and impatience of journalism. No wonder one comes to Russia, for the shock and the excitement and the anxiety; and no wonder that Russians, oppressed by too much of another kind of deadening reality called material need, and by a long-suppressed history, read Marques.

When you are travelling there is the poetry of coincidence. Things and people happen, seeming to make a pattern or to enlighten your way, even if you travel, as I have done on this Volga voyage, with no preconceived interior purpose. Repeatedly on the Volga, for instance, we passed under monumental rail and road bridges. Trains and cars passed overhead and there might also have been a plane in the sky as we passed underneath. The moment offered up such a densely packed image of progress that I felt called to account by the Futurist world as movingly as Wordsworth by nature.

At Syzran, below Samara, there is a particularly famous bridge which is often compared to the Eiffel Tower for its nineteenth-century ironwork, and was once the longest rail bridge in Europe. The radio was playing the last movement of Beethoven's Choral Symphony as we passed underneath. The moment was happy; the cause the music; the prompt for noticing it the bridge or the coincidence of the two.

The present moment matters. Perhaps there is something mystical in that conviction of mine, though I am not concerned with whether coincidence or some divine immanence lies behind it. Only that we should give it our full attention. To read about a different world while travelling, to plug oneself into recorded music, even to write letters home, is virtually to send back the ticket.

Under the Syzran bridge, then, I felt called to account. Beethoven's voices wanted to unite the world behind virtue and justice, or maybe they just strained to make their antiquated selves heard above the static of trains and boats and planes. I could hear both things happening, grating the centuries against each other, setting them at cross purposes like wild dogs. The faith behind love of reason and belief in higher purpose may be an illusion, but it makes life bearable, and even joyful. In any case, how could anyone bear to be in Russia without it? I don't believe in Him, but I often thank God for humanist art in this godless wasteland which observes no graces in the struggle for life. Yet I believe in comfort and convenience, too, and wish them upon Russia to make life easier. I believe in the material progress and the human independence which have pushed God out of the picture.

I'm left staring at the water. Then comes a very pleasant feeling of solidarity with all of Russia around me. I feel I'm caught up in a massive drive for psychic health against the repression of seventy years. That is the cumulative impression of eight days of talking and watching.

12

Strong Men
of the Zhiguli

SOUTH OF Ulyanovsk the Volga is suddenly forced east by the 300 metre (1100 ft) high, deeply forested Zhiguli hills. Swinging dramatically and picturesquely back on its south-ward course through more than a right-angle, it describes a huge loop known as the Samara Bow. Two Russian brothers called Chernetsov, amateur painters who made the first Russian 'artistic' Volga journey in 1838, compared it to the shaft-bow which stands upright on a horse's harness. There are many of these real bows, ornate, carved and painted, in museums along the Volga. To me the Samara Bow looked on the map like the bulb of a spring onion laid horizontally, or a cross-section of the female pelvis. It was reputed to be the most beautiful stretch of the Volga but, since the liners passed it in utter darkness, how could we know? The secrecy arose in Soviet times because there was much industry here, besides the beauty of nature.

Before the Revolution an Italy-loving hereditary aristocrat, Count Orlov-Davydov, ran the peninsula as an efficient private estate, dealing in timber and sheep and agricultural machinery. In 1927 the estate became a nature reserve. Photographed from the air, the Zhiguli hills seem themselves like a great green animal with a prominent bare backbone. The trees are lime and oak and the occasional pine up high.

In prehistory, before the creation of the Volga, this whole region was under water. In geological upheavals, consequently the subject of legend, twin peaks erupted, ancient Jurassic highlights rising above the general long range of limestone hills which also emerged to run east–west and make up the Zhiguli proper. One stood on the right bank at the entrance to the Bow and the other lower down at Volzhsky, where the river Sok enters and the Volga turns south. The Molodetsky Kurgan and Tsarev mountain were latter-day names for this ancient geological couple uniquely linked by their fault lines. Other weird shapes were formed, too, like the Stone Cup at Shiryaevo.

More or less at the entrance to the Bow of the little river Sok is the Zhiguli Gate, by nature an especially narrow and perilous channel, and a great opportunity for bandits who exploited the perverse winds to multiply sailors' fears. The robber bands, who thought of themselves as looting the rich to help the poor, gave their names to Karaulny Bugor, the Look Out Rock, also at the mouth of the Bow, and the Sheludyak cliff just beyond and opposite Tolyatti. They exacted levies from ships as they entered and left the Bow. Those who resisted, according to one source, were flogged with lighted birch twigs, whence perhaps the name Zhiguli – *zheguli* suggests burning. In the thick Zhiguli woods all the infamous Russian pirates, many of them Cossacks, waited to pounce. First Stenka Razin, then the Cossack hetman Kondraty Bulavin, then Pugachev personally terrorized the Middle to Lower Volga. Samara was founded in 1586 to maintain government control over the river, but the campaign had still not succeeded two centuries later.

Here at Zhiguli the Volga resembles the Rhine of the Lorelei and the Danube of the Wylies. Its giants seem to live and its peaks to express primeval dramas: between man and woman, between oppressors and revolutionary oppressed. Legend associated the Molodetsky Kurgan, the 'young lad's rock', more intimately with its smaller neighbour, the Devichy Kurgan, 'the rock of the young girl'. Either the girl hurled the boy who betrayed her into the river, or both fought with Stenka Razin and, trapped by government forces, jumped. Locals also used to claim that Peter the Great had carved his name on top of the Tsarev rock, but when the gullible Chernetsov brothers climbed it they found the 'writing' illegible.

Industrialization has drowned some of this legend. The sleepy old town of Stavropol has become the efficient car works of Tolyatti,

and the Zhiguli, with its sailboat mascot, has become a car better
known in the West as the Russian copy of the Fiat 124, the Lada
(after *ladya*, a poetic Russian word for boat). Tolyatti on the left
bank and another recent industrial town, Zhigulevsk, lie opposite
each other along the upper edge of the Bow. Zhigulevsk processes
goods derived from the oil industry and is the site of another vast
hydroelectric dam from the fifties. Tolyatti, the third largest
automobile factory on the Volga after Nizhny and one outside
Kazan, has been producing cars for home use and export since 1970.
Special Volga 'despatchers' used to float the cars to distribution
points, though in 1993 the high cost of oil and the privatization
of container shipping had pushed car transportation on to the
railways. Tolyatti's other product is the four-wheel-drive Neva,
high off the ground, chunky and the chicest of Soviet cars. In
1966 the Soviet government paid the Italian company Fiat one
billion US dollars to build this plant, then the world's biggest, in a
town named after the Italian international Communist Palmiro
Togliatti, who died in Yalta in 1964. I once owned a Zhiguli. My
Moscow-based Japanese colleagues had to warm their cars' frozen
parts with small electric fires lowered from their apartment windows
with extension leads when real winter set in, but there was never
an occasion when the Zhiguli didn't start unaided. This triumph
didn't interest me personally, but for Russia's sake I had to let them
know, for Russia, so ambitious, is one of history's greatest instances
of national wounded pride.

Tolyatti, as foreign-sounding a name to the Russian ear as
Zhiguli to the English, swallowed up Stavropol when the Kuibyshev
reservoir raised the water level and the hydroelectric dam and the
car plant were built. Stavropol still existed on the *Komarno*'s 1959
wall map of the Volga, but since then it had suffered the fate of
Kalyazin. In Stavropol there used to be dachas and healing establishments for tubercular patients, though only on a village scale. Volga
Stavropol, not to be confused with a more important Stavropol on
the Russian side of the Caucasus, was founded in 1738 when St
Petersburg decided to divide Kalmyks from the south Volga into
baptized and non-baptized, and to move the baptized ones to the
new 'town of the cross'. There Russian peasants would teach them
how to work the land. *Seichas pryamo!* So misguided was this

ukaz that after only four years all the Kalmyks were transferred again to the steppe lands of Orenburg province, where thirty-five years later they would join Pugachev's army. Stavropol remained a town with a missionary name taken straight from the Greek into Russian. Without a *raison d'être* it quickly dwindled to a resort, like Plyos.

Then Repin came to paint. The rocky Zhiguli has never commanded Romantic treatment in painting. Minor Russian painters, quite alien to the world of Levitan, more affected by Turner, preferred to discover dramatic landscapes in the Alps or the Bay of Naples. There is a rare Volgascape by the realist, later Expressionist champion of the steppe and the Don, Arkhip Kuinzhi, which suggests an origin here. Alyosha reminded me with reference to Pushkin and Lermontov in the Caucasus that Russians loved mountains, and found their heights liberating after tightly collected Russian life and stifling urban *mores*. Yet Russians have not reacted to their mountains as, say, Ruskin, Turner and Nietzsche did to Switzerland, nor even as the Lakeland poets responded to the Fells. Indeed, the aesthetic sublime seems always to be dwarfed in the Russian context by ethical and social concerns. The music of the Zhiguli was not Bruckner and Richard Strauss but the 'Song of the Volga Boatmen', famous in the West in Shalyapin's rendering, and much appreciated by Gounod, but still not a world-class symphony.

Repin was world-class, though. He was a kind of documentary Rembrandt *en plein air*, at the centre of the Russian realist tradition, who painted the survival of rounded Russian humanity in appalling social conditions. Ten years after the Emancipation of the Serfs he chose as his subject their last surviving brothers on the Volga, the *burlaki*. Repin studied over thirty living characters and filled two albums with sketches from life before embarking on his prizewinning picture *The Barge-haulers*, exhibited in Vienna in 1871.

Burlaki first appeared in Russia in the fourteenth century. There were about six hundred thousand of them in the early 1800s, comprising all kinds of social oddments. They either fled to the river as runaway serfs, or at the spring *burlak* fair were hired out for summer profit by their masters. Free peasants, like Gorky's grandfather, also sought out this work to keep their families. One of the last of their number was the distinguished social historian of Moscow Vladimir Gilyarovsky, who died in 1935. The Volga provided food, and, for the fugitives, shelter on its banks and in its forests, and a reassuring loss of identity. According to Haxthausen a journey from Nizhny to Rybinsk, a matter of 473km (300 miles), could take from two to six weeks, depending on the wind. There were human barge-haulers in England too, at least on minor rivers, into the twentieth century, so it wasn't a marked matter of social backwardness. But the *burlak* had a very distinctive social character in Russia. His *alter ego* was often a robber or a hermit, and here he joined forces with that permanent Volga army of the discontented and dispossessed who would invariably support an insurrectionist. The *burlaki* were obvious symbols for a suffering people.

Repin's 1871 picture shows an *artel* straining at their yoke, with a tall-masted ship in tow. The yoke strapped the men's arms to their sides so that they couldn't waste energy, and they marched in the *burlak* step, setting the right foot forward and dragging the left. The *shishka*, the 'big wheel', set the pace and rhythm, helped by general singing. In the 'Song of the Volga Boatmen' the refrain *Ei ukhnem!* signified the *burlak* groans. Other *burlak* songs were collected by the Nizhny-born composer Mily Balakirev. In the round there was a rhythmic chorus to be repeated: *seno-soloma* – 'hay and a thatch-atch'. That long stress on 'hay' makes the ancient burden palpable.

Repin's first trip to the Zhiguli in 1870, with his friend and fellow painter Feodor Vasiliev, suggests that in their twenties they were overgrown boys from a distant age of innocence. They would sketch and read Homer and 'play' the Trojan War beside the river. When he envisaged his picture's chief hauler Kanin, the *burlak-bogatyr*, a giant hero from Russian legend, Repin recalled the Romans over-running the Ancient Greeks. He imagined Aristotle wearing the chains of a slave and being given hard labour comparable to the *burlak*'s, without losing his noble countenance. His Volga at Zhiguli became the backdrop for a dream of eternal Greece, a Golden Age of Humanity, even as the Russian dispossessed sweated and staggered to tug along a tall ship flying the Russian red, blue and white tricolour.

Where Repin left off in *The Barge-haulers* Alexei Tolstoy in his Civil War trilogy *The Road to Calvary* (1922–41) picked up, hallowing the noble rational man whose spirit was untouched by bodily enslavement. Eisenstein worked in the heroic tradition and so did Cecil B. de Mille. In *The Volga Boatman* de Mille captured for the silent screen that crusading fairy-tale spirit which in Russia united the world of the *Burlaki* with the philosophy of Ancient Greece and really powered an uprising against injustice. De Mille's detailed attention to the painful feet and bodies of the boat-haulers scarred by their harnesses perfectly illustrated the sense and provenance of the Soviet battle ethic.

Extraordinary. I owe it to reading about Repin, reading early Soviet fiction, and looking at countless war and Civil War monuments in Russian towns, that never before this Volga trip has the classical heroic world seemed so relevant to Russia, as if this were the form the Russian Renaissance took, four hundred years late. Now as we approached Samara came the final conjunction linking those ideals: steel. On the Volga shore going towards Samara there is a steel obelisk, built as late as 1971, called the Monument to Glory. It soars upwards out of a formal garden commemorating the city's war dead. Steel was so attractive as an early Soviet metaphor that Nikolai Ostrovsky called his model propaganda novel of 1934 *How the Steel Was Tempered*. The Georgian Josef Dzugashvili adopted the name 'Stalin' or 'man of steel' to become a man of the Russian people. Steel, the perfect product of modern industry, forged the link between Greek warriors, Repin's Greco-Russian heroes and those of the Soviet Union.

The purpose of Ostrovsky's novel was to help engrain a fabricated proletarian ideal of complete devotion to Party ideals into a resistant Russian peasantry and disgusted, anguished, frightened intellectuals. It was the barely fictionalized autobiography of a Ukrainian worker's son expelled from school for putting tobacco in the priest's cake, drawn at fourteen into the Civil War, and at sixteen fighting for the Red Army. Later, though badly wounded, its hero Pavel Korchagin battled for the Party and to rebuild his country as Soviet Russia. After the Second World War a West German critic called this novel 'inhuman and soulless' and said it reminded him of Nazi ideals. Fair enough. But this story shows a man physically and emotionally wrecked by Heroism. It hardly bears a literal reading today, but rather it shows Soviet ideology, Party loyalty, as just one more instance of Russia's perennial waste of human talent. The Soviet ideal was not noble in practice. It wasn't worth coming back on one's shield for.

13

Bread, *Kumiss* and Civil War

SAMARA, the most easterly Volga town, sprawls for more than 15km (10 miles) on a long crest bisected by a Volga tributary. The un-Russian-sounding name originates with the Bolgars, who maintained contacts with Baghdad and traded with Persia, Central Asia and India, and whose empire reached its southern limit here. The shacks and woodpiles visible in old photographs have disappeared, leaving a shoreline lush with deciduous trees and in August bouffant with dark green foliage. The Volga left bank is not naturally always wooded this far south, and Samara was conspicuously treeless to visitors at the end of the last century, so it has been well planted. A cluster of tall, thin, redbrick chimneys, the nineteenth-century brewery, rises out of the trees, its funnels still steaming, and its red and white mock-Gothic appearance enlivening the riverside and recalling Nizhny. Nearby stands a vast municipal swimming pool, in concrete with an imposing façade of recessed angular columns. The beach reaches into the town centre, with rowing and sail-boats, wrought-iron umbrellas and tables and wooden benches on the sand, and a painted metal water slide. This might be Nice if the bluish water sparkled more.

Locals mourn the passing of the Voskresensky Sobor, the Cathedral Resurrection church of 1894, from the ships' approach. They say the sight of this gold-crested thanks-offering for the life of Alexander II, with its twelve blue cupolas, used to bring admiring steamer passengers out on deck, while in the town all municipal and family life had its roots and its meeting-place here. But in the early 1940s, when the Moscow government made Samara, initially far from the German front, its wartime seat, the Voskresensky Sobor became an ideological embarrassment. It was the town's most prominent wartime architectural casualty, blown up in stages, at night. Children scoured the streets next day for coloured fragments from the cupolas and frescoes. Post-war Samara built an opera and ballet theatre on this church's foundations and a House of Industry with its stone, while the catacombs and tunnels under the church were converted into a wartime bunker for Stalin. The bunker is said to be open to visitors nowadays, though on our first visit no time remained and on our second the ship arrived too late for us to check.

There are many tensions in the recent history of this city. From being Samara, a county town of wheat and camels and horses, it became the industrial city of Kuibyshev in 1935. During the Civil War General Nikolai Kuibyshev led Samara's Bolshevik forces, fighting alongside Frunze and Chapaev. When the Reds, deployed along the Volga in 1918–19, wrested back Samara and Saratov, Simbirsk and Kazan they effectively won the war for the future Communist state, for they kept the Whites under Kolchak from joining Denikin's forces east of the Volga. Thus this city and many small places were renamed in Kuibyshev's honour, notwithstanding that Stalin soon had the man murdered. Closed to the world after the Second World War, the city Kuibyshev went on to produce rockets and aircraft, including the Tu-154, Russia's more than adequate answer to the Boeing 727. Electronic equipment, machine tools, bearings, building materials, clothes and processed foods, ultimately almost everything the Soviet Union needed to survive was made here.

As we approach I can hear one aspect of the tension by imagining a competition between Shostakovich and Wagner. I think of Shostakovich in part because he was among the artists evacuated to the wartime capital after the siege of Leningrad, in part because the music suits my metaphor. The bleak Seventh Symphony, finished here, received its premiere in Kuibyshev in spring 1942. I think of Wagner because the Monument to Glory recalls his grandiose world of heroes. The Monument is like the prow of a ship in steel or a Flying Dutchman of the air. I hear a conflict between ideal Soviet reality, represented by a totalitarian Wagner, and what really happened, represented by a skittishly suffering Shostakovich.

The captain barked orders I could never quite hear over the radio, guiding the *Komarno* towards the harbour wall and priming the sailor to spring ashore with the first rope. A dull thud and a moment's gentle impact against the rubber tyres of the wall beneath the river station, and we had docked. We moved our watches forward an hour from Moscow to Teheran time, since Samara lies on longitude 50°1'E, the same as Bahrain and Eil in Somalia, East Africa. The longitudinal comparison with Tver, on 35°E, and Moscow, on 36°E, shows how far we have already travelled. Then, spoons jammed in our wooden blinds, money strapped to our bodies, still in our shorts, because the heat was unremitting, we joined the queue at the gangplank to disembark. Russians don't queue well, and if you don't elbow your own way forward like everyone else you will be last to set foot on land. Nor will anyone admire your politeness and forbearance. Still, we weren't in a hurry. Had Alyosha been woken by banging on the captain's cabin door in the night? I enquired. But he hadn't, and as we shuffled over the spread dishcloths and deck mops crossed like swords to draw sand off the feet of returning passengers, so I put the incident, suddenly remembered, to the back of my mind.

The quay, paved and planted with conifers, was gay and colourful, with a trade show like an old-fashioned fair in progress. Under a small obelisk of ugly, rudely jointed concrete, and displaying a tribute to Lenin's kin with the words: 'In 1889 the Ulyanov family arrived in Samara', a stage had been erected as if for a life-size Punch and Judy show. A man and a woman appeared. He had a guitar and she, blonde, in a silver lamé coat and black mini-dress beneath, was singing a song, urging people to buy-buy-buy . . . sweaters, T-shirts . . . buy-buy-buy and make life better. Beside the stage stood the players' battered yellow bus, at least twenty years old mechanically and more in design. Quite a crowd had gathered, of men in jeans and T-shirts, and women in all variety of dresses and skirts. Prematurely old women, with traditional peasant headscarves knotted under the chin, screwed up their eyes from a mixture of sunshine and puzzlement and consternation. Whoever had money in Russia was not here.

This was a Monday, no special trading day, but beyond the stage, behind the river station, there stretched out for perhaps half a mile stalls, issuing from open car and lorry boots, selling all kinds of food and drink in tins, clothes, electrical and kitchen equipment. The spectacle was ugly, but the crowd compelling. We paid high Western prices for bottom-of-the-range Brazilian instant coffee, and found Russian *varenie*, the fruit-rich runny jam essential for eating with *kasha* and which the restaurant had stopped providing. Somewhere my ear or eye caught the Russian for Pepsi, the choice of the new generation. In 1847 the economist Haxthausen spoke of 'the unhappy spirit of imitation'. It makes me unhappy to see Russia being handed Western cast-offs: anything from worn-out advertising slogans to unsaleable fashion clothes sent in a job lot from a Spanish department store, something I would notice in Saratov. I want to pursue some notion I have of the 'real city'. But Alyosha's new to shopping. I have to take his arm to drag him away. 'Sorry,' he says, dutifully.

The natural ravines in Samara's limestone hills have been filled, unlike in Nizhny. Steep parallel roads lead up from the railinged embankment with its formal gardens. Viewed from the top down, these roads give Samara the quality of a wide-open, exotic resort, which indeed it was in Baedeker's day. Dacha owners did well renting their properties to foreign visitors. Trotsky, an intellectual, found this town outstandingly philistine: without a university, obsessed with money-making and devoid of aesthetic concerns. Perhaps he was too harsh, as intellectuals often are. In his day one of Samara's assets was cosmopolitanism. Before the Revolution the official figure for Germans living in the province was 3.5 per cent, lured with government subvention to farm the surrounding black soil lands. There were also Estonians and Ukrainians and as many Tartars as Germans and Ukrainians put together. A cynic might say that the German presence is why the beer, named Zhiguli and since declined to a watery proletarian brew, was so good in those days.

We climbed the slope closest to the river station, past a line of traditional traders. These fruit sellers, mostly kerchiefed older peasant women, stacked their tumblers of greengages and laid out their apples and tomatoes and watermelons in neat rows on the four-foot-high wall dividing two levels of the escarpment. Samara used to be famous for its fruit as well as its beer, though large-scale market gardening has always been hampered by the severe continental climate. Life by nature is well provided but not easy here.

I was considering vegetables for our lunch when I noticed a youngish woman with her head down on the stone wall. 'Overcome with her burdens?' I tugged at Alyosha's sleeve.

He laughed. 'She's drunk, that's all. You think people would show their grief in public? *Seichas pryamo!*'

I twitched, feeling reproached for being ready to imagine too much sadness. I can never muster enough sympathy for people close to me. It's much easier with strangers, easier still when it's inappropriate. With that muddle in my mind we arrived in the imposing rose-coloured main commercial and business square of Samara.

The statue in the middle used to be Alexander II. He did so much for Russia in liberating the serfs and defeating the Turks in the name of Pan-Slavism that there was no greater public hero before Communism, and he was particularly loved and commemorated in this town. But like liberators right up to Gorbachev, with the freedom Alexander brought his country he endangered himself. A violent populist who wanted to give the land to the peasants finally succeeded in assassinating him in 1881. Gorky remembered the cathedral bell in Nizhny tolling and the reaction of people around him: two days of whispering, long secret conversations, many visitors, then silence. The adults hid the newspapers from the thirteen-year-old boy who was told: 'You are not supposed to talk about such things.' Samara claims to have been grief-stricken, partly because its great church was still being built. Alexander remained a symbol. Through the Civil War when the Reds prevailed they boarded up his statue in this square, and when the Whites prevailed they removed the boards. Finally after the Revolution, as in other Soviet cities, Lenin took the Tsar-Liberator's position.

The Lenin statue in Samara, erected in 1925, a year after Vladimir Ilyich died, shows him every inch the proletarian official, in flat cap, and waistcoat and jacket over shirt and tie. The people's fashion for omitting the bourgeois tie had not yet arrived. His right hand is in his pocket, the thumb of the left is hooked in the waistcoat. 'It is a myth spread by Gorky,' said Alyosha, 'that Lenin often stood in the F-position.' This doesn't translate well into English. The Russian expression, meaning arms akimbo, describes a human being in the stance of the Greek letter *phi*, a vertical through a circle, and though it does suggest smugness, I can't turn this bumptious statue into more of an obscenity than it already is. But did I say there is something funny and faintly obscene about the name Kuibyshev? It sounds to Russians in a hurry like calling an English city Fluck Yew. Alexander Zinoviev showed in his novel *The Yawning Heights* how much the Soviet Union was a hilariously self-deflating place, especially when it didn't intend to be.

I wonder how long this statue will remain. In every Russian city Soviet monuments are currently under threat. But why not preserve this one, Samara, to commemorate the pomposity that ushered in a tragedy? This was proletarianism, and, in the name of the Party, it would virtually destroy the social fabric of Russia over the next seventy-five years, setting small-time worker-bureaucrats against peasants, disregarding their superior knowledge of their own affairs and as much depriving them of the land as under the tsars. The weapon would be collectivization.

As we crossed Lenin Square, now Alexeevsky Square, against the tide of people hurrying to work, it was a beautiful morning and good to be free to analyse Lenin. But we couldn't sustain the mood. Alyosha asked a man the number of Samara's inhabitants. One and a half million, came the answer, which a woman walking behind us picked up. 'One and a half million alcoholics, more like,' she muttered. Off the square a middle-aged man, in a pink nylon shirt and an evident drinker, waited outside a bank, where his pay should have arrived, but had not. Disgruntled and battered, when we prompted him he sounded off ferociously against the miseries of perestroika and Gorbach, a corruption of Gorbachev's name meaning hunchback. He was one of the few Russians I couldn't have understood without Alyosha. This worker said he wouldn't care if Samara reverted to being a closed city, if only the standard of life recovered. Gorbach and Yeltsin should be shot.

This conversation took place where Alexeevsky Square became Frunze Street, a place always busy with trams and trolley-buses and private traffic. It used to be called Dvoryanskaya after the word for gentry, and contains some of Samara's best older stone buildings. Outstanding is the *style moderne* Philharmonia Hall, formerly known as the Olympus Theatre, which once housed the circus. The adjacent pedestrian shopping street, which has reverted to its Ukrainian name, also for 'gentry', Panskaya, also has some potential grace. The flaking, crumbling, provincial classical buildings – all broken pediments, decorative plaster architraves, and pastel and white colouring – are mostly under reconstruction. Off one side of Panskaya a perfectly restored neo-Gothic bank marked a recovery of capitalist *temps perdu*. I never found out what happened to the old Stock Exchange.

They called Samara a Russian Chicago because, still small in 1850, it very quickly grew with the railway into a mighty provincial industrial city. From St Petersburg and Moscow the Trans-Siberian Railway crossed the Volga at Samara. The first major stop was the Bashkir capital, Ufa, and by 1917 the route was complete all the way to Vladivostok. Samara was also the beginning of the line south through Cossack Orenburg to Tashkent and Samarkand. The development of Volga shipping further demanded Samara's expansion.

Before Soviet times, prosperity depended on grain. From yields within the parallelogram formed with Kazan to the north and Ufa and Orenburg to the east, Samara, along with Ukraine, made Russia the world's biggest grain exporter by 1913. From all around Samara province, and neighbouring Orenburg province, peasants and gentry landowners, travelling by horse and cart, by sled and by camel, delivered winter wheat and rye, also oats, barley and millet. The grain was stored in some two hundred and fifty silos along the Volga and the Samara, and international spring sales followed. The most lucrative crop was premium durum wheat. Its exceptionally high protein content made it superior even to the products of southern Italy and elsewhere in the Mediterranean.

Grain brought wealth but also disaster. From Kazan to Samara and Saratov the Volga region was prey to famine, caused by excessively hot summers and insufficient rain. When the crop failed the poor suffered most, because they had insufficient land for their needs. Crisis years were 1874 and 1891, when the summer temperature in Samara hovered between 43 and 45°C (about 110°F). Famine meant typhus, dead cattle, dead children. In his story *Nikita's Childhood* Alexei Tolstoy remembered his mother standing at the window and weeping with relief when a rainstorm finally interrupted the broiling summer they experienced at their country home. In another early story he painted an opposite picture of careless plenty, with the very rooms in the house of a declining landowning family ankle-deep in grain. That was the extreme rhythm of Russian agricultural life, with terrible political consequences.

When Rozanov's steamer left Kazan in 1907 he was puzzled by men in rowing boats close to the ship, waving their arms and shouting, and never dreamed that they were starving. They begrudged the passengers the money spent on river cruises. 'Into the water with you!' they cried. Rozanov could only wonder at this cursing in a supposedly civilized Russia. He was born in 1866, only two years before Gorky, but his roots were entirely in the humanitarian nineteenth century, which is to say he was closer to the Russian Communitarian Alexander Herzen than to Lenin. By the time Rozanov died in 1919 self-elected representatives of the powerless had killed the Tsar and taken control of the state. Rozanov died of hunger and Russia was faced with the worst Volga famine in memory.

Harvests had been failing since 1917. Many Volga peasants supported the Bolsheviks in spring 1918, believing they would give them grain. Tensions grew up between peasant farmers wanting a return to the pre-war free market and the landless extreme poor who could not feed themselves. War requisitioning enforced by Bolshevik military food brigades tipped the balance when the crops failed again in 1920.

Arthur Ransome reported back to the *Manchester Guardian* on 11 October 1921 as today a correspondent might file from Ethiopia or Somalia:

> We went down to the shore of the Volga, past booths where you could buy bread, and not a hundred yards away found an old woman cooking horse-dung in a saucepan. Within sight of the market was a mass of refugees, with such belongings as they had retained in their flight from starvation, still starving, listlessly waiting for the wagons to move them away to more fortunate districts . . . I shall never forget the wizened dead face of a silently weeping girl, whose feet were simply bones over which was stretched dry skin that looked like blue-black leather. And she was one of hundreds . . . In the morning of the second day we called

at one of the 60 children's houses in Samara, so that Ercole could photograph the famine orphans. The plain courtyard was full of children, lying in the sun under the wall, ragged, half-naked, some with nothing on whatever but a shirt. . . .

Such a terrible blight has not hit the Volga again, yet under Communism it has never recovered its position as a world leader in grain exports. The problem has been collectivization diminishing individual incentive, coupled with an exaggerated stress on high yields. The Volga was famous for its hard wheat, but the emphasis on quantity – remember all those five-year plans, photographs of Stakhanovite workers, and heroic production figures in the Soviet media? – led to a preference for growing soft wheat. This was prey to fungus, had a far lower protein content and was worth less on the open market. Not only Soviet export potential but the quality of daily bread steadily fell, in taste, in appearance and in nutritional value. Meanwhile productivity did not rise. From 1913 to 1973 Russia went from being the most powerful world provider of grain to being a superpower in need. Instead of exporting 20 million surplus tons of grain it needed to import up to 60 million tons from the United States. Both Khrushchev and Brezhnev knew repairs to the agricultural system were required. For their successors it was too late. Meanwhile, the durum wheat which made Samara's reputation was almost extinct.

Trotsky was right in some respects. Late nineteenth-century Samara was dusty and dirty and smelt. Camels, traded at an annual market in September, added to the aesthetic discontents. Samara also dealt extensively in dead animals, earning fame for its lard and hides, and intensifying the certain foulness in the air. There were horse fairs, and the Bashkirs excelled as breeders. The town had a racecourse with a Moorish pavilion. Another course organized an annual showjumping competition at which hussars, Orenburg Cossacks, gypsies and Tartars competed. The new middle class amused itself with open-air skating to live music, skiing and tobogganing, cycling and tennis, a lending library and a theatre (where Gorky reviewed plays for the local newspaper). Trade generated money, and leisure became important. Samara was well advanced along the bourgeois road.

Yet a great mix of Volga peoples and settlers populated Samara, with diverse arrivals from further east by train. The social ambience was unpredictable. Lenin, who set up the first Marxist caucus here in the 1890s, made converts from among the unsettled immigrants: ethnic minorities, students on holiday, prisoners returning from Siberia, Old Believers, disgruntled Cossacks. Marx's group met on a bench in the Strukovsky Gardens, laying the foundations for the Socialist Revolutionary (SR) Party to establish itself in Samara in 1902. This was the same elegant spot where Baedeker recommended Western tourists to listen to the band of an evening. There were many colourful costumes about the streets, including those of the Bashkirs who wore faded quilted robes and long-eared caps. Perhaps it was also an exciting town.

Today along the Volga promenade stroll Tadzhik refugees from 1000km (600 miles) away in Dushanbe, showing off their brightly coloured national costumes and begging for money; and there is me, a mobile modern Western woman in a T-shirt and Reeboks; and there is my hybrid Russian friend in his American washed-silk shirt, which was probably made in China. Imagine how much more varied Samara was then!

The passion for sanatorium cures boosted the European presence here in the 1880s and 1890s. The staff in Samara's four decent hotels spoke French and German and English, and worshipped superior foreign ways. (The first infatuation of Alexei Tolstoy's heroine in The Road to Calvary was an Englishman on holiday in Samara.) Baedeker recommended two kumiss establishments where tuberculosis sufferers might live in isolated cottages two-thirds of a mile from the Volga and drink pints of faintly intoxicating 'milk wine' – anything from two to five bottles a day. The fermentation of mare's milk produced lactic acid and carbonic acid, both of which eased digestion, and 1–3 per cent alcohol, which eased the tedium of waiting for health. Leo Tolstoy and Gorky were among the takers.

The naturally kumiss-drinking Bashkirs thus brought Samara sophistication and added to its prosperity. Leo Tolstoy, though, suspicious of sophistication, insisted on visiting them on the steppe,

116

only passing through Samara *en route*. He liked the healthy, open-air ways he found among this people from east of the middle Volga. They seemed to have more vitality than the jaded Russian nobility and, part-Christian, part-Moslem, they courteously shared his interest in discussing God, Christ and Mohammed.

The Tolstoy who really belongs to Samara, however, is Alexei Nikolaevich, only a very distant relative of Leo. We entered a weed-filled yard where several wooden buildings showed signs of recent carpentry. A woman in her thirties, with a postgraduate degree in Alexei Tolstoy and very conscious of her official role, led us through what until 1983 had been a small block of Communist communal apartments, apparently without indoor facilities. We were the Tolstoy Museum's only visitors and at first the combined power of the postcard and ticket seller, the cleaner and the guide, all sitting idle, would not admit us because we were fewer than ten. 'How much is it then for ten?' asked my Russian friend. Came the answer: 250 roubles, by current rates all of 25 US cents. So we bought tickets for a complete phantom delegation.

There were photographs in books under glass and on the walls. Alexei Nikolaevich, born in 1882, looked thick-set and plump, with faintly puffy eyes, sagging cheeks and dark hair. He was a sensualist, who liked women and food and drink. It is always good to know there are a few around. Just as in his written style, so probably in his personality there was something markedly soft and feminine. The face in a 1925 snapshot of him wearing a boater suggests Tartar origins through the Turgenevs of Simbirsk, something that the genealogists have mooted but never proven.

The house was full of beautiful objects, of the kind seldom seen in present-day Russia. Most families long ago pawned their heirlooms if they were not looted by the revolutionary proletariat. Only chance secured them in official cupboards. Perhaps because Tolstoy accommodated himself to the Communist regime and Stalin he was lucky. The furniture here was mahogany, ebony and that Russian preference, Karelian birch, a pale, mottled timber like a cross between walnut and bamboo. There were French novels, parasols, Turgenev family porcelain, a Singer sewing machine and a Remington typewriter. On the desk in the stepfather's study stood a fine black abacus and an ink-pot with the labelled face of Gutenberg.

One woman's memory helped decorate the apartment in its original style in the nick of time. She was the last family governess, who died in 1992.

Tolstoy went to Petersburg on the wings of his early success with the Volga stories, which described that non-intellectual life made up of horses, trading, grain, country living, quirky relationships between masters and servants, sexual looseness, superstition, overwhelming summer heat and famine. At the outbreak of hostilities in 1914 he became a war correspondent for a liberal Samara paper. In time the Bolsheviks seized the Samara house, and Tolstoy fled with his wife to France in 1919; but after a meeting with Gorky in 1922 he returned. How interesting, dramatically, that meeting must have been, with both exiles ambivalently longing for the motherland!

Count Tolstoy, as he was, wrote historical novels, about Ivan the Terrible, about Peter the Great, which kept him in touch with his roots and made him politically acceptable. *The Road to Calvary*, covering that great sweep of history by which Russia passed from being the land of Leo Tolstoy to the land of Lenin, won him the Stalin literature prize before he died in 1945, infamous for his collaboration. Like Gorky, Alexei Tolstoy made his pact with the world he knew, though that world had gone over to the devil. The way the Civil War divided and wrecked Russia was his most profound personal experience, and he showed how appallingly Samara suffered. The Volga was chock-full with bodies. Human flesh and mortars flew through the air. Women wielding parasols beat to death any unprotected wounded enemy they found on the embankment.

In 1936 he came back to see his old house in Kuibyshev. His granddaughter is the contemporary writer Tatyana Tolstaya, who herself now lives mainly abroad.

Lenin and Alexei Tolstoy were never aware of each other in Samara. Lenin, a generation older, came in 1889 to live in the nearby countryside with his mother and siblings and elder sister's husband. As a political agitator, arrest would have awaited him in Kazan. His mother sold up and, with the new son-in-law, bought a large property with land 30km (20 miles) from Samara. Part of her wished to turn Volodya into a farmer to keep him out of political trouble. But he couldn't get on with the peasants, not being one of their kind. He spent his summers on the farm studying and improving his physical strength on a set of parallel bars in the garden. After taking an external law degree at St Petersburg (the authorities would not allow him to attend any university in person) he worked as an advocate in Samara until 1893, when Alexei Tolstoy would have been eleven. He translated Marx's *Manifesto of the Communist Party* and studied *Das Kapital*. His clients were petty downtrodden criminals and he lost every court case he undertook. But the famine of 1891 sharpened his revolutionary's sense of how to mobilize the masses. If they were hungry, so much the better.

Something about the Volga dispossessed nonplusses me, all the more so as a large unpredictable element makes politics dangerous Russia-wide today. The Volga downtrodden could in theory have been recruited to any cause that paid, as were the *burlaki* and the Cossacks. In the age of Ivan the Terrible a Central Volga pirate called Yermak was persuaded to change sides and fight for the Russian state in subduing sixteenth-century Siberia. In another chapter of Volga history the merchants who paid the *burlaki* to drag their ships could never be sure they would not side with the pirates, so just before Zhiguli they fed them well and paid them extra. Everywhere from Kazan to Astrakhan, it seems, the Bolshevik Revolution was able to exploit such opportunism, born of lack of belonging.

Yet no one could predict what would happen here in the Civil War. Alexei Tolstoy showed families split and characters unsure of which side to join, just as did Sholokhov in his Civil War portrait of the Don. Meanwhile, Samara was of such strategic importance that it was bound to see terrible bloodshed.

The intensity of peasant desire to control the land, plus good political organization, ensured that Lenin's SRs assumed power in 1917. But when Bolshevik state dictatorship loomed, Samara declined central allegiance. Instead there came into being the anti-Bolshevik Samara government of 1918, supported by the Whites. Fighting ensued on the Volga in earnest. Samara fell in October, but local anti-Bolshevik uprisings continued. Roaming marauders terrorized those Bolshevik food procurement detachments whose work helped induce famine. Not until 1921 did a kind of peace descend.

On the way back to the ship we passed another statue, another tribute to classical heroism – this time to Chapaev. It showed soldiers in action, with bayonets mounted, rifles loaded, led by a mounted Cossack brandishing a cutlass. Soviet Russia espoused the aesthetic splendour of the warrior kind, a Greek ethic of glory, though let's pause for one more thought about 'flexibility' here. Russia destroyed the independence of the Cossack clan of fighters to establish its own warrior ideal. Authorities say real Cossacks no longer exist. Soviet Russia also destroyed millions of its own people; and decades of its history. No wonder its cities seem disjointed and uprooted.

14

Is the Englishwoman Prim?

L UNCH IMPROVED after we bought tomatoes and peppers and apples and plums in Samara. To double portions of buckwheat, millet, rice, pasta or boiled potatoes we added jam at breakfast and vegetables, oil and cheese at lunch and dinner. The dining room lent us a bowl. Almost everyone else was bringing in vegetables and fruit too. The wife of the reader of the pre-revolutionary encyclopedia prepared for every meal a feast of glistening tomatoes and cucumbers. Over-compensating, we began to feel very well in our skin, though meals were now more like picnics.

We passed Samara's limestone caves. These were believed to be haunted, and attracted many stories of mysterious disappearances, deaths, suicides and sightings of a strange boy with red hair. The boy was originally one of two local schoolboy brothers who, having whetted their taste for adventure by reading *Tom Sawyer* and the English fabulist Mayne Reid about the Mississippi, decided to explore the caves at Red Glinka and were never the same again. One died insane, the other became a ghost. The spectral cold surrounding the spot is still blamed in this highly superstitious country when tourist bonfires won't light. Just after the last war the Interior Ministry intelligence service, then called the NKVD, predecessor of the KGB, became worried that enemies of the people were hiding in the caves and posted a round-the-clock guard. The caves were filled with loose rocks to put an end to uncertainty in a certain socialist world.

After our exit from the Samara Bow I went up on deck. The left bank, prelude to the steppe, was monotonous, with flat sand and a thin line of trees, but the right was changeable and animated. Rather humble, shed-like dachas punctuated scorched, close-cropped shallow hills, and here and there a small town reached back up the broad valley. There is a rhythm in this landscape from the Ice Age, and also a sense that life has barely changed for centuries save for the arrival of the odd minor manufacturing plant. The dramatic low-level undulations and plateaus to the water's edge offer grazing to a few chestnut cattle. Mostly this is sanatorium country, with its centre in the town of Khvalynsk. When it was founded two hundred years ago this place became another mecca for Old Believers. Behind, extending south and west, the land generally forms a vast low table of between 180 and 270 metres in height (600–900 ft), separating the Volga from the Don. That river, a little over half its length but the most loved in Russian literature after the Volga, descends from central Russia to the sea of Azov and through to the Black Sea. A line drawn across to it from the Volga at Khvalynsk would form the base of an inverted triangle. The two rivers slowly converge to meet in Volgograd, another 615km (400 miles) downstream.

At the time I wasn't sure where we were. The captain, a man in his late forties, appeared at the rail; I asked him, and he came and treated me to his arm. His breath suggested a big drinker. He had rough hands and a sagging waistband on his tracksuit bottoms, and evidently he couldn't get to sleep that broiling afternoon. *'Kayuta nomer? Nummer Kabine? Number? No Alexei. Alexei good boy. But no Alexei.'* Offered a cheap necklet of particles broken off my beloved Russian and German and English languages, I thought of the forfeit that passengers once paid to pirates on leaving the Zhiguli gorge. Then Captain Krainev, twenty-eight years on the river, and pictured in better shape in the official photograph on the main deck, not too old for me but far too unappetizing, looked down at my hands on the rail and saw that they had formed two clenched fists. He was shocked. He said so. I was, too. He left abruptly.

Alyosha laughed. We applied coconut oil to each other's backs and lay side by side on the wooden benches on the sundeck which he had reserved with a towel before his afternoon nap. 'For every five women he asks one will say yes, of course.'

'Maybe.' I recalled yesterday's night-time banging on Krainev's door.

Alyosha went on: 'Sex could be very simple if one wanted it to be.' ('Sex' is a very funny-sounding hybrid word in Russian.)

'It helps to like the chap, that's all. Old brute.'

We lay reflectively soaking up the sun. At length Alyosha muttered: 'I want to get brown like you. And I don't want to hear again that you went to Greece. You know a place like Greece is an impossible dream for us.'

The left bank continued low, broken and rather wild, with many sandy clumps and bosky islands. Black dead tree stumps poked up from the surface of the water like a network of traps for the unwary. Before the Volga was widened they constituted frequent hazards to shipping. We had 429km (270 miles) to traverse from Samara to Saratov, most of it steppe to the east, with the river following a relatively narrow course.

There was something comforting about Alyosha and me enjoying our separate dreams side by side. He'd written a poem saying he was missing someone. I saw it on his table.

On Tuesday, 16 August we woke up on what seemed like a desert island: a Robinson Crusoe asylum, without philosophy, without sex. The ship had a scheduled Green Stop – a chance to enjoy the countryside – at 7.30am. An infinitely sandy beach hemmed by trees stretched up- and downstream. Tipping ourselves out of bed, we swam with gusto, and from the inevitable beach-sellers bought some sourish late-season cherries and more apples. Pre-breakfast some of our travelling companions were already gnawing at piscean skeletons with golden smoked flesh. The bream here was nicely displayed, with a garnish of parsley.

I ran barefoot along the shoreline. We had twenty minutes left, so ten minutes out and ten minutes back. Magpies dominated the trees, small silvery-white finches flitted across the sand. Sunflowers lauded it over a too serious world and their slight roots made them easily portable. The boat was out of sight, and other beach enthusiasts were long past, when I saw Man Friday footprints in the sand. A dark youth in swimming trunks appeared out of the trees to tend one of many fishing lines with invisible owners. Now I could see the roof of a tent. 'Hi! What's the fish?' I asked.

He screwed up his face, unwilling to smile: 'Pike-perch, *bakleishka*, bream . . . and who are you? Where do you come from?'

'London.' I arrived back at the gangplank with minutes to spare, clutching the sunflowers, feeling I had been somewhere secret and achieved something.

Our programme ahead was physically undemanding though Alyosha might find it emotionally so: we had barely two hours to spend in his home town of Saratov before sailing on to Volgograd. Since we intended to spend several days in Saratov on our return there was no pressure to sightsee, and multitudinous human intercourse took over. My companion was on deck as we approached, waving excitedly at his wife Yelena in a black and white and gold trouser outfit, carrying a bunch of dark red roses, his thirteen-year-old rake-thin blonde daughter Ala in eye-catching purple, and his suntanned parents. Yelena with her fluent English worked for the Peace Corps of America which was helping to set up small businesses across Russia. Ala was fast catching up with her mother's English skills and knew every Russian pop group and Swedish and British ones too. Alyosha, burdened with messages, rushed ahead to the *Volga* editorial office, stricken at being briefly dropped back into work in the middle of a holiday. The rest of us strolled along the embankment.

Saratov immediately resembled Samara in being well appointed along the river, with flowers and benches, tiered promenades and clean flagstones. Alyosha's parents looked well and prosperous. They would have reminded me of the American pensioners on the *Chernyshevsky*, had they not been more restrained and discreet. 'You've been to Russia before, so you know what's what,' smiled his father, who held the Order of the Friendship of Peoples, the equivalent of a British MBE, for his work in agriculture. His mother was a well-presented woman with a gold tooth and a good figure. Marx was wrong about the proletariat. It's the class that owns its own home and cares for a family and strives to stay in employment which has common economic interests worldwide. The middle class is united. Alyosha's parents were just like mine.

At the *Volga* office the parents melted away. *Volga* is one of the thick journals like *Novy Mir*. Since democracy it has happily dedicated itself almost entirely to literature, plus an interesting archive of materials concerning the Volga. On the literary side its reputation stands high. It first published Shalamov's *Siberian Tales* and part of Solzhenitsyn's *Gulag Archipelago*. Among its published translations into Russian have been Alexandre Dumas' travels on the Volga and, now that it is free of censorship, Henry Miller. At the bare, dark office where this work proceeded we walked into a feast. For eleven of us the women – of course – had laid tables end to end. Plate after plate of fresh-looking salami and pliable yellow ('Dutch') sliced cheese, black and white bread, pickled cucumbers, pyramids of fragrant apples and bowls of giant beef tomatoes were offered up to the twin gods of Russian social life, hospitality and adversity. Even if people starved for days in secret, the social table would still groan. There was beer and vodka, fake Amaretto and cola. The occasion was the birthday of the editor's secretary Valentina Ivanovna, handsome in a red and black dress, with dark hair and a suntan brought back, along with this fruit, from her dacha. Our arrival coincided with hers at some middling age. The scene reminded me of the set for Chekhov's play *The Wedding*.

The vodka was from Germany – since the demise of the Union no one trusted familiar labels and there was no consumer protection against the fake and dilute products which plagued a money-hungry young market. Not because it was bad, but because it was 40 per cent proof, one tablespoon of this liquid nation-killer (Bear Vodka!) clamped the back of my neck and made my hands shake. It was too early in the day and we hadn't been eating enough. I swallowed as many counteractive cucumbers as I could, realizing I had to speak. An attentive, encouraging, listening silence came over the table.

There were three writers, a translator and university teacher, three secretaries, and a young woman critic all behaving well before the editor. All addressed him, and the bosses addressed their secretaries, politely with first name and patronymic. The editor, also a writer of fiction and literary criticism and called Sergei Borovikov, seemed a kind, suffering man. Boyish-faced, he had made it his human mission to be jolly. My fellow guests leaned over encouragingly and would have spoken my words for me if they could, and in any case quickly took them over. 'We notice you like

Valentina Ivanovna's cucumbers.' 'So you are writing about our Volga – I think *I* should write a book about the reever Tyems.' 'Have some more cucumber! Valentina Ivanovna made them herself. She has everything in her garden. Eat! Eat!' 'I know nothing about London except there is a lot of fog.' 'I am translating Lawrence Durrell. I do not have so much practice in speaking. But I would like to talk with you.' 'Don't you have cucumbers in England?' 'England is just a small country, I think, but it has everything.'

'Yes,' I finally gasped, like Chekhov's wedding guest from Greece speaking of his own country. 'Yes, in England we have everything.'

An English writer addressing herself to the river Volga seems plausible enough. The river is an established cultural entity. Yet she is so far from home, so exotic in a city that was closed until recently. 'Does anyone know of Russian writers visiting Britain, to compare?' I cried. No one did. The British are a faraway people for the Russians, more so than the Russians are to us. They are more curious about America. But they do have a view of us as emotionally distant, over-controlled, given to diplomatic dissembling and unkindness to children. Our society is deeply influenced by tradition, they believe, not realizing how much has crumbled away in the last thirty years.

Alexei Tolstoy reported in 1916 that individual emotion, inspiration and virtue in Britain were invariably suppressed for the general good. Except that even then, apparently, we no longer knew what that good was or why we should uphold it. Also we had a very simplistic notion of Russia. Evgeny Zamyatin, in the north of England a year later, also found a life-draining, mechanical society. He encountered middle and upper classes desperate to paper over any crack in the fabric of a smooth life. Ivan Goncharov, author of the man-in-the-dressing-gown novel much liked in England, *Oblomov*, said back in 1853 that we had nice houses and shops, but everything was too clean and orderly, and the streets too quiet and the people too private. By the same token virtue, inspiration and goodness were never allowed to shine with a bright individual light, having long been drafted into the general timetable of the ordinary day. Yet Russians do feel drawn to England, and particularly in the Soviet period they were fascinated by a country where the past is pre-eminent. They loved *The Forsyte Saga* on television and remain Dickens readers.

I offer these thoughts because they are the framework in which Russians will judge my Volga enterprise. I think they realize we come to Russia because the emotional life is more intense and palpable than at home; that we see them, as they see themselves, as a suffering people also addicted to suffering. I'm not sure the emotional life is more intense, but certainly the show of it is. What really grips me is the way ideas have wrought such havoc with reality. In that way, yes, I am fascinated by a country where tradition carries so little weight.

On the lighter side, Russian stereotypes for Englishwomen include being tall, prim and ugly. I'm neither tall nor particularly ugly, but I may be prim, prepared to be the essential maenad I am only in the right company. One thing here: I can't get even mildly drunk because that way I would lose my ability to speak. I'm on duty, wanting to communicate. I'm often like that elsewhere, too. That dedication to alert consciousness does tend towards the prim – though not in the mind, believe me.

15

Stenka Razin, Progress and a Dying River

WE WERE BACK on the *Komarno*. Alyosha cried: 'Why didn't they bring the dog? I miss the dog.' The dog? Alyosha, you sound like me losing my rag over domestic details at home, fussing over the shopping list. Today's brief call at his home town had upset our smooth working relationship. I thought we might have a row. Still, I remembered in time how grateful I was to my literary sherpa. He was – unlike me – almost English in his undemonstrativeness, also buoyant, funny, persistent and perceptive. I left him for the afternoon to mull over his home thoughts.

After Saratov the Volga was memorable. Four and a half hours out, at Zolotoe on the right bank were strange rocks which reminded the Russian pre-revolutionary travellers Lepeshinskaya and Dobrynin of cottage loaves. Beyond another small village called Bannovka, a sheer, crumbling cliff half covered in vegetation and riven with gullies bore the name Stenka Razin. Here, according to legend, the Don Cossack pirate would sit and watch the tall ships go by. If, when he waved his white handkerchief, the sailors did not halt, then with much shrieking and whistling twelve boatloads of young men would climb on board and the merchant could say goodbye to his wares and his head. Stenka's cave, the ravine where he kept his prisoners, his 'table', his 'chair' – all these were named places in the surrounding rock beside the river.

The Stenka rock was less impressive than the history of a class warrior two centuries before Marx. Stenka, who claimed to retain his Cossack loyalty to the tsar, but to hate tsarist officials and landowners and their defenders, claimed, like Lenin, the support of serfs and peasants from all over Russia, exiles from officialdom such as Old Believers, and the Moslem minorities. Whenever he captured a merchant ship, or later a town, he would say to his victims: 'You are free. Go where you wish. I won't force you to stay with me, but whoever wishes to may do so and become a free Cossack. I have come to fight the boyars and the rich landlords, but with the poor and humble I am prepared to share everything.' There is a foolish legend that Stenka is not dead, but waiting to reappear when his hour comes.

The beginnings of Stenka's story encapsulate the fate of the Cossacks in the seventeeth century. The Cossacks were not a people bound by blood or land, but an order held together by a chosen badge of identity sworn upon military oath. Their ancestors had been steppe nomads, with their most distant history in Mongol Central Asia; they were distant, left-behind sons of the Golden Horde, or they were Tartars, Turks, Finns, Little Russians, Great Russians, Mordvins, Lithuanians, who came into the pay of the Russian government as fighters because only Tartar could subdue Tartar; Russian forces alone could not. Thence came Cossack 'loyalty' to the tsar, and in the Revolution and the Civil War it was mortally splintered, as Sholokhov showed in the third and fourth books of *Quiet Flows the Don*.

We think of Cossacks as belonging to the Don, but they also settled or were moved beside the Caspian, along the Lower Volga, in the Caucasus, beside the Yaik and Terek rivers, and in Siberia and Mongolia. In Siberia they represented the last traces of Russia's conquest of that region, led by Yermak. Wherever they went the Cossacks took from their new home the name of their 'host', the military body that was their collective identity, and they welcomed newcomers accepting their code. The Don Cossacks, however, of whom Stenka was one, received in the mid-seventeenth century a new influx far too large to contain economically. A new Russian law on serfdom in 1649, entailing the death penalty for desertion, caused thousands to flee to the Don.

Stepan Timofeevich Razin took advantage of the new swell of men. Incensed that tsarist forces had earlier killed his father for disobeying Moscow orders, in 1667 he recruited hundreds into a pirate army. A year later, a large number of Cossacks having joined him in search of booty, he had three thousand men. Moving from the Don to the Lower Volga (where many victims of his pirate sallies also joined his army) he attacked Persia from the Caspian, murdering and plundering on a vast scale. He returned to the Don with heavy losses but a grand reputation and much booty. Meanwhile refugees from serfdom still streamed in. To support themselves in such large numbers Stenka's men began a new round of adventures. Their banner cause was social justice, its sincerity doubtful.

Tsaritsyn's poor opened their town's gates in April 1670, and Razin's men slaughtered the officers and merchants. Following the same bloody pattern Stenka took Kamyshin, Cherny Yar and Astrakhan, which became his temporary court. Then, supported by one pretending to be the recently deceased Tsarevich Alexei, he resumed the Volga trail, aiming ultimately for Moscow. From the countryside, now in open revolt – Soviet historians called it the Peasants' War of 1667–71 – up to two hundred thousand men joined Stenka Razin. They took Saratov and Samara, but were driven back by the Russian army at Simbirsk. Like Pugachev a hundred years later, having retreated, Stenka was opportunistically handed over by fellow Cossacks to meet his end.

Tsar Alexei Mikhailovich had Stenka quartered on Red Square in June 1671, an ignominy that was bound to enhance his subsequent reputation. After his death he became a Robin Hood figure – or, to Alexandre Dumas, Fra Diavolo – charged with mythical good deeds and just powers. His rhetoric lodged in the minds of Russians, who love charismatic popular heroes. One of many folk songs in which Stenka features, 'Stenka Razin's Cliff', ends like this:

Now that cliff stands
Preserving the secret thoughts of Stepan
And now and again shares its memory only with the Volga
    of the brave life of the ataman.
But if there is in Russia a man somewhere who has had no
    truck with profit
Who has not lived dishonestly nor oppressed the poor

Who has loved freedom like his dear mother
And acted in its name
Then let him go boldly, let him approach that cliff
And put to it his deftly tuned ear
And the cliff-giant will pass on to this bold fellow all the
    thoughts of Stepan.

Two hundred and fifty years after Stenka's death he was as important to the early Russian film industry as Ivan the Terrible or Boris Godunov or Pugachev. In 1928 the director Viktor Tuzhansky, exiled in Czechoslovakia, made a silent classic called *Volga Volga*. Stenka, worshipped as a father by the peasants, was shown Christ-like. As portrayed by Hans Schlottov he was tender, severe and restrained; physically very strong and imposing. A Dutch sea captain, Jan Straus, who sailed the Volga in the warship *Orel* and reached the Caspian at the time of Stenka's raids in 1669, left a similar description of the real man. In Tuzhansky's film, a modest intensification of an extraordinary reality, Stenka gave his love to a woman and a child, was the victim of treachery among his own men, and appeared to die crucified on his ship's mast when Russian troops attacked. The marvellous crowd scenes, with their mingling of Kalmyk Orientals, round-faced Russians and Cossack tonsures, and the entrancing, exotic Volga scenery of tall ships, windmills and fabulous Eastern palaces on the Caspian, radiate the seductiveness of the Stenka legend.

Gorky in the 1920s also tried to write a film about Stenka Razin, actively drawing the parallel with Lenin. Interesting that both heroes had been moved by an execution in the family: Stenka his father's, Lenin that of his elder brother. But Gorky's idea failed owing to the extreme, contradictory, hard-living character of the earlier leader. For Stenka was both abstemious and abandoned, devoted and open to temptation, whereas Lenin was cool, calculating and ascetic. Stepan Timofeevich murdered the woman he loved, according to Tuzhansky's film and to another famous Razin ballad, 'There Is a Cliff on the Volga Overgrown with Wild Moss'. For taking a woman into his fighting life, against the Cossack military code, his men challenged their ataman. Obedient, he abandoned his captive Persian princess to the depths of the Volga. Stenka's inner world may well have been like Dostoevsky's in *The Idiot* and *The Devils*. It was certainly not that of Lenin, nor of Nikolai Ostrovsky.

As the Volga and the Don drew closer to each other, the bare rock was pale and close-ribbed like the bones of a skate. At Shcherbakovka the sheer drama of that ancient structure took over. The denuded cliff was fabulous for 10km (6 miles), like a huge, flat-topped table with its side to the Volga in high relief. The ship slowed for passengers to observe all the details of those rocks which contain fossils from the Tertiary Period up to 190 million years ago. Their formation began an aeon before the Ice Age, and from them geologists named an era after the Volga.

The almost sheer stone falls in pleats into today's smooth, bluish water. The late afternoon sun highlights the crest of each fold, gradually moving up the white rock curtain and leaving the water an ever darker mirror. The local name for the range is the Columns. That does not capture their strange animation. Occasionally separate figures break away from the formation to suggest pillars and towers. But mostly these are serried ranks, rows of *bogatyr* heroes now standing as if with bedouin head-dresses, now sitting tightly pressed together, knees folded in a perfect line. Nature has become heroic sculpture and is narrating a mass fate. The sea which once lapped here has vanished, leaving behind the vast sandstone tombs of a lost civilization, studded with quartz. Or it has provided a prehistoric model for a hydroelectric dam.

The ancient rocks continue less steep, more varied, sometimes covered with sparse vegetation, for 60km (35 miles). Among them the Urakov mountain, descending in three distinct tiers, marks the spot where Batu's Golden Horde first crossed the Volga from the East to yoke the Russian principalities to the legacy of Genghis Khan. Named after a pirate predecessor of Stepan Razin, it is close to Kamyshin. That is where the great rock epic abruptly ends. The Volga reaches the Caspian Depression, the vast dry bed of that former inland sea of which today's Caspian and these cliffs are the remains. At Kamyshin an English naval officer called John Perry, in the pay of Peter the Great, first measured the flow of the Volga in 1700. Salt encrusts the soil round about.

After Kamyshin we passed Dubovka, which may well have been a town where the Bolgars once lived. The Don and the Volga enclose a narrow fertile strip with its north end at Dubovka and its southern tip, formerly marked by a small natural river, now the beginning of the Volga–Don canal south of Volgograd. Before first the railway, then the canal, supplied the cross-route for transferring goods from one river to the other, Dubovka was the reloading point. In the mid-eighteenth century Cossacks were deployed there to guard the Lower Volga, and took the name Volga Cossacks, but when they went over completely to their nominal enemy, fellow Cossack Pugachev, they were transferred to the upper Terek river and other settlers introduced. Early this century Dubovka, with its churches and picturesque wooden houses, its flowers and fruit, made a scenic short stop on the steamer route. A unique speciality then was oleander, which the women sold on the quay. These days Dubovka is famous for its watermelon, which the Russians salt for eating as a delicacy beyond its season.

With the sun allowing us the grace of an open-air life we took a clean warm shower on deck. Dinner, as usual, wasn't much of an occasion. We had to mark out the football coupon for tomorrow's food while eating today's, and the whole meeting at the trough was over in fifteen minutes. The father and son alongside us routinely ate with the same physical attitude as others would dig a hole in the ground. Alyosha warned: 'Leave it. If they don't want to talk, don't try. You won't change anything.' Russians agree that public civility has been a prime casualty of Bolshevism. I drank the Spanish wine with excessive moderation, flaunting the bringing of the bottle in and out of the dining room. Moderation, I hoped Russians would see, was a better solution than fake temperance.

After dinner we were still digesting aspects of our flying visit to Saratov. Yelena had explained local entrepreneurs' hostility to American business advice in the new Russia. 'Just give us the money, we know what to do with it,' they would say, apparently unaware that no Western entrepreneur would be so easily convinced by their patriotic pigheadedness. From the hostility of the Cold War a good percentage of Russians had moved to thinking that the West should simply hand over its money to them, as if they were victims of a disaster not of their own making. A few remained proud. On the other side Yelena mentally divided her foreign employers into those who genuinely wanted to help post-Communist Russia, and those who had come for personal financial gain. I thought how galling it must be to live in a country where all outsiders seem to be either charity workers or profiteers. (I speak, of course, as a spiritual profiteer.)

Alyosha seems to me a little condescending about his wife and whether she can hold down an important job. I don't know whether she minds, because this is pre-feminist Russia and relationships have a different basis from what educated and economically independent Western women require. Women are expected to appear passive and inferior, and there's something wrong with them if they don't conform. Even my admired Slava, just before his departure at Volgograd, suddenly asked: 'Why aren't you married? Don't you love anyone?'

There were moments when I felt so lonely being a woman in Russia. In some of the big cities Western women involved with Russian men have formed support groups. They regard themselves as a deprived section of the community. Actually, men and women so need each other in order to survive in Russia that there can't be a sexual revolution. So women continue dressing for men, wearing non-functional clothes despite the dusty, pot-holed, unmade-up streets, and generally mask their appetites and subordinate their careers, while we Westerners stride in working men's boots along streets paved with velvet.

Russia after Communist prudishness and hypocrisy is nevertheless experiencing a sudden liberation, like the 1960s in the West. Playwrights like to get their characters into bed and have them use four-letter words. Thirty years of social revolution compressed into an instant has led commentators to use the expression 'wild' about the cultural atmosphere. The contraceptive pill would become widespread if only it could be widely obtained.

Yet much of Russian life is still susceptible to muddle-headed folk wisdom: everything from overwrapping children and constantly fussing about the cold to believing that both Stenka Razin and Yury Gagarin, the first man in space, are still alive. The sheer foolishness is depressing.

Russia also brings its pathos even to permissiveness. Alyosha has something to say about *The Joy of Sex*, Alex Comfort's 1972 classic which sells, with a couple of outdated Western flower children on the cover, on every post-Communist bookstall from Kazan to Samara. *'Russkii seks? Seichas pryamo!* A Russian woman will just smile to herself when she reads *The Joy of Sex*. Where should she get the food, and the wine, and the lighting, and the music, and the room, and the privacy and then finally the time and the energy, having spent a week procuring the material setting? Thanks, Alex, for the thought, but this wham-bam country is short of all luxuries, and dedicated to the Joy of Nothing.' We smiled rather weakly at each other as Alyosha told this story.

Alyosha felt both proud and mournful about Russian women compared with those from the West whom he had met. 'They deserve your understanding if they over-dress and over-makeup. For years they have had nothing. Now they want to try everything. You may have noticed – though how can I say this to you – we have the most beautiful women in Saratov. If they wear evening clothes in the day that is because they only have two outfits in their wardrobe. You must understand.'

'I do. Of course.'

Actually, in awe of beautiful women anywhere, I had not wanted for objects of passing admiration this trip, though most had been young. But I let Alyosha's tenderness remind me of Gautier. The Frenchman was describing the third-class passengers on his trip from Tver to Nizhny: 'The women were hardly pretty, but their gentle and resigned ugliness had about it nothing disagreeable. Their vague smile allowed fine teeth to show and their eyes, although slightly restrained, did not lack expression.' Then he noticed the women sellers on the quay 'dressed in skirts up to their armpits. It is easy to imagine the hardly gracious effects of this constant depression which finally fatigues the firmest of contours.' To write about women like this you have to love them.

I like the Russian attitude to things: things which are precious because so rare, things which are infinitely susceptible to mending. While ours is a consumer society, theirs has been a repair economy through most people's living memory. Alyosha bought Yelena a cherishable Harley Davidson T-shirt. She was on a business trip for the Peace Corps when it was stolen, along with her money. To get home she had to pawn her antique earrings, another gift from her husband. It was a small recent family disaster, big enough for him to want to tell me.

But all these things, the contemplation of which enriches Western life, and reminds it of its excesses, alas help determine Russian despair. Tonight Alyosha, who, the last time he drank, drank the warehouse, tells me whom he has promised not to drink for three years. He has promised himself. He has promised death. He has had that possibility sewn up inside him in the form of a drug, rarely used in the West, which has a potentially lethal reaction with alcohol. If he drinks he plays *Russky avos*, Russian roulette.

Social backwardness, superstition, and every variety of spiritual, material and physical deprivation: is this what we are supposed to admire about Russia, and what they admire as 'national' about themselves? As a matter of fact I think Russia will lose quickest of all this addiction to nationality now it is free. There is no people – a nineteenth-century idea, if ever there was one; there are only people. One thought, then: will the Volga become less of a Russian sacred river? Probably. There is a case for national psychoanalysis, which might take the form of dragging this 'poetic' river.

One of Russia's most famous contemporary rock stars, Boris Grebenshchikov, has gone some way in this direction. Alyosha sang me Grebenshchikov's hit about a dying river – and a sick country – as he told me the tale of alcoholism and its cures.

> From a long way off the river flows
> About three more years remain to live
> In black embrace all round she dies
> And you say nothing
> There on the mountain behold three aspens
> There a half-idiot walks
> He chews a rotten orange
> And spits out the peel on the path ahead.

The river could be the Volga and Grebenshchikov asks the question: why has Russia poisoned itself? It is, of course, not primarily meant as a question of ecology.

Ecologically, though, the Volga *has* become 'another body'. The river no longer cleans itself. Moreover, more than a third of its hundred and fifty thousand tributaries have disappeared, with many of the rest overgrown and dirty. Chemical substances collect visibly. Rubbish sticks to the bottom of the reservoirs. In the reservoirs of Rybinsk, Samara and Volgograd the fish population has decreased 70 per cent, infected by tapeworm and other intestinal parasites. The figure hovers betwen 80 and 100 per cent destruction around Nizhny. The bream cannot swim in deep water; they hug the shore 'as if seeking human help', says a 1989 exposé called *The Pain and Misfortune of Russia*. The slow water flow encourages disease to spread. Pike, pike-perch and sterlet have all died in huge quantities. The hydroelectric dams and reservoir locks destroy fish life because of sudden water pressure and changing levels, and because some fish, most notably sterlet and Caspian herring, are reluctant to swim over the fish ladders. Land has also been lost to agriculture through the broadening of the Volga waterway: up to 4.8 million hectares flooded. But, mainly as a result of pollution, the Volga has thirty-six towns in Russia's ecological black book. They include Astrakhan, Volgograd, Volzhsky, Saratov, Samara and Tolyatti.

I have not myself seen dead fish or chemical waste, but I accept what fishermen say, from source to mouth of the Volga, that the stock has almost vanished. People in this country keep telling me I look well and young, and I cannot but repeat that this is mostly because many Russians look ill, badly nourished, overweight, prematurely aged, and ravaged by poisons. They have a poor environment and diet and no surgical luxuries. They are prone to prominent birthmarks and odd external growths. There is a Russian saying 'to be on the water but without water', which is apt in today's Russia for both fish and men. The feeling is that life is so poisoned that no human being dare take what he needs from nature to survive.

The Volga illustrates the adulteration of all nature here. It parallels a physical dehumanization and it suggests itself as an obvious metaphor for the decay of the Soviet regime and the spiritual pollution of the Russian populus. Without openness to a larger world, without the free circulation of opinion, the old Soviet Union could not cleanse itself. It stagnated. The organism became mortally infected. Or, to intensify the metaphor, by ignoring nature and turning Russia into 'another body' a monster was created. (This was the theme in 1925 of Bulgakov's *Heart of a Dog*.)

The Pain and Misfortune of Russia is that this country, staring into the Volga, has become anti-Narcissus, gazing into the water at its own ugly reflection.

16

Stalingrad

A T 5.30 AM with a jolt against rubber tyres we had entered the lock of the Volgograd reservoir, beside the new town of Volzhsky. The extinguished engines no longer subliminally encouraged sleep. I pulled open the yellow curtains and wrestled down the nail-breaking wooden blind. The sky was pale grey-pink, an ethereal backdrop to the row of tall fir trees that the dawn rendered almost black. We seemed to be in mid-countryside in perfect stillness, yet the largest hydroelectric dam on the Volga was only minutes away. The industrial town of Volzhsky was built in 1951 to locate this power brace on the map. Named after the Twenty-second Congress of the Party, the exemplary dam, topped with a row of pylons like metal horns, has a capacity of 2.5 million kilowatts, though it runs these days below full power, as do many hydroelectric stations, bowing at last to ecological pressure to restore the Volga to efficient flow.

I closed the blind against early morning promenaders on deck. The table was pretty with sunflowers, apples and cherries. For days I have wanted to write that the Volga, so laden with Russian woe, is the saddest of rivers, but that is not the whole truth. Sometimes it is merry, sometimes joyful, sometimes beautiful. It is not only Levitan's river, but also Kustodiev's and Kuinzhi's; lyrical, dramatic, epic; ancient and modern; romantic and futuristic. From the indefinably varying colour of its water and the sky, filtered through its moods, from the vastness of its life as an inland sea, the Volga draws a sublimity which makes almost painful the sight of tiny rubber fishing dinghies bobbing about upon it. Maurice Baring said in 1913 that the Volga looked by turns like every other river he had seen. Perhaps it is the universal river.

The human life that the Volga spawns has its own universality:

lazy, comic, frighteningly inefficient, unconcerned and bare of social nicety. You can see some or all of those qualities in Alexander Ostrovsky's plays set on the Upper Volga. *The Woman Without a Dowry* is a disturbing comedy of neglect and callousness, two vices of merchant life with its premium on survival. The woman kills herself. Katya in *The Storm* goes the same tragic way. There is an excess about behaviour on the Volga; perhaps the water multiplies existing Russian excesses by a small factor. Of extreme but less tragic behaviour, Gautier recorded the duel between a husband and a lover on his steamer, which ended with the lover being tossed into the water. No one objected or did anything – except the lover, who swam ashore. Oliphant observed the captain of his ship throwing the pilot into the water at Samara. I thought of our own captain and of the *chiaroscuro* of life on our ship: filth and darkness downstairs, light and natural beauty on the upper deck, and the place of light and darkness in the souls of all of us travellers. Rozanov strove to understand an aspect of the universal in every small incident on his cruise, and to relate it all to God.

In his cabin Rozanov too wrestled with the wooden blind, which also worked badly eighty-six years ago. He cursed Russian passivity which permitted shoddy workmanship and impractical design. I had not read his essay when I tripped over the hump of carpet in the corridor outside my cabin, once, twice, and visually many times more, but I had reached a similar conclusion, that if this were my ship, my home, I would cut the carpet either side of the deck rib and nail it down with treads, leaving the edges neat and the rib exposed, not rest with a botched job like this. My impulse, probably a general Western one, is to order where I can, despite the insights of psychoanalysis warning me not to overdo it. I'm bound to ask: what is this terrible Russian carelessness, which has no merit whatsoever – not spiritual, not material, not aesthetic? Why must they make such a mess of civilization and parade it all along the Volga too? Who are these Russians, that, unlike the entire Western world, they lack housepride to the point of squalor? Can it really all be blamed on the Byzantine heritage of Eastern Christianity and Russia's lack of contact with the Renaissance? Why is it that a high degree of spiritual culture does not affect material standards?

Communism has worsened the carelessness, but it has always been in place, even as the substratum to excessive luxury.

The physical decrepitude of Russia is well known and incontrovertible, yet it is difficult to reconcile with the sight of Volgograd, the great temple of Stalinist classicism, a monument to order and permanence in the face of the wanton vandalism of war. We disembarked at 9am, climbed the wide wave of paved steps behind the Volgograd river station, and mounted more triumphal steps. At the head of these reigned twin colonnades topped with sculptures, while two rows of globe-shaped ornamental street lamps divided them vertically to make up the usual Communist-cum-classical opera set. Straight ahead, across a little used road, rose the Avenue of Heroes, softened by trees. Wet patches from a recent hosing were visibly shrinking in the already hot sun. To the right, at a distance and angle dictated by totalitarian city design, stood the tall, square and solid Communist Party Headquarters, displaying on the rooftop the city's red and gold Order of Lenin.

As Stalingrad this place became the most famous city on the Volga in post-war history, because its miraculous defence changed the course of the Second World War. It is such an open, flat place, on the edge of steppe and semi-desert, that the advancing three hundred and thirty thousand-strong Nazi German army discounted the difficulty of seizing it. Already in the summer of 1942 Hitler presumed control of the Volga. But the Russians, having never expected an attack here, defended it with such vehemence that the Germans, though hugely reinforced, never crossed the last 200 metre (220 yard) strip between their front line and the river. One of the Russian battle cries was: 'The enemy will be halted and defeated. Beyond the Volga there's no land for you!' Russian losses are not quantified on maps and brochures available in the city, but the Germans, who had not quite twice as many men, more weapons and more than twice as many aircraft, eventually lost up to two hundred thousand men and vast quantities of arms, planes and motorized vehicles. In practice many died when the retreating Germans, like Napoleon and his army leaving Moscow not quite a hundred and fifty years before, faced starvation. Russian losses included many civilians. Fifty thousand inhabitants of Stalingrad formed a citizens' army. Along the Avenue of Heroes, vertical tablets display the names of several hundred holders of the military decorations of Hero of the Soviet Union and Order of Glory. They lead into the centre of the modern city with its population of one million. Stalin, who led the Red defence in the Civil War and had his suspected enemies summarily executed on a barge in the middle of the Volga, gave it his name in 1925. After his disgrace it was renamed Volgograd in 1961.

It is an efficient, showcase city, that was open to foreigners during the Cold War. It rarely draws attention for its more peaceful past as Tsaritsyn; powerful memorials to the 1942 battle and a unique architecture of the future from a 1950s' perspective overwhelm. The Slav Woman leading Russia into battle from the top of Mamaev Kurgan, the small hill where the 1942 battle raged, brandishes her sword, beckoning troops from behind towards the Volga. Of the heroic two-breasted Amazon variety, this Battle Mother stands dramatically visible to every approaching ship, though she has been thoughtlessly dwarfed by pylons. Her counterparts in daily life are the massive buildings which shape the esplanade and the fine blocks of dwelling-houses closest to the river.

These buildings' imitation of Antiquity has given the Soviet Union almost its only comfortable and durable constructions. Virtually anything else of quality in other towns predates the Revolution. Sixties' jerry-building of box-like blocks of apartments, a style popularly named after Khrushchev, is as dire a failure in the domestic sector as is the seventies' plate glass and concrete style which has shaped civic building. These shambles derived from modernism contrast so strongly with the preceding classicism that the relationship between political freedom and humane domestic architecture seems inverse.

You are meant to think of Greece and Rome. The summit ambition of Russian culture for many centuries has been the idea of the Third Rome – Russia as successor to the ancient legacy after Byzantium. At the same time this architecture expresses the will to order, the triumph of humanity over evil, the aftermath to *Götterdämmerung*. Its roots lie again in the Wagnerian nineteenth century, a German notion of a revived classicism for a new modern age. As an expression of man's relationship to nature, too, the achievement is plain when you step from the flat stillness of the water, and the endless flat steppe, and feel here the vulnerability of civilized life. I faced the hero-city with dread but found it bearable and even beautiful, as if its misery were effectively purged in pillars and porticoes and pediments. Here Communism has functioned like scaffolding. Once removed, it has left good-looking buildings to stand independently. Stalin classicism's borrowing from the Antique world was direct and naive, not oblique and tongue-in-cheek as in the post-modern West. It also pretended to civic pride, which covered up Russian slovenliness.

The battle, which began in August 1942, continued with an uninterrupted eighty-two-day bombardment by the Germans. Then in November the balance changed: the Russians went on the offensive in a campaign lasting until February 1943. In those six months the pre-war town was destroyed. I lined up my local map, trying to find shadows of older streets, and Alyosha looked on me pityingly before becoming irritated. The banks of the Volga, where smokestack industry used to reach to the river, are still a devastated Champ de Mars. Memorials occupy the centre, but towards the south, where the shrunken tributary the Tsaritsa flows into the Volga, gapes an unnatural flat empty paved space, with grass poking up between the stones. We spent half an hour looking in vain for Pushkin Street, which had some pre-war distinction. The intricate re-creation of the past in a fabricated dimension, such as one might find in a Paul Celan poem, clashed with the demands of our timetable and energy. We found a rotunda-shaped café with stained glass windows, Doric columns and marble floors. Open, but with its white-coated, gossiping female staff not anxious for business, and certainly not offering coffee, this elegant fifties' palace of proletarian refreshment had recently changed its name from Tashkent to Mayak (Lighthouse), just because name-changing was in the post-Soviet air. Its windows were outstanding, showing the town crest with yellow, white and green fish and a boat on deep blue, a memorial to the inspiration and local pride of a naturally rich Volga town.

Tsaritsyn originated in 1558 as a Russian outpost on a now vanished island in the Volga. It embodied another stage of Ivan the Terrible's conquest of the Volga and its men were Cossacks, ordered to shoot other Cossacks and pirates endangering river traffic. Despite

143

the sound the name was Tartar, from the same word for yellow as named Saratov. It meant yellow walls, or island, or sand. Another Tsar, Peter the Great, stayed briefly on his way to fight Persia. Before him Stenka Razin and afterwards Pugachev left their mark on a town sympathetic to their rebellion.

Tsaritsyn, with a pre-revolutionary population of sixty-seven thousand, used to be a capitalist bastion, where hotels, private residences, de luxe shops, restaurants, clubs and telephones existed provocatively alongside poverty and ill-kept streets. After the Civil War, by the 1930s the good life had returned. Viktor Nekrasov's novel *Vo okopakh Stalingrada* (published in English as *Frontline Stalingrad*) set a pre-battle scene with Studebakers, those vast American tourers of the 1930s, lining the streets. Musical comedies played to enthusiastic audiences, the cinemas were full, and from its building with a balcony over the Volga the public library lent copies of the adventures of Jack London, one of the best-loved foreign authors in Soviet Russia.

Like Samara, this non-university town had grown with the railway. Its peak of success came from the 1870s onwards, from the vastly rich business of the Nobel Brothers in mining, refining and shipping crude oil. The black gold came up from their Caspian gushers by ship to be stored and freighted on, by camel and sled and steamer, later by diesel tanker and by pipeline, across Europe. Not Immanuel, who built a munitions factory in Russia and developed underwater mines, nor his middle son Alfred, the inventor of dynamite, but Alfred's brothers Ludwig and Robert and Ludwig's son Emanuel created one of the world's richest firms, with an oil supply network from Poland to Vladivostok, Azerbaijan to Finland. The story of their Russian business, so long suppressed by the Soviet Union and under-publicized in the West, is told in a book by the American historian Robert Tolf, *The Russian Rockefellers*. Tsaritsyn was one of the Nobels' largest oil storage bases for crude moved in barges from Baku. The mile-wide Volga allowed ample manoeuvring and docking room and was free of ice from late March to late November. Storage tanks were built of ironplate produced in Tsaritsyn, and a barrel factory was established using American technology. For the oilmen, shipbuilders and metalworkers, and their families, the Nobels built a village with schools, health care, electricity and telephone. Nobelites enjoyed some of the best working conditions in 1890s' Europe. Their labour built the world's first oil tanker, the first pipelines and the first diesel-powered barge; and it revolutionized drilling techniques. By 1900 nearly 60 per cent of oil moved on the Volga was in barges owned or chartered by Nobel Brothers, and Russia supplied more than half the world's oil needs.

When the Bolsheviks seized the Nobel assets it was convenient to dismiss the achievements of the capitalist outsider as exploitation of the workers. But it would be enlightening to compare conditions at Stalingrad's Red Tractor Plant, the largest in the Soviet Union, built near the Nobel site in 1935, with the Nobels' achievement forty years earlier. Their workers formed self-management committees in 1905, but the current of revolution never made them violent. Was Nobel organization not exemplary for Soviet industrialists? The irony cuts both ways. Tolf suggests that the Nobel distribution network was ideal for clandestine use by the authors of Lenin's revolutionary newspaper *Iskra*, based in Baku.

The Nobels paid their last dividend at 40 per cent. In 1918 the petroleum industry was nationalized. Emanuel fled Russia disguised as a peasant. A deal was struck to get his two brothers out of a Cheka prison. The Nobels lost a fortune to the Bolsheviks, who after the Civil War had the oil industry rebuilt by Americans and then successfully ran it themselves, with no word of Nobel involvement, nor a penny of compensation.

Going north along Sovietskaya Street, broad, pleasant, bustling, busy with trams and some cars, we diverted into the glass-walled Central Market, full of babushkas in black headscarves printed with bright flowers. No Volgograd citizen could complain of shortages, only high prices. For salad oil you had to bring or buy your own bottle, of course, for milk your own canister, and for everything your own bag. We found a man selling empty bottles. I wondered how they were washed. The sunflower oil came from an under-counter flagon behind a curtain. The Spanish cooking oil scandal of the late 1970s came to mind. What guarantee existed that we wouldn't be poisoned by bottle or oil? In Russia there is no consumer protection; everyone is family. In fact this oil, sampled with tomatoes and purple basil leaves, crisp green onions and ridge cucumbers, was the gastronomic milestone of the trip: cold-pressed virgin sunflower oil, chestnut brown in colour and as nutty as a mouthful of succulent seeds. Never have I tasted such oil anywhere. Volgograd was a feast.

The market continued outside, with native watermelons and imported bananas, and whole stalls of dried oily white fish called vobla or Caspian roach.

'What do you do with it?' I asked.

'Do with it?' echoed the woman seller. 'Nothing. We just chew it. Like this.' She broke off a dried pinkish grey cheek.

To save me from eating more than a flake of this sun-fried flesh I described in detail the Breton *brandade* I envisaged.

Then Alyosha who takes such a vicarious pleasure in my modest drinking habits, had a surprise. He remembered Volgograd's Georgian wine shop. The quality was high, the prices absurdly low, the same for decent wine as half a bottle of Coca-Cola. Was it really because the Russian sweet tooth reduced demand for dry wine? I never did find out why this shop, unique in all my Russian experience, was here, except that the Lower Volga has a small tradition in wine-making. From the white-coated staff who ran the sterilized establishment like an operating theatre we bought as much as we could carry.

These diversions didn't exactly ready the spirit. We passed fine solid redstone apartment buildings with rounded balconies and classical balustrades. The geraniums on the balconies speckled the façades with brilliant vermilion. At a stroke we seemed to have moved west to Central Europe, yet that was an illusion, for Sovietskaya Street suddenly brought us out on to Lenin Square and the Panorama of the Battle.

It was an uncanny event in military history, and Kuznetsov attributed the miracle of Russian victory at Stalingrad to an infectious sense of national belonging. The leading character in his novel, the architect Lieutenant Kerzhentsev, quotes Leo Tolstoy to support his gut feeling about *narodnost*, which is as impressive and unprovable as the British Dunkirk spirit. To the victory it secured

146

here memorial sites are dedicated throughout the town, but most eloquent is the ruined flour mill before us on this square, with the Volga as its backdrop. The mill represents, like the Frauenkirche in Dresden, like Coventry Cathedral, the wholesale involvement of the town in its fate. The stone is a deep brooding red, of local derivation and dramatically apt in its suggestion of blood and fire. From the five storeys of the burnt-out mill rows of windows gape black like empty sockets. The mill has been given the surrounding space for impact, with a smooth green lawn. Eventually to the fore are tanks and guns and planes from the battle on permanent display. Someone has daubed one with a CND sign. To one side lies the entrance to the large glass and concrete roundhouse of the Stalingrad panorama, a modern building of rare high quality and finish. Visitors to the town rightly besiege this museum where a life-size panorama conveys the experience of the battle from its very midst on Mamaev Kurgan.

We moved, strictly marshalled, in a slow circle from one hellish vantage point to the next. Tatyana, about thirty, was our Virgil. To the east we could see the snow-covered steppe, to the south the Volga turning almost at right-angles away from the city. We travelled from one group of stricken men to another with our serious, dedicated eyes. Who could come here in any other mood? We might ourselves have been marching through the snow-covered terrain, with the river and sky about us traduced by mud and fire and smoke, and occasionally lit by hazy sunshine. Nothing in sight was green.

After the tour I followed Tatyana with my questions. In every museum this summer the guides have been happy to talk, free of old constraints, but lonely in their work, because the old system has effectively blunted Soviet visitors' curiosity and/or made them unwilling to stand out in public. Tatyana told me her mother had been born in a house on today's museum site, her grandparents' home, and was six when the battle raged. The mother remembered as a child dashing out and scooping up spoonfuls of flour from the torched mill to make something to eat. The grandmother eventually died of hunger. The child's only other memory was of the Volga on fire. The river was oil-drenched after shells pierced the storage

147

containers. The subsequent blaze not only melted the ice, but, added Alyosha from his own family's memories or legends, the steam was visible in Saratov.

Cast back out into the sun, we stood staring silently out over the river.

'It's good to hear people's personal memories,' said Alyosha.

But we didn't want to speak. We boarded the bus back to the harbour in silence. Only I noticed some graffiti out of the window: Why not let our city be called Stalingrad still? We're proud of it! The strength of Russian pride may be unequalled in the world.

And yet it goes hand in hand with a deep-rooted lack of honesty. The kind of honesty I mean has many names: loyalty, authenticity, genuineness, integrity, conscience. It implies a commitment to do one's darnedest to describe the world as it is, to say what is so. The cultural roots of that commitment are in Plato. No Western mind can avoid their imperious flowerings, though it may of course reject them. I mean, where have we been today? Volgograd, Stalingrad, Tsaritsyn? And what is the condition of the large early twentieth-century suburb Nobelgorodok that no one, East or West, has heard of it? Forgive them, Lord, for they know not what violence they do to people's spirits with their careless revision of nomenclature. Renaming is why Russia does not have a past. Renaming is part of the spiritual pollution, the disregard for history, the susceptibility to ideology. It also indicates a cruel insistence on names over substance, precipitating a crisis which only poetry and memory can resist. Renaming streets and towns happens in continental Europe. But isn't the phenomenon much more exaggerated in Russia? Or are my objections another form of primness?

On Volgograd's Lenin Square – just look at those names! – I bought a brochure called *Volgograd in the Names of Its Streets*, which listed lost names and reproduced old photographs and engravings. It was an evident fruit of the new freedom to revivify the uncensored past. The author was still cautious. He quoted someone else on that terrible standardization of Soviet street names which means that Moscow and Volgograd probably have at least 30 per cent of names in common, with some towns overlapping by 70 per cent. He listed what happened to Tsaritsyn's nine churches – one turned into a garment factory, another a baker's, a museum, a social club, and so on – but no Nobel-related names occurred in his book. In Russia you can feel truth trying to establish itself sometimes, fearful and moving crab-like.

It was when I was looking for a cat to which to feed my chunk of unwanted *vobla*, and we first felt the weight of the Georgian wine in our bags, that Alyosha led us unwittingly to the spectacle of Soviet conceptual displacement.

'It's all right to eat, you know. We used to chew it with vodka, and then when there wasn't any vodka, when Gorbachev imposed virtual Prohibition, we washed it down with eau de cologne.'

'Lord, Alyosha. No wonder people look sick here! Promise me you'll stick to wine like this in future.'

'If I can get any. You know what happened with that 1987 anti-alcohol campaign? They destroyed Georgian and Moldavian vineyards to save the nation from poisoning itself and not doing any work.'

'But it's not wine-drinking that's to blame! It's fake port and madeira and Amaretto. And vodka!'

'Yes, but some department had to cover its backside. And they didn't want to interfere with Russian vodka and drinks that make money.'

'So they destroyed what was good and genuine in order to leave the rotten untouched.'

'Right.'

'Aaagh! No!' People do it, governments do it: move the target, then claim to have fired on course. Soviet Russia must have almost exhausted the possibility of conceptual trickery with seven decades of propaganda war. I plus my two wine bottles jumped up and down on the pavement in rage.

'What are you making so much fuss about? The whole of life is a lie here.'

We walked for a bit, thoughtfully, then Alyosha began again: 'I think that's why people have affairs, to relieve the stress.'

'More lies, then. Is there no way out?'

'No, there's no way out.'

We maintained two minutes' silence for our lives here. I can only record my general thoughts. The Soviet system discouraged every kind of honesty. It doctored photographs, spread disinformation, discouraged self-knowledge. Conceptual edges were deliberately blurred. It was the kind of system in which anyone committed to integrity would either rejoice to be a criminal or as a social Buddhist long to get off the wheel. That at least is how I imagine it, and in this city supposed to commemorate a great victory for humanity, it makes me sick at heart to spell out the impossible choices men have sprung upon men in Russia.

We looked over our postcards of Stalingrad in the evening, sitting at the open cabin window, behind the wooden blind and the yellow curtains.

'They are less than the reality,' I said. 'The dignity of those terrible losses has vanished. These are just ruins.'

'Do you care about the quality of a photograph? Really? No Russian would notice.'

'Yes, I do care very much, if it affects the quality of memory.'

17

Lost Peoples: Mongols, Germans and Kalmyks

VISITING VOLGOGRAD, with its history and industry, it is easy to forget the surrounding land. The babushkas selling cashmere-like shawls the colour of mud, meeting every ship, give one clue to local resources. The province of Volgograd, on both sides of the Volga and reaching down from north of Kamyshin to the top of the Volga–Akhtuba plain in the south, is famous for its local variety of sheep, the karakul, cross-bred with a French strain to give this high-quality, fine wool. The coarser wool makes the fur which for centuries has been exported worldwide via the Volga and which we call astrakhan. Volga boatmen, Old Believers and Cossacks earned fame among foreign visitors for wearing karakul made into tall, brimless, chimney-shaped head-wear. The rich used it for collars and cuffs. The Soviet Politburo had a passing passion for not so tall astrakhan hats.

Volgograd province stands for all the riches of southeast Russia. The northwest is a black soil region, where the sunflowers, wheat and corn grow; the drier southern part is where the sheep graze and the mustard flourishes. Across the Volga, between it and the Medveditsa river which runs into the Don, there is natural gas and oil and grazing for livestock. All along the river there used to be abundant fish. These products went north by the river, while timber was shipped in for the treeless steppe to the east. Today's leading industries have capitalized on natural wealth. The Volgograd oil refinery, its large metallurgical plant and tractor plant, together with the Volzhsky cement works, have helped Russia progress into the twentieth century. There are food, footwear and leather industries, and many others. Only the fish have gone.

The turning off to the Volga–Don canal passed. One hundred and one kilometres long (60 miles), this artificial waterway begins just south of Volgograd, branching west where the Volga turns sharply east. Between 1948 and 1952 forced labour completed the pre-war project, another issue of Stalin's great 1931 plan to revise the Russian waterways. But the idea of a Volga–Don canal was at least three hundred years older. The Turks tried in 1568, before Tsaritsyn was a Russian stronghold. Impatient with the awkwardness of unloading and reloading cargo bound for Persia and Central Asia across a mere 5km (2 mile) land gap between the Don tributary Ilovlya and the Volga tributary Kamyshinka, Sultan Selim II ordered seventy thousand Turkish soldiers to cut a water channel. Insanitary conditions and Russian conquest of the lower Volga stymied its completion, though the so-called Turkish Earthwork still remains beside Kamyshin.

Peter the Great took up the idea a hundred and thirty years later, shifting the site a few hundred metres south. A Dutch vice-admiral, Cornelys Cruys, was charged with a project overseen by the Paris Academy of Sciences and put into practice by a German colonel called Brekel, who fled Russia in terror when his first sluice gate gave way on testing. On a fact-finding mission to England Peter then invited John Perry, that engineer and former naval officer who had served in Russia's army, to try his hand. Perry moved the site a fraction south again, worked for three years with up to ten thousand men, but still struggled. The Governor of Astrakhan, representing the Tsar, decided that God did not will the two rivers to meet, and though by 1701 Perry had finished some sluice gates and part of the water course, Peter stopped the work when war broke out with Sweden. Perry's plan nevertheless became the foundation of another attempt to link Volga and Don, this time from the Don's source to the river Upa at Tula 230km (150 miles) away. The project began in 1702 and presumably would have led from Upa to Oka and thence to the Volga at Nizhny. But sixty-eight years and twenty-four stone sluice gates later this work too was abandoned when the Turks regained the Lower Don. Twenty-two more attempts to link the two rivers would fail before Stalin's final triumph.

The finished product has three reservoirs on a much smaller scale than the Great Volga. Its architecture tells a continuous story of Tsaritsyn from the Civil War to the Stalingrad battle. In good times, unlike the sluggish present, the Volga–Don canal ferries mainly coal from Donets to the Volga and timber and petroleum products from the Volga to the Don. At its Volgograd entrance there prevails a large statue of Lenin the pseudo-proletarian by the prominent Soviet sculptor E. V. Vuchetich. The Don joins the upper part of the canal at Kalach-on-Don. This way large ships can reach the Sea of Azov and the Black Sea, along a vital arm of the Six Seas project.

Having exhausted her Volga supply, the kiosk lady on the *Komarno* now gives me *Rechflot* postcards of the Don Canal for change when I buy mineral water.

In bed with sunstroke from our Stalingrad visit all afternoon I can hear children playing, some with guns, some with psychological weapons. A little girl cries. A boy's voice says: 'Aw, come on, Katya, I was only playing.' He will grow into a man and he will still be saying the same thing, I speculate grimly. There is the tinny sound of metal triggers being pulled. Russian adults are talking the way they never used to about shopping, comparing prices from one port to the next. Volgograd contained many bargains, some say. Others allege the cheapest prices will be in Ulyanovsk next week, or tomorrow in Astrakhan. I heard the story of one *Rechflot* captain who was so ashamed of his ship disgorging avid consumers that he hid to dissociate himself. On the return from Astrakhan passengers hardly had room to sleep in cabins overloaded with bags and boxes and buckets. Gorky showed pre-revolutionary peasants living like this, carting their sacks from port to port. The decks were so crowded it was often difficult to move. Today's packed Russian buses, underground trains and aeroplanes suggest that not much has changed on any modern transport, though Volga overcrowding only happens in private now, after a 1970s' law forbidding more than personal provisions aboard passenger ships. The story of the too modest *Rechflot* captain continues, though. Moderation was on his side, because before each cruise ended he would observe that the produce rotted in the hot cabins. From my sick bed, having damned relations between the sexes in their infancy, and the future of Russian conversation in a market economy, I now saw a parable of Russian agriculture at large plagued by bad organization and waste. There was surely a health risk, too. At least in this last respect I wasn't wrong. On the *Komarno*, beside the fruit-washing trough a huge poster warned against the danger of typhoid.

By six, however, I was feeling better and went on deck. The Volga had turned abruptly east and we were sailing along one of its few sections unchanged from nature. The idyll – or so it appears to the naked eye – lasts from Volgograd to Astrakhan, and for most of those 500km (300 miles) both banks are tree-lined, flat, sandy and still. Where the Volga irrigates the land in spring, lies a deceptive strip of vegetation.

The river Akhtuba leave the Volga just above Volgograd and flows parallel to it, creating a flood plain until the Caspian delta merges their last strands. On the far bank the nomadic Kalmyks grazed their cattle and sheep here in winter before Russian settlers took their space in the last century.

There is a distant memory of local anti-Russian warfare. The slightly elevated land running alongside the Volga before Volgograd continues southwards, becoming the Yergeni chain of small hills. These move southwest, ever further from the Volga. The right bank, therefore, lies as flat as the left. Only once does the Volga have a cliff, where, always tending right, it has relentlessly eaten into the edge of the harsh, flat, barely populated steppe to form a steep overhang at Cherny Yar. Here was a Cossack outpost from those seventeenth-century days when Russia found it impossible to subdue the mixed local population, to which Kalmyks and Kirghizians, Don Cossacks and Yaik Cossacks, Tartars and Bashkirs, and Russian runaways belonged. A series of fortresses attempted to police the river between Tsaritsyn and Astrakhan; Nikolskoe and

Enotaevka are the best-known after Cherny Yar. But Stenka Razin seized them all.

The still deeper memory is of an ancient, fecund civilization. One of the great vanished cities of history, the Golden Horde capital at New Sarai or Sarai-Berke, built in the mid-thirteenth century by Berke Khan, stood near the top of the river Akhtuba, on its left bank. The nearest name on the map today is Tsarev and in a recent Soviet Volga guidebook it gets one line, a measure of how sensitive still is the memory of the Mongol domination of Russia. To Sarai the Russian princes paid their dues in money and in service, which involved living at Sarai and possibly never returning. Only in 1395 when Tamburlaine, in rival Mongol fighting, sacked New Sarai, together with the other Mongol capital Old Sarai, at today's Astrakhan, did Russians become hopeful. That fissure in the vast Mongol Empire was the beginning of their liberation.

New Sarai was a trade and industrial centre straddling the route linking the West with Persia, Central Asia, Mongolia and China. Rubruquis of Brabant, who left in 1253 from Constantinople and made his way to the Gobi Desert, was one of two early visitors to leave an account. In 1838 the Chernetsov brothers found a site extending over 40km (25 miles) but marked only by ugly holes and heaps. Serious excavations did not begin until the 1920s. Since then archaeologists have uncovered traces of pottery, metalwork, textiles and coloured tiles – enough to give the hint of a picture, though too little to warrant the name of a Volga Pompeii.

A more recent civilization to disappear from the Lower Volga is that of the Germans. There are many sites, mainly radiating from Saratov, but one that stands almost alone, in the crook of the Volga on its sandy right bank beside the river Sarpa, was called Sarepta. It disappeared from Russian maps after the Revolution, though it is still mentioned as a railway halt on the line from Volgograd down through southeast Russia towards Krasnodar. That halt lay 8km (5 miles) from the German colony which economic engineering created in 1771 and political engineering swept away roughly a hundred and fifty years later. An old photograph shows a pretty, tamed landscape, ruled off into manageable portions with wooden fences and bounded by maple and poplar trees. The skyward towers of a Protestant church speak for the community's moral and economic aspirations. Alert to Russia's permanent need to cultivate its resources better and live in a more orderly fashion, and seeing vast areas of good agricultural land untilled, the German-born sovereign Catherine the Great invited her former countrymen and -women to come to Russia as settlers. They received land and paid no taxes for thirty years. The result was such a stark contrast to Russian life that native eyes could only describe it as a dream.

Those Germans who settled in Sarepta came from the Herren-huter pietist sect. They fished, they kept livestock. They grew mustard so successfully that it was mentioned by Baedeker, and by Alexei Tolstoy as a skill that the Russians could not emulate. How strange it must have been for Russian muzhiks to encounter these quiet, orderly, non-drinking, non-dancing people who even in western Europe were unusual. The Germans pursued a thoughtful, disciplined existence, maximizing whatsoever was fruitful and good, and expressing their spiritual energy in song. At home the Herren-huter ideals of inner cultivation so deeply touched the German mind that the greatest literary figures of the age, first Lessing and then Goethe in *Wilhelm Meister*, had written in their praise. They brought their high moral standards to the southern Volga in the same years as Pugachev brought his barbarity. The Lord later inflicted a ghastly fate on both, but that of the Herrenhuter community was longer drawn out. Russia's twentieth-century conflicts with Germany and Stalin's severity either starved them out of existence during the Civil War or despatched them east to Siberia, and Sarepta disappeared.

The Germans' positive thinking, their desire to beautify the world, seems to live on in the heaven-struck names of two other places where they lived beside the Volga: a colony called Raigorod, which means in Russian 'Paradise Town', and a small town known today as Svetly Yar, 'Bright Bank'. For Russians, the places the Germans cultivated were holiday spots before they became towns to live in.

*

The *Komarno* anchored at 'Bright Bank', which appeared now to be a large Russian village of well-spaced pretty wooden bungalows, open meadows, grazing cattle and maples and poplars. The people of Svetly Yar had set up stalls under a few trees on a clearing beside the Volga, and streams of plump Russians in cotton dresses were ascending the slope from the boats to inspect their produce. In the early evening the nature here might have been painted by the older Gainsborough, so delicately picked out was the incandescent white of handkerchiefs on peasant heads. The young Constable of Flatford Mill might equally have painted a scene of such pastoral calm, dominated by the natural tints of water, soil and sky. I stood watching this picture in which the sole modern elements were low wooden telegraph poles, a jeep and a few motorcycles and outdated cars. A family of pigs wandered over from the fields and loitered under a maple tree, curious about the guests from the river. I don't say no one wanted to leave this chance to live in another time, but one older woman almost missed the *Komarno*'s departure. The gangplank was already up. A little girl cried out tearfully from the deck beneath: 'Babushka, babushka, don't get left behind!' No, don't! I thought. It's not really paradise. Conservationists say the water here is more polluted than anywhere on the Volga, with the filth of the Volgograd and Astrakhan industries and pesticides from intensive agriculture, especially rice, washing into the river.

Now the time of the Volga's end is near geographically. As high up as Kamyshin it receives no more tributaries. It slows and spreads, soon to lose all sense of direction and purpose. Hay floats on invisible platforms waiting to be towed downstream. There are rafts of shale and a rusty hull on the sparse green and sandy bank lined with trees. The river trickles this way and that, forming scrubby islands.

After Volgograd, with the exception of the Akhtuba flood plain and the immediate Volga right bank the steppe becomes semi-desert in both directions. Not far to the east lies the border with Kazakhstan. The railway junction and town of Akhtubinsk, formerly the busy trading post of Vladimirovka, exists to service the important salt lake of Baskunchak, almost on the frontier. There are other salt lakes, like those newly left by the semi-dry Sarpa on its course south, but this one at Baskunchak is old and, with a circumference of 70km (45 miles), vast. The salt, which automatically belongs to the state, is said to glisten like a winter landscape in the sun. The valuable underground strata must be broken up with dynamite, picked at and the salt raked into piles. It is unpleasant work, damaging to health, and in 1911 Lepeshinskaya wrote that Russians shunned it, leaving it to Kirghizians, Tartars and Kalmyks.

From the 50km (30 mile) train ride between Vladimirovka and Baskunchak it used to be possible to view two huge, ancient rocks, the Great Bogdo and the Little Bogdo, the larger of which the Kalmyks regarded as sacred. I can't be certain that these honeycomb remnants from the larger ancient Caspian still rest in the flat, empty steppe, but if I were passing again I would search for them, thinking of the night Dumas pitched his tent by Baskunchak, did half a tour, spent his evening writing, and felt for the first time since Paris immeasurably happy to be free. I would think of him in this barren place, a great, spirited and infectious traveller, one of the best whom Russia has ever attracted, and never doubt the attraction of expeditions to this ungraspable, always unpredictable country.

Dumas became particularly interested in the Kalmyks who settled either side of the Lower Volga and around the Caspian in 1630, having made their way from Mongolia. By the time he visited in 1858 their meagre fringe existence had long intertwined with that of the Nogai Tartars, who were the remnants of the Golden Horde, and the Kirghizians. Dumas found them 'placid and law-abiding', though this is not my impression from reading of their relations with Russia. Soon after arriving from Mongolia the Kalmyks organized themselves into warrior communities and became Cossacks alongside the Tartars. Living partly by plunder, they supported Stenka Razin's campaign in 1670–1, a fact so crucial that Tuzhansky was bound to include Kalmyk faces when he filmed Stenka's entourage for *Volga Volga*.

So powerful was the Kalmyk contribution to warfare on the Lower Volga that another popular rebel Don Cossack leader early the next century, Kondraty Bulavin, failed to make headway up the river when they refused to join him. The Kalmyks held the power balance until in 1771 they moved back to Central Asia to help their kinsmen against China. After that, Russia tightened its hold on the Lower Volga. The remaining Kalmyks were a subordinate, impoverished people. Their serf status was not lifted until 1892. The Kalmyks have exotic flat faces, narrow slanting eyes and straight black hair. They were traditionally horse and camel riders, farmers of livestock and eaters of horseflesh which they cured by placing it between live animal and saddle. Of the fine meat of Kirghiz fat-tailed sheep called *kurdyuk* they were connoisseurs. They were also *kumiss*-drinkers; and finally, as Dumas was delighted to discover when he watched them hitch up their loose trousers and ride bareback, Kalmyk women a hundred and fifty years ago possessed a freedom that Western females could only dream of. This tent-dwelling people, with their kaftans and four-cornered yellow hats, were among the best encounters a traveller on the Lower Volga could hope for.

Dumas ventured that judgement even before they sprang upon him surprises like a horse race, a wrestling match with the local Prince Tyumen and a singsong and dance round an imported piano. Ten thousand wild horses were rounded up and driven across the Volga before his eyes. Falcons were unleashed with deadly accuracy on local bird life – swans and herons. The latter sight horrified him, but he was infatuated by the living colour. Another traveller, the Englishman E. D. Clarke, arrived in 1816. He thought the Kalmyks the most unusual-looking people and among the most culturally distinguished in all the Russia that he saw. They organized life around their love of the open air and their dislike of houses. With exquisite logic they called the venereal disease which plagued them 'the house disease'. Lepeshinskaya dwells on the filth that inevitably accompanied their impoverished life, but to a traveller like Clarke they brought a vision like Coleridge's in *Khubla Khan*.

The closer one comes to the nomadic peoples of the open air, like the Bashkirs and the Kalmyks, the more they suggest certain formative influences upon Leo Tolstoy, and thus perhaps on Russia generally. It is not enough to say that Tolstoy, opposed as he was to the pseudo-civilization of towns, had read Rousseau. Tolstoy too could have used 'the house disease' as a portmanteau term for a world of decadent appetites which his fiction decried and his aesthetics ridiculed. Did he not die a nomad in pursuit of a pacifist, non-bourgeois, non-capitalist, rural life? I know he was influenced by the Bashkirs; possibly by the Kalmyks too.

The Kalmyks' Lama Buddhism was a great rarity in Russia. It defined their architectural contribution to the Lower Volga, with a number of wooden pagoda-like Tibetan temples. Baedeker mentioned a temple at Kalmytsky Bazaar, once the chief Kalmyk settlement and trading post for cattle and fish, on the right bank of the Volga directly opposite Astrakhan, now subsumed into the larger town. But only one *khirul* remains. Standing at Rechnoe, on the Volga left bank, it was built in stone by the same Prince Tyumen whom Dumas visited, and when Rechnoe was still Tyumenevka.

Prince Tyumen was commander of a sabre-wielding regiment which famously inflicted woe on Napoleon's retreating army in 1812. He built a temple as an honourable home for the regimental flag. In its obvious European style it was the beginning of his people's undoing. Tyumen himself gave up the nomadic life.

The Kalmyk descendants no longer dress in native costume and are no longer nomads. Their Buddhism is as watered-down as Tartar Mohammedanism. Under Russian pressure to settle, they acquired first a region, then in 1935 an autonomous republic with a capital at Elista and ports on the Volga and the Caspian. Stalin deported them in 1942 on suspicion of collaboration with the Germans, just as he deported the Crimean Tartars, the Volga Germans and the Meskhetians from south of the Black Sea. The Kalmyks alone were allowed back from Siberia in 1957. They are another stateless people now virtually absorbed into atheist (post-) Soviet life.

A final twist to the Kalmyk story came with the plan, still being put into action at the end of the 1980s, to irrigate the Kalmyk steppe with a new canal to be called Volga–Don 2. This latest Soviet challenge to nature would have obviated forever a nomadic culture necessitated by the arid semi-desert. Livestock farming would have given way to intensive cultivation of food crops. But with the ecological damage already caused by the widening and canalization of the Volga and its power stations and the first Don canal, public anger mounted. Protest found its voice under glasnost, and work on Volga–Don 2 stopped early in 1991.

*

In the night before Astrakhan we completed one more round of invisible sightseeing. We passed Old Sarai and Itil: the Golden Horde capital from the thirteenth century and the far more ancient Khazar capital from the fifth. The Polovtsians, nomadic people from Asia, usurped Itil from the Khazars. The Tartars took the Polovtsians' place. Itil was just seven kilometres north of modern Astrakhan, and for the first time in history that name appeared.

When the Russians finally conquered the Lower Volga they were building on 1500 years of lost civilization, as well as laying the foundations for a modern world which has still not quite arrived.

18

Astrakhan and the
Gateway to India

STRAKHAN, with its vanished Asian past, may be the best place to try to understand the complex Russian Oriental heritage. Russian dreams of the East are bruised by the Mongol occupation, yet they feel as strong a sense of belonging to the Orient as to the West. The Oriental heritage affects politics. The Merchant Afanasy Nikitin, departing down the Volga from Tver, was the first to fulfil the Russian dream of reaching India via the Caspian in 1466. Three centuries later the same dream cast a shadow over relations with England, the imperial power in India. The quest for 'warm waters' still haunts extremist contemporary politics. The Russia that might be the Third Rome, inheritor of Byzantium, is a Christian Slav world with its roots in India. The Volga runs like the axis through that global dream. Moscow is the token Asiatic capital by contrast with St Petersburg, but Astrakhan is the real gateway to Asia, as Kazan and Samara are to Siberia and ultimately China.

Velemir Khlebnikov, a wayward modern genius born in Astrakhan, and fascinated by the geographical complexity of his inherited culture, called the Volga an Indo-Russian river. He wanted to see a statue of Nikitin in Astrakhan, also one to Ivan the Terrible in Moscow for his Eastern conquests, one of world-record height to Yermak at Samara for subduing Siberia, one at Kazan to the soldier-writer Kurbsky, and two more at Samara: a colossal monument to Planet Earth and a configuration of human life and nature featuring Adam and Eve. He also wished to ornament the rivers Volga and Don, and thus, curiously foreshadowing Stalin and Soviet Russian monumental culture, to mark in grand style the frontier with the West. Monuments, he believed, spoke directly to the people of their history.

Khlebnikov, born in 1885, was firstly a natural scientist and secondly a passionate student of Lobachevsky's non-Euclidian geometry at Kazan. His father was a natural scientist who studied the traditions and lore of the Kalmyks, and Velemir's early life was spent in their midst, in the only stone house amid tents. From these sources he acquired his strong feeling, backed up by scientific, geographical and historical fact, of Russia at the East–West crossroad. The mathematical background may seem odd here, but like many of his literary contemporaries, outstanding among them Andrei Bely, Khlebnikov associated Euclidian geometry with the rational West, while that stranger world where parallel lines converged and two and two no longer made four he associated with Russia's non-West. Folk literature from Russia's Eastern ethnic peoples also from an early age fed the imagination which would finally emerge in literature. The family lived for some time in Simbirsk province, where the ten-year-old boy came to know Mordovian folklore. He wrote poetry, progressing from the Symbolists to the Futurists, and alongside Mayakovsky strove to invent a new language transcending space and time. His true domain was speculative anthropology. He wrote a short 'supersaga' in verse, expressing the historical and eternally present life of the Volga, called *Otter's Children*. It evokes an otherwise impossible condensation of Frazer's *Golden Bough* and a history of Russia through its battles.

The link between the East and the new geometry, between the West and the dying age of limited reason, dominated the silver age of Russian literature. Bely's *Petersburg* teemed with Eastern themes which challenged 'Western' lines of reason, order, logic and control. Khlebnikov with his notion of Planet Earth as the fusion of Russia and the East (China, India and Mongolia) was geographically specific. After the Revolution Zamyatin used the mathematical aspect of the new thinking about Russia to oppose the 'final' revolution which Bolshevism threatened to impose. Lobachevsky's geometry expressed infinite change. The East–West opposition is not part of Zamyatin's 1929 text, though still one can see the

October Revolution's coercive fixtures as running parallel to Western rationalism, both suppress that side of Russia which belonged to the non-rational. The greater truth about all humanity and specifically about Russia could not be expressed by reason alone. Much Russian truth lay with the East.

Momentous and long drawn out in the mind, our arrival in Astrakhan seemed similarly to stretch on for miles. It looked Russian enough, but the jumble of different ages of man and radically different styles of human activity left the impression of unresolved identity. On the right bank the wooden shacks, rows of beached rowing boats and dinghies, piles of timber, pencil-thin factory chimneys spewing deceptively pure-looking white smoke, ugly metal hoists and pulleys, and small boat stations were dragged into the twentieth century by the presence of tall cranes. Children and cows pottered and paddled along the sandy shore. Over the left bank, reigns the originally sixteenth-century white kremlin. The bell tower and square Uspensky church with its five green and gold domes protrude into the otherwise uneventful skyline from amid a dense belt of trees separating town from water. From some angles the kremlin's small perimeter towers with their wooden triangular roofs are also just visible. Two tall apartment blocks are sited without regard to aesthetic planning. The big ships moor two kilometres or so south of the fortress at a turquoise-painted traditional wooden river station, with lacy fretted eaves and a big pre-digital clock indicating the wrong time. Close by stands the concrete and plate-glass Lotus Hotel.

For us footsoldiers the way into town led through a leafy park past a postcard site called Swan Lake. There were swans, and altogether Astrakhan, monstrously dusty by nature and polluted by traffic, tried to offer some green and shade in central pedestrian areas. But the signs were not good. We passed a statue of two Pioneer children skipping through a glade. They had been mutilated. The bright hope of Soviet humanity just a few years ago, figments of false goodness from the official youth movement, now danced with severed limbs. Khlebnikov was right to say that statues in Russia perpetuated a continuing dialogue between people and government. But his optimistic young mind (he died at the age of thirty-seven in 1922) never took in the possibility of that relationship becoming as cruelly distorted as it did under Communism.

In its centre Astrakhan has many stone buildings as well as a good number of wooden shacks. Several better-known stone piles show 'Indian' and 'Persian' touches added to Russian provincial classicism. But jumble is the word. The eighteenth-century Catholic church and the White Tartar mosque look Orthodox. When the Armenian church existed with its two tall spires it looked Lutheran. This is a strange meeting place of cultures which has not produced riches. The best remaining architecture coincides with Astrakhan's pre-revolutionary wealth and a generously conceived *style moderne*. Piece for piece, it might belong in any continental city from Brussels to Riga, though the pieces are few. The Gubin family house on the river Kutum embankment, which became the Soviet Pioneer Palace, has lovely wrought iron balconies. The former Stock Exchange is a whimsical, opulent construction of 1906. A tropical garden in the foyer of the 'Moderne' cinema, albeit long since renamed 'October', has continued to ply the message of luxury all century.

Real living standards struck Alyosha as exceptionally low. We stuck our heads into a stone courtyard and quickly removed them again in horror. When Bertrand Russell arrived here in 1920 he was horrified to see no drainage and excrement piled up in the centre of town. What we saw was virtually the same mess, though covered from sight. A basement where local *biznismeny* ran an antique-cum-junk-cum general shop was dark and damp, full of blank tapes, old heavy furniture and a working bicycle at inflated prices. Alyosha found the perfect pair of earrings for Yelena, but that good fortune hardly cleansed from our experience the obscene air which hangs over these new oases of so-called capitalism. It is as if by grotesque exaggeration some power is determined to dissuade Russia from joining the world market. Money is as squalid as it was in Dickens, Zola and Marx. The reality of Astrakhan's material condition is appalling for the end of the twentieth century.

The mid-nineteenth-century Ukrainian poet Taras Shevchenko passed through Astrakhan on his return from exile and found it a filthy heap crowned by a white castle. Astrakhan being on the penal route as well as the trade route west–east, Nikolai Chernyshevsky also lived here in second-degree exile after Siberia. His little white house is near the kremlin. The kremlin itself is large and bare, surrounded by pleasant formal gardens with more mutilated statues of Communist heroes. Guidebooks draw attention to the intricate Baroque mouldings of the church and the bell tower, and the light inside. Externally, both show signs of excessive nineteenth-century restoration.

Lenin's father, Ilya Ulyanov, with a handsome statue beside the kremlin, was born here. You can see it in his son's face. There is also a statue to Sergei Kirov, the man who against Trotsky's advice refused to abandon Astrakhan in the Civil War. It was an heroic stand, though the Germans on the White side never quite arrived from Elista. Yet only a Soviet source would describe this as Kirov's main significance. His action helped elevate him to Stalin's second-in-command, and when he was assassinated in Leningrad in 1935 Stalin used the arranged murder of his rival to initiate the Great Purges.

Astrakhan used to be more attractive for visitors, with its melee of costumes, languages and religions. Baedeker met Kalmyks, Kirghizians, Russians, Tartars, Caucasians and many others. Today the art gallery, opened in 1918, holds out the best prospect of colour. Housed in the Uspensky church in the kremlin, its presiding native genius is Kustodiev. An active man crippled young, Kustodiev painted the life he was missing. He refused to include those everyday elements such as mud and dust and drunkenness which inescapably accompany all Russians sojourns out of doors and all merriment. The result is a world hovering between the symbolic and the real: brighter and cheerier and more individualized than Russia has ever been, with gorgeous spreads of food, pure white snow and a range of colourful street types. Kustodiev loved the colour red, the traditional hue of Russian peasant shirts. He painted Astrakhan types and scenes, which include the town from the Volga and the Tyumen temple. Beside his canvases hang works by Malevich and El Lissitsky. Once again, in Russia, with Kustodiev and with Khlebnikov art offers an oasis in a desert.

Russell, not knowing the work of these men who were his contemporaries, simply called Astrakhan Hell. So many flies circled the table where he ate that he had to hold his food under the table cloth. Here was a nadir for humanity. Could Communism, the otherwise promising marriage of Mohammedanism and the French Revolution, do anything to upraise such filthy life? With hindsight one must declare: hardly.

19

The Delta

WE TRACKED down the local newspaper, called *Volga*, and asked for advice on how to get to the delta. Six functionaries and two buildings later and we still had only the vaguest of directions and no practical assistance. The *Volga*'s editor, a dead-eyed, middle-aged man with a gold tooth and a shallow expression combining hostility, stupidity and contempt, was a bureaucrat intent on deflecting curiosity. So much for his fashionably 'independent' newspaper, I decided. 'Why not visit the kremlin?' he breezed. Instead we part walked, part rode to the bus station, installed in an Orthodox cathedral. The deconsecrated result, polluted by exhaust fumes from the ancient charabancs which pass for public transport, and candy floss and pop music, was profoundly ugly. The midday temperature was approaching 100°F, and the only bus had just left.

Alyosha negotiated the price of a private taxi and I kept my foreign mouth shut. We travelled shrouded in dust, through heavy traffic. An oil refinery passed. The air was thick with petrol. I remembered a visit to Baku when the air was equally saturated and poisonous. But when we got out the air was good enough. It only ate nauseatingly into our sinuses in this fancily curtained, poorly serviced Zhiguli. The driver, hearing we were off the Volga boat, described to Alyosha the trip he recently financed with a sack of Volga roach bought in Astrakhan and sold in Samara.

Beside the long straight flat road leading out to Ikryanoe on the western side of the delta stood rows of wooden houses mostly painted turquoise, with dusty gardens. Pretty colour, I ventured. No, said Alyosha. The shop only had turquoise paint. Even when we crossed a canal lushly bedded in rushes the scenery was dull. A

168

journey down the prongs of the Volga's final desultory course by rowing boat would have been better, of course.

The delta is vast. From Astrakhan to the Caspian is at least 100km (60 miles), depending on where across the sprawling breadth of marshes you measure. The area closest to the sea is a nature reserve, founded in 1919 by Khlebnikov's father. Today's official figures record more than 270 species of bird living in the wind-ruffled, myriad waterways, including cormorants, coots, herons, swans and pelicans, 56 varieties of fish and 280 different plants. The prize among the plant life is the lotus, the deep pink Caspian rose.

Ikryanoe, less than halfway into the delta, brings none of these natural wonders obviously into view, yet offers once again an almost medieval scene, with cows fetlock-deep in the water and, on the opposite bank of this Volga backwater, long-limbed boys diving from a high wooden jetty. Rowing boats bob beside more blue bungalows. The road bridge divides the water in half, leaving many tethered motor launches called *barkaty* to float perfectly still, while in the distance, on the broader water called the Bakhtemir arm, occasionally a glamorous *meteor* zips by. These hydrofoil river buses are used everywhere on the Volga for local passenger traffic. 'Couldn't we catch one back, Alyosha? It would be better than the car.' My attempt at enterprise was left unanswered in the enervating heat.

The driver left us at the Volga collective farm about a mile on. That establishment, with its abandoned performance tables and quietly rusting boards of hero workers, showed no sign of activity. Hero workers used to be called Stakhanovites for toiling to emulate a legend now himself exposed as a forgery. Communism was a manipulative religion, promising rewards from the gods and punishment from the devil. Stakhanov was another *deus minorus* gone. While Alyosha sought help, I meditated on these things in the small, shaded, crazy-paved grove which doubled as an open-air waiting room. Another long walk followed. Beside the road on one side stood low wooden houses, too humble for bungalows, with outhouses of wood or corrugated iron. This was the collective farm where there was fishing in season, but otherwise the workers turned their hand to tomato-growing, rice-farming, building and labouring.

The Russian countryside is not an idyll of the western European Rousseauan kind, simply a worse place to live than the town: socially and intellectually cut-off, poorly supplied in economic terms, and for more than half the year bogged down in mud.

'I couldn't live here,' said Alyosha. 'I once wrote a play set in a bus shelter like that.' We had passed a wall of concrete and a carved-up blue bench. 'In my play the bus never comes. People realize they never wanted to go anywhere anyway. It was a comedy called *Russian Boredom*, but when I took it with me to the United States no one laughed.' Alyosha spent an instructive month at the Eugene O'Neill Center. My reply was, well why shouldn't Westerners find Russia bewildering? Its countryside combines the negative sides of rusticity with the desolation of a run-down inner-city estate, and Russians find it funny.

There was no smell of fish, no sign of water. In a dark interior, a mixture of peasant and Soviet austerity, two women at a baize table accepted our unannounced visit. The blonde, in her thirties, with a clear tanned skin, brown eyes and yet another immaculate white dress, had a degree from the Astrakhan Fisheries Institute. We had missed the morning catch, she explained (in fact there had been a TV crew present to film it today), but we could talk to the head nurseryman, Vanya, and tour the farm. I liked and admired Ekaterina Mikhailovna instantly. Here at last was a good communicator and a human being.

The fish-breeding farm at Ikryanoe was founded with six others in the early 1960s when it was first realized that the Volga hydroelectric dams, particularly the one at Volzhsky, interfered with the slow-swimming sturgeon's spawning cycle and threatened its life. Both the caviar and fishing industries were endangered. The farms compensated for about one-third of losses precipitated by the Great Volga project and general industrial pollution. The hybrids they developed mostly spawned locally, thus avoiding the perilous fish ladders on the Volga dams.

The farms are by and large a Soviet success story, therefore, for which their legatees can be grateful. Vanya and Ekaterina Mikhailovna's farmed sturgeon, sterlet and beluga, and descendants of these fish bred in other countries, already appear on smart restaurant menus the other side of the world. Our hosts recently had the pleasure of refusing to sell their farm to Americans. Still, they face ever-new environmental misery. A recently built sulphur works in Astrakhan, a gas condensate plant and untreated sewage are the greatest present threats. As with the anti-alcohol campaign, so with ecology – the system sets one interest group against another to produce painful anomalies, the effects of which still endure. The gas condensate plant was established directly opposite a purpose-built haven for fish idyllically called 'Upper Swan Rest'.

Caviar is less likely to make the fish farmers' fortune, despite its preciousness on world markets. When the Soviet Union was breaking up caviar became a free-for-all, with rampant poaching, but now, like vodka and icons, it is again controlled by the state. No private caviar export licences are given. Poachers face fines of a year's salary, though it is not clear to me that that will deter them. This is Mafia business, and unlike Vanya and Ekaterina Mikhailovna *mafiosi* stand to get very rich indeed from the wealth of the old Soviet Union; if they can stay alive.

If Vanya acquires even an easier life I don't suppose he will change now. Around fifty, he has features so weathered that his character seems beyond detection. He wears his khaki shirt belted over his trousers, Russian style. His mouth flashes gold teeth, as he laughs away what has been a long struggle to survive. The fishermen have an exceptionally hard life. I have heard them say on television that their kind rarely live to pensionable age, being prone to bronchial and arthritic diseases. The size of the fish, the constant wading and working in freezing salt water erodes their health. In previous centuries many of the fishermen were, like the salt-miners, Kalmyks.

The main fishing time for caviar is late March to May, with lesser seasons in July and October in pursuit of the whole fish. It takes place with both line and net, and the state regulates the seasons.

We saw the breeding. Some spawning and fertilization takes place in the wild, but many fish are inseminated indoors, in a chain of white-tiled laboratories with concrete floors. The incubator nurturing the fertilized eggs imitates the river rocking. First in plastic washing-up bowls, then in large round concrete vats in rows under a high tin roof, the young fish swim, graded by age. One hybrid, a cross between a beluga and a sterlet, is called *bester*. This cross-breeding happens in nature; human exploitation has followed. The chromosomes are right, and they produce a fish doubly distinguished for culinary purposes. Another hybrid, which marries the Russian sturgeon *Acipenser guldenstati* with the beluga, cannot reproduce but is valuable for its flesh.

Ekaterina Mikhailovna donned a white coat and gave us each a six-month-old *bester* to hold. Translucent grey-blue and white, it was about twice as long as my hand and already had a magnificent crest and powerful tail. The sturgeon all possess an upturned whiplash tail to thwack to and fro in defence against the fishermen. They grow nearly two metres long and take at least eighteen years to mature. Nature made them so complex that they cannot dart away, nor survive in turbulent water. Of crests, that is those lateral scutes along the backbone, the sterlet, the Russian sturgeon and the sevruga own the grandest. The sevruga appears with its crenellated back and long nose on the blue and silver export caviar tins. It is an iconic fish for the Volga. Not all the sturgeon have it, but the sevruga and the sterlet do: that step-down, long, slender nose which reminded Gorky of the elongated prow of a Volga sail barge. Possibly there exists between the shapes of the great river fish and the forms of pre-motorized ships something of the same relationship that occurs between mushrooms and the folk life.

The delta made Astrakhan wealthy. In 1914 Baedeker saw its living gods, the fish the fishermen caught, displayed in a large tank on the Volga esplanade. The revenue from caviar built the town. Best-known among the businessmen were the caviar merchants Sapozhnikov, first father and then son, who gave hospitality to the German geographer Alexander von Humboldt in 1829 and to the English traveller William Spottiswoode almost thirty years later. By that time the younger Sapozhnikov, A. P., had become mayor and owned the 'Regent Street' of Astrakhan. The family's most extraordinary possession was Leonardo da Vinci's *Madonna of the Flowers*, called today the *Madonna Benois*, the most valuable painting ever to be housed in Astrakhan. Proud of his home town, Khlebnikov wrote about it in the national press. After the Revolution the painting was appropriated from the Benois family, into which it had passed by marriage, to hang in the Hermitage in Leningrad.

An Astrakhan fish merchant's wealth also paid for the canal to be built, creating a third water arm around the city kremlin. This in turn laid the communication basis for an extended town in the eighteenth century. The Varvatsiev canal, named after its Greek-born patron, only lost its personal name after the Revolution. Alexander von Humboldt described 'Major' Varvatsi as the owner of the largest Volga fishery.

The common folk of other parts of Russia were spellbound. Much like the idea that the streets of London were paved with gold, it was said of Astrakhan that a man could catch sturgeon there with his hands.

Maybe in the remote delta this is still true. For this, suddenly, unexpectedly, is the magic of Astrakhan, its copious nature. Today at Ikryanoe we have enjoyed meeting two people devoted to farming that nature, and held a young fish in our hands. When this hectic day was done, that experience stayed with us. The same tender love of Volga life we felt with the fish reminded me of the fishermen's ballads I had heard.

Against that the walk back to Ikryanoe town seemed interminable. Alyosha was so sure that no bus would come that we did not bother to wait. I wore shorts, which he had warned me against in the backward countryside. A Russian girl passed us in shorts. 'Ah, so I'm out of touch with my own country,' he said forlornly. When we could hardly go on, a café appeared unexpectedly: its walls were decorated with mosaics of women harvesting grapes, and there was some quite tasty meat and mashed potatoes to eat. About those viticulturalists in passing: all older accounts of Astrakhan speak of its abundant grape harvest. John Perry included them in his account of Russia in 1716. A century later Humboldt found the fruit superior to any he had seen in southern France or Spain, though he did not compare the resulting wine. Dumas drank the wine from goatskins, and observed that others found it a great delicacy, he not. It is a question for a future visit to Astrakhan: what has happened to the grapes? In this unusually clean café we were the sole clients, chatting in Russian while husband and wife proprietors conversed in what was perhaps Armenian. The bread was superb.

'Goodness, Alyosha, taste this!'

'Yes, yes,' he said. 'You're always making choices. It's just bread.'

We finished with apples and mineral water from my bag. Their weight hadn't helped on the long walk. But I chose to carry them. The food gave me strength. You're quite right, Alyosha, I come from a world where market, personality and philosophy are all built upon CHOICE, and I love it. But he just looked, and in the heat again I subsided.

Should we have retained the driver to wait for us? I would have paid, but the idea never occurred to Alyosha, so now we were stuck. We held up our hands (not just thumbs in Russia, but whole hands held upright, like policemen on point duty). But there were a dozen other supplicants, mostly women with shopping bags, and though hitching is normal adult practice in the Russian provinces, with their infrequent public transport, no one stopped for any of us. Eventually a bus came, lurching on its uneven springs and so old that all the angles of its coachwork were in the rounded immediate post-war style. Squashed upright inside, I tried to laugh at the idea that this bus was even older and rounder than me, but by now I felt terribly sick from the sun. It was easier to take the lurching sitting down. An old woman shouted angrily when our bag fell on her lap. We had not looped it over the hook provided. 'Sorry,' I said. Good Soviet citizens have always been very keen on rules, which ought to please me with my craving for order, but actually irritates me with its aspect of sucking up to teacher. With closed eyes I thought fondly of the little *besteri* germinating in the rocking cradle of the incubator. I fell asleep. Then it was time to walk back again from the bus station. On the way we desperately wanted a swim and oh! so encouragingly I caught sight of a man bathing with his dog. But even that spectre of the private civilized life that I had first noticed on the Moscow canal, which came back to me now as I met its double at the other end of the river, failed to tempt me into this Volga of ill repute. We slumped in our cabins in dock.

*

The Caspian Sea, into which the Volga finally flows, is larger than Japan and at least 570 million years old. It is salty thanks not to the receded ocean but to the Volga, which transfers minerals from the Urals. Its pre-Cambrian bed is very shallow – no more than 10 metres (30 ft) deep in the north. The shallowness increases when the intense summer heat causes evaporation. Khlebnikov called it the sea of forty names, amongst which I have come across the Blue Sea, the Sea of Khvalynsk (Khwalis) and the Sea of Derbent. Alexander von Humboldt came to measure the water level and the magnetic inclination and to collect zoological specimens. Geographers come a hundred and sixty years later with the same curiosity and excitement because of a curious, as yet unexplained phenomenon today. For more than thirty years the Caspian, already below sea level, had been sinking, but in the last fifteen years it has become the world's fastest-rising body of water, threatening the lives and livelihoods of three million people dependent on small towns on its western banks. In the bizarre behaviour of the Caspian the Volga plays a part. Despite increased precipitation in the 1950s the water level fell, threatening the fish with excessive salinity. The finger was pointed at the Volzhsky and Kuibyshev dams, which then reduced their output. But the Caspian rose disproportionately, suggesting a longer-term pattern of behaviour for this exemplary prehistoric sea. An Earthwatch expedition set out from Astrakhan in August 1990 in pursuit of more precise data.

The author of an interim report of the expedition, Christopher Leahy, had this to say of dawn on the delta:

> A prodigiously flat, apparently limitless expanse of reeds stretches away in all directions. The air and water are filled with birds. A fleet of twenty Dalmatian pelicans lifts ponderously into the air and sails with impossible slowness across the top of the marsh. On a spit perhaps a half-kilometre away, a white-tailed sea eagle stands majestically calm – digesting an early duck breakfast?

Such words ought to ensure the world's active interest in the fate of the Caspian: sea of rare nature, sea of lucrative oil, sea of magical fire. Fire belonged to the Caspian before oil was discovered.

In Baku fire-worshipping priests had for centuries tended a Zoroastrian fire temple, where flames burned out of the ground. Robert Nobel, who made the family's first investment in Baku oil, encountered this temple which is still in existence today. Khlebnikov made fire-worship a motif in his supersaga of the Lower Volga, *Otter's Children*. The Nobels named their first three tankers the *Zoroaster*, the *Vandal* and the *Sarmat* after the fire-worshippers and the early peoples of the Caspian.

20

Highway of Energy

THE *Komarno's* radio operator played Vera's theme song from *Volga Volga*: 'Beautiful river, national river, river of freedom mine' – and leaving Astrakhan what an evening we had! Alyosha preceded dinner with a wordless pagan grace, inhaling the scents of the basil, the nutty sunflower oil and the Georgian wine. He reminded me of culinary modernism, that bold attempt to escape nineteenth-century bourgeois manners and mealtimes and rediscover the essential, child-like pleasure of food. I discoursed on this subject dear to me until I realized out loud that all this sensual-artistic finesse depended on affluence. The poor don't play with food. 'You don't have to tell me!' he said bitterly. I felt guilty, as if playing the superior foreigner without wishing to. I squeezed his arm and I hope we ate in peace.

We sat on the warm sundeck, crowded now by night too. The August sky was animated with shooting stars. 'Make a wish!' cried Alyosha. 'When you see a shooting star you must make a wish.' In Tuzhansky's *Volga Volga* Stenka and his bride also see a shooting star hereabouts. Later, as Stenka gives up his Princess's lifeless body to the Volga, another star shoots across the dark vault, and he knows that a soul has just entered heaven.

Astronomers know the phenomenon as the Perseid Meteor Shower. Shooting stars are debris from the Swift Tuttle comet which returns every one hundred and thirty years, and which generates a peculiarly hectic activity of comet dust in August and December. The absence of towns between Astrakhan and Volgograd to cause light pollution makes the dust particularly visible from the Lower Volga.

Vera, also star-gazing tonight, joined us with an older friend called Zoya. Zoya wanted to talk about London. Alyosha, left alone with Vera, whom he finds unattractive and naive, promptly disappeared. He himself may not be naive, but he's certainly superstitious. 'Do you realize how superstitious Russians are generally?' I wanted to call after him. I haven't observed so many people making wishes and touching wood and not counting their chickens since I was a child, by which I mean this is another way in which this country is old-fashioned.

But Alyosha has a real grudge against Vera, a former Marxist economist who cannot explain to me its basic concept, the theory of surplus value, the very source of the idea that profit is wicked. 'Paah, no wonder our economy collapsed, with schoolgirls like that running it.'

In the night there was a storm, with lashing rain and thunder and lightning. I heard the flipflops of a sailor running down the deck past my window and thought the engines sounded peculiar. Volga travellers have suffered worse fates. The high winds which blow up on the large reservoirs can apparently turn a ship over. Or there might be a fire or a collision. On the *Chernyshevsky* Mikhail told me that in 1984 a liner like ours took the wrong course and sailed under a bridge that was too low, killing more than a hundred people. With our storm, to my astonishment I woke up thinking of how Turgenev nearly died in a shipwreck. The drama of a great writer had transmigrated to waken anxiety in a very minor one.

'We got stuck on a sandbank,' reported Alyosha at breakfast.

'Yes, I knew something was wrong. Who did you hear that from?'

'Why, from Vera, of course. She knows everything.'

'She can be useful, then.' I felt a sudden sisterly inclination to defend her, but he wouldn't budge an inch.

The storm inclined me to restate my reasons for travelling. Excitement, of course. Dumas said he travelled in pursuit of love and action, and who could better that? For me Russia means unpredictability, wild behaviour, endless talk and despair. It speaks simultaneously to the pioneer and to the philosopher, to the

178

adventurous spirit and the reflective, so low are physical standards and so skewed and raw and vital is the world of ideas. I know those who hate it. But perhaps those Russia-loathers have belief or excitement elsewhere, or do not dare look beyond fragile things like reason and civilization.

I was also aware that I had seen the whole Volga now. I had seen the whole of a great river, though from this flat, hot semi-desert flanked by steppe it was already hard to remember the narrower, green, wooded banks of the Upper Volga, with their neat villages and pastures, the scenic variety between wooded Kazan and rocky Zhiguli, and those stark prehistoric cliffs before Volgograd. The contrasts are great, but because this mighty waterway runs in its entirety through Russia, and historically has marked and defended Russian boundaries, and also has acted as that vital food, trade and transport artery which entitles it to the name of 'Mother-Nourisher', it can lay easy claim to an overall identity, transcending the vicissitudes of climate and landscape. The language and the very name of the river bear this out. Those who live on the Volga anywhere are Volzhanye, 'citizens of the Volga'. There are the Upper, Central and Lower Volgas; there is the Transvolga and along the banks flanking Volga towns the Povolzhye, 'the Volga lands'. Finally comes the delta, not a demise, exposing broken force, but a gracious old age; not a brutal end but a gentle dispersion and a return to the creative source. The Volga is Russia, and the delta its eternity. It is not what you might think, a suitable metaphor for an exhausted ex-Soviet country. Russia flows on.

When Khlebnikov died so young of penury and poor medical care during the Civil War, his friends buried him as the Prince of the Earth, who like his friend Hiawatha cared for all living things; but, unlike Hiawatha, they said, Khlebnikov cared for them everywhere in the world, not just in America. That sly criticism of America is not worthy of discussion, though Khlebnikov remains of interest. One of his inspirations was his father, who insisted that the family should not spend all its life in one place or even country, and took them to live not only in Astrakhan among the Kalmyks, and in Simbirsk province among the Mordovians, but also to Volynia in Poland, into the cultural sphere which has often spread to the Upper Volga. Khlebnikov learned another Russian world again in St Petersburg, and rightly saw the Volga as a highway of energy, with signposts pointing in all directions of the human compass. It was the breadth of his vision and his love of the natural world, coupled with a desire to express all this in a new poetic language, which his friends prized as regal. I erect a little invisible monument to him on my Volga now as we retrace our course: through Nikolskoe, where we had a Green Stop and swam, and through Akhtubinsk, where our fellow passengers cleared this apparent ghost town out of bread. Akhtubinsk used to be on the Akhtuba, but the risen water level has brought the Volga to its doorstep. Alyosha once again muttered: 'Lord, I couldn't live here.'

Khlebnikov's friend and fellow linguistic revolutionary Vladimir Mayakovsky boldly called the Mississippi the American Volga. This was a provocative description, considering the competition between the two young countries. But there were similarities. A grand river flowed through the heart of the country, bringing prosperity and supporting life. The flat Mississippi basin flooded annually. At 3760 miles (6000km) the Mississippi was over a third longer than the Volga, but it had the same relatively lazy flow and shallowness. The paddle-steamer was its ideal vessel, from where the idea spread to the Volga. Until the mid-twentieth century Volga shipping also took much of its expertise concerning safety and payloads from the mariners of the Mississippi. Then there was the sympathetic figure of Mark Twain, once a Mississippi pilot and eternally a writer of the people, also a chronicler of the many varied peoples and their local dialects along the river. Twain further endeared himself (and was to remain a highly popular foreign author in Soviet times) when on a visit to Russia he expressed democratic hopes for the 1905 Revolution. Gorky, singing Twain's praises for Russian readers, established for himself virtually a twin, and opened up a folkish, fresh and anti-bourgeois America. Twain took his pen-name from the sailor's call when he measured the depth of the shallow Mississippi. The same call in Russian figured in Gorky's stories. I half-regret there is no need to shout 'Mark twain!' in Russian today, for I would like to hear the sound.

Today the Mississippi, the American giant, still makes a more viable comparison abroad for the Volga than does Rozanov's hieratic 'Russian Nile'. These are secular times. Yet Rozanov's plea for the Volga's sacred nature, kindred to the Nile, turns on the names Volga Mother and Volga Nurturer which still inspire the conservative Russian heart. The two interpretations of the river encapsulate Russia's modern political and social dilemma. The Soviet attitude embraced a dedication to secular progress, always close to and competing with America. 'A Russian Mississippi' was right. Rozanov, on the other hand, hallowed the cyclical, praised the God-given, and saw man as essentially humble in his dependence on the gifts of nature. He expressed enduring Russian piety.

Our captain articulated a far cruder Russian conservatism, nothing to do with Rozanov's, when he came for a drink. We had to invite him because we needed his help. His conservatism was based on national pride. He had the feeling that Russia was being drained, sold off to foreigners. We were conversing with another political hardliner who would have shot the reformers and closed the country if only he could have had Soviet prosperity back: 'Shoot Gorbachev! Shoot Yeltsin!' Alyosha observed later that this man was like so many Russians, demanding order, but disorderly and unreliable himself. He sat poised on Alyosha's bed, holding his glass primly, as if he had never before held anything so delicate. He never once sipped, though he kept pestering my friend to drink, just one, just a little one, and I had to stifle a fierce desire to assault him. We were all uneasy, including Vera, who had come by for a parting drink and to return the Bible.

We needed the captain's assistance to change our tickets back to Nizhny, and feared we weren't going to get it. After he left we sat and commiserated.

'You think you've seen Russia? You don't know the half of it. We could try to get you a third-class ticket. Then you'd see. You know, when I was in Nizhny there was an American missionary at the ticket office, insisting on a first-class ticket, and there weren't any. The woman said to him, "But father, why not travel third-class, and be among the flock?"'

'You want to test me?' We foreigners in Russia are provocative: all of us.

'Yes.'

I smiled, though, and waited for Alyosha to mellow. This time he did.

'OK. So we want to stay together. We could share a luxury cabin for two – there is one on each ship.'

'Mmm. That sounds like an excellent idea.'

'We'd be the talk of all the passengers, not being married.'

'Huh! Where are all the good Bolsheviks when you need them? Wasn't the Bolshevik Revolution about sexual liberation? I don't care what the other passengers think. Let them think!'

'Free love? Huh! *Seichas pryamo*! That idea soon disappeared.'

Actually, since we almost shouted the exchange and our daring soon evaporated, I suspect we wanted to stay as we were. Anyway, the captain surprised us by delegating his sozzled substitute to write a letter to a colleague purser on another ship. We handed over a bottle to this executive, and all was well.

We called again at Volgograd, for a second meeting with Russian pride. This time we ascended the battle hill itself, Mamaev Kurgan. From here the Maternal Figure leading Russia into battle with her shoulder-high sword dominates the town. Mamaev Kurgan is a pilgrims' way, culminating in an eternal shrine guarded by young, fragile-faced soldiers with bayonets. Looking back, away from the great statue, the view in steps down to the blue, hazy Volga is dream-like in its grandeur. Heavy single heroic figures punctuate the central aisle of the pilgrims' walk down to the water. Postcard sellers tout for business and children younger than ten have improvised soft-drink stalls to earn a few roubles. The more interesting wall sculptures either side comprise the faces and bodies of scores of men in action, grouped together to petrify the rhythm of battle and the determination behind it. The resulting stone resembles those pre-Cambrian Volga cliffs called the Columns north of here. It is as if the sculptor has dug deep into the native earth to bring out its eternal secrets, doing in stone what Khlebnikov intended in words with the supersagas, to create a continuous

Russian identity along the Volga from nature to art and people. Mamaev Kurgan is worth taking seriously, despite the commercial degradation, which never would have been allowed in Soviet times. Russian shrines are still private; they still do not speak deliberately to foreigners, and in that they retain their mystique.

We were gliding away from Volgograd harbour when the tannoy suddenly crackled with Schumann's *Träumerei*. All the pensioners at once appeared on deck, some with their medals, and small children crowded forward to the rails, watched or held by parents. The children had flowers in their hands. The air resounded with soldiers' songs from the Stalingrad battle, including a famous one sung to the tune of 'Stenka Razin'. Sounds of guns and shells, air-raid sirens, Rachmaninov's Second Piano Concerto and church bells betokening resurrection bombarded our ears. Stalin's right-hand man, Molotov, announced the German defeat, which was followed by a crackly command: 'Hands into the Volga!' The children had been waiting for that. They tossed their garlands into the water. Behind us, as behind every departing liner, coloured blooms lay strewn on the water. The recording then boomed: 'Remember! Remember! Remember!' The *Komarno* hooted its bass foghorn in respect for the Russian dead in the last great defence against the foreigner. I the Englishwoman with Alyosha the Russian patriot am the foreigner.

21

Saratov and a Writer's Life

W E DISEMBARKED at Saratov and I missed the subliminal rock of the boat and the wide-open vistas. Nabokov has a theory, voiced in *The Gift*, that Russia's wide open spaces bred the opposite habit of close community. My theory about the Volga is the contrary: that Russians love the broad river because it redeems their crowded, indoor lives, and they love it more than we ever could, because their lives are more swaddled against the weather and generally more crushed, involving forever queuing in tight formations and bending forward into tiny kiosk windows to get information or tickets or, lately, to buy goods in the new commercial kiosks in the street. Some aspects of Russia remain impenetrable to me. Who can tell me, for instance, why the kiosk windows are always tiny, no bigger than eighteen inches square? No Russian can understand why I ask, so I am left to speculate that perhaps these Alice in Wonderland apertures lose less heat, and are easier to close when staff goodwill is exhausted by demand on the other side. Psychological health is at stake, but the little windows make people crowd each other all the more. They are a trivial, miserable part of living in a punitive bureaucracy, a symbol of a place which offers no beauty and no freedom and no space to the soul which is not mere emptiness. That is why the wide open Volga counts for Russians.

Dzhina the collie dog greeted Alyosha. He was homesick and proud. He lived just off the old centre of Saratov, in a leafy area reflecting Saratov's late nineteenth-century prosperity and the wooden house was so old that the staircase was dangerously worn away.

'How do you like my *old* house?'

'Lovely,' I said, longing for us all to relax.

There was a small park laid out with an athletics track beyond Pugachev Street. I ran round the soft, pitted and puddled track while two drunks jeered from the rusty, once pale blue, spectators' stand. Sport is another discredited Soviet ideal. I swore at them in my own language, went home and showered by pouring a bucket over myself in the bathtub. The disadvantage of old houses in Russia is that they have not been modernized, nor barely maintained. Still, the weather wasn't cold. It was Sunday and the *Volga* writers had invited us to lunch in dacha country.

Dachas gird Saratov, and more holiday homes and old trade union holiday camps reach south along the sandy Volga. Sitting in a steep amphitheatre bordered by the Volga, it is naturally picturesque and last century attracted a whole minor school of painters, including even one from Milan. The Sokolov hilltops now entertain monuments to the war dead. Further inland a steel obelisk marks the spot where Yury Gagarin, who trained in this town and regarded it as his second home, landed after making man's first space flight in 1961. The landing was planned for further east in the Kazakh steppe, but the wind or the gravity of emotional attraction intervened. Now the twentieth-century industrial town, enriched by natural gas and with a reputation for making good fridges, has also crept up the hills, bringing post-glasnost accusations of bad planning. But where there is still greenery there are numbered dacha areas, which are suburbs of wooden houses with gardens, and some wooded areas. We were headed for 'dacha area one'.

Fish from the former Gulag capital Magadan on Siberia's Pacific shore, marinated boletus mushrooms and other stewed wild mushrooms, gathered by our hosts and home-prepared, a delicious kind of Russian ratatouille, black treacly Borodinsky bread with coriander seeds, stewed courgettes from the garden dressed in oil and garlic, cooked meat, boiled potatoes, pears, apples from Voronezh, plums, tomatoes, cucumbers, parsley: we were eating all afternoon. The proper order of a Russian meal is to follow an assortment of hot and cold hors d'oeuvres, including salad vegetables, with meat and potatoes, and then something sweet, but as the first courses are always superior they make up the greater part of an extended meal. To drink there were wine, vodka, brandy and whisky. The Russian way at table is to treat fortified drinks, spirits and table wines all in similar fashion, as accompaniments to food. Once the bottle is open it should be emptied – 'squashed'.

'We Russians eat too much, eh?' called over Sergei Borovikov, Alyosha's editor.

'Rather,' I said, modifying my views to be polite.

We sat, twelve of us, around a huge oval table in a pretty wooden dacha decorated in rustic style. Our host Volodya was a philosopher and novelist, his wife a writer and currently the editor of a children's magazine. They had two daughters, ten and twelve, whose English confirmed my impression that languages are well taught in Russia. With the steady flow of alcohol, conversation appeared endless. The men went out to smoke, so did some of the women, and those with no alternative made their way to the privy at the bottom of the garden. 'I shouldn't bother if you can help it,' whispered Alyosha. Our hosts had already apologized for the lack of conveniences. In Russia writers are poor these days, they moaned, whereas writers in the West are rich. I disabused them of that notion.

We talked, as is usual among Russian intellectuals, about art, and politics and religion. I must have caught the Russian germ for I suddenly raised the subject of the Holocaust. In the West the Holocaust is a benchmark for modern writing and poetry. With the systematic destruction of Jewish lives Western humanity lost its last Enlightenment hope that mankind was essentially reasonable and good. But I had tried talking to Alyosha about this landmark and concluded, all the more after talking to a Jewish critic, that it was not the same in Russia.

'Don't remind me! I *am* Jewish!' he – let me call him Glazer, from Moscow – cried, swaying, wagging his finger, sucking air between his prominent front teeth, and delivering his words with a projectile nasal twang. 'What matters to us is why sixty million people died in Russia as a result of the Purges. That is the problem for us. And what about the millions of Russians who died in the war? How dare you say "our war"?' Well, I hadn't, but there didn't seem much point in continuing this exchange. Russian 'conversation' may be of legendary intensity but it isn't always pleasant or enlightening, as I have often found.

Volga editor Borovikov was more interesting, in that he had recently published a book called *Words at a Standstill*. From him I learned post-Communism had precipitated a peculiar new fear for Russian writers. The changes had trashed billions of their words overnight; very little Soviet literature was now worth reading for its artistic merit; so could they be sure of what they were doing? Well, perhaps that's why the afternoon collapsed on us. All the men except Alyosha got drunk and ate too much. Yelena was tired. I was bored. I mentioned Gorbachev. That set Glazer off. One moment pale and angelic in his pink shirt, the next breathing dragon fumes from a nicotine-stained mouth and firing darts with his Rasputin eyes, he looked to heaven and cried: 'Why, oh why, did he ruin my beautiful country?' His argumentative forward lurch pushed me into a flowerbed. (Dostoevsky was right to find in Russian intellectual life something quite farcical beside the deadly earnest.) Later he apologized. I decided my foreignness just reminded him and everyone else of the present crisis. How shall we change? What shall we be?

We returned from the dacha by stopping a car. The driver named a modest price. Though it had been more difficult in the countryside a few days ago, there has long been this genuine cooperativeness about Soviet Russian life. It will surely vanish now, as people acquire more, and define their individual lives by defending their privacy. In neighbourly terms the old way was better. Russia senses that. Russians see that in the West already exists, flawed and violent and alienated, the society they must become. Or can they avoid it? Like they tried to avoid capitalism altogether? It's uncanny how little the world has moved on from the October Revolution in terms of where Russia stands in relation to the West.

Alyosha makes a related observation over the next few days when I see him, though desperate to work and rest, constantly harassed by the telephone and, even worse, by many unexpected visitors to the house. Ah, but it's the Russian way, he says. The Russian way is to welcome everyone, to turn no one away, even if it is the middle of the night, for he or she may need to talk.

And Yelena? Will she be relieved if Russians get the filofax mentality and start to make appointments? She tells me she does not remove her make-up until after 11pm, for fear people will come. She is also strained when people like the drunken Glazer and his beautiful wife do call, partly because she is short of time, working long hours for the Americans, partly because there is a yawning cultural gap between her work environment and her Russian life. My arrival only adds to the tension. Our first evening Alyosha snapped: 'Oh, for God's sake, everyone wants to tell me how to live: the English way, the American way, the Russian way . . .' Our second, over dinner, when Yelena burst out sobbing: 'But I love my country!' Later in the week this resurfaced as a little English jingle on Alyosha's lips, which he would pronounce with a sympathetic smile, recalling his wife with affection.

22

More Tormented Writers' Lives

I SPENT Monday and Tuesday getting to know why Saratov – a place of just under a million people, rich in gas, oil and manufacturing industry, with a flourishing intellectual and artistic life and an already well-restored centre – was different from other Volga towns. The answer was mainly the very strong German influence. The main street until the Revolution, and again now, is 'German Street'. In between it took the name Kirov Prospect and the Catholic church was converted into the Pioneer cinema. The façade of the moviehouse is Soviet new concrete, but at the side you can still see the solid redbrick walls of an ecclesiastical building from another civilization.

German Street, Nemetskaya Ulitsa, a modern pedestrian precinct, with globe lamps, well-restored provincial classical and *art moderne* buildings, pavement cafés and trees, offers a mixture of order and gaiety. Living up to its name, it has a Central European, not a southern or Oriental feel. At the eastern end it culminates in the neo-gothic Music Conservatory on Chernyshevsky Square. There are booksellers, grocery shops, ice cream stalls – only no coffee in the cafés.

It is a cultivated town, with a German-built university, a splendid art gallery, a theatre where Alyosha's plays are performed, and an art nouveau covered-market sometimes compared to the original Halles in Paris. The whole slopes gently down to the always impressive river, and there sits in a stone armchair, the most famous Saratov-born modern writer, Konstantin Fedin. Through him the

German influence makes itself felt as a particular kind of intellectual independence, and ultimately a mute Russian tragedy.

Fedin, hailed in the West in the 1960s as Russia's answer to Steinbeck, wrote a Soviet classic in 1924 called *Cities and Years*. It possessed that steely objectivity with regard to recent Russian history which qualified it as socialist realism before the term was even invented, though before the end of the twenties it clearly did not fit the mould. Fedin became an acceptable figure not by recanting this novel about the agony of adjustment from pre- to post-Revolution, but by henceforth trimming his artistic sails. Born in 1892, he was a near-contemporary of Gorky, and like Gorky's, his later life, in which he became First Secretary of the Writers' Union through the Khrushchev Thaw, was diminished and confused by ideology. During the war he had reported from the front line, but his ideological bravery was less marked: in the mid-1950s he deserted his friend and dacha neighbour Boris Pasternak over *Dr Zhivago*. For these reasons Fedin does not excite interest in Russia today, though his talent will one day be rediscovered.

In *Cities and Years* two men, a Russian liberal idealist and a German painter, were great friends until the war broke out, followed by the Revolution. When they met again the German, once a fanatical patriot, had been converted to Communism as a prisoner of war. But the Russian was bewildered and disillusioned by the violence. Eventually the German had his former friend killed for helping a counter-revolutionary escape.

Soviet critics accused Fedin of sharing his Russian protagonist's doubt, a contention likely to be true given that the German hero's name was '*Wahn*', that is, 'madness' or 'delusion'. The Revolution was madness; madness of German philosophical origin. Fedin went along with it, and turned his fictional attention to peasant life and Russian suffering.

Much of Fedin's work, especially the trilogy of novels that were mainly written in 1943–8, concentrated on the life he knew in Saratov as a child, 'a town of gingham, retired generals and flour kings', and on his experiences of western Europe. He had been studying German in Germany and was interned there when the First World War broke out. One of his later novels deliberately echoed Thomas Mann's *The Magic Mountain*. Fedin died in 1977 and in that stone armchair looking out to his beloved native Volga seems to sit wrestling with his soul. To reconcile the demands of political reality with his true beliefs and the uncompromising requirements of art was impossible.

Chernyshevsky, who gave his name to our first Volga boat and was born the son of a Saratov priest in 1824, is this town's other famous writer, whose fate is so caught up with Russia's still that he can't be ignored. He was a Social Democrat, a Proto-Marxist, and a dangerous simplifier. He attacked unproductive idealism on the part of Russian intellectuals and called for a new age of reason in Russia. A novel called *What Is to Be Done* and a doctoral thesis called *The Aesthetic Relations of Art to Reality* purported to make clear what he had in mind. Work hard, don't succumb to love or jealousy, and don't worry about art, was roughly the message.

Russians dislike this man so much now they are free to reject him that like so many museums in 1993, the Chernyshevsky Museum in Saratov was reorganizing to save its life. The fine villa with its Volga-facing balcony, where the family lived and Nikolai Gavrilovich died, was also in symbolic crisis. Chernyshevsky's great-granddaughter, aged seventy, curator for decades, had recently fallen to her death from that pretty wooden balcony and the town was talking of suicide, triggered by the shock of perestroika. It could also be observed openly now that there had been mental instability in the Chernyshevsky family since Nikolai's son Sasha. Vladimir Nabokov once imagined Chernyshevsky senior calling his son 'a big ludicrous freak'. The father too was very odd, though communism made his oddness a norm, which Russians today are all the keener to repudiate. So they love to talk of his wife, Olga, whose marriage to a man whose instinctive chastity and long incarceration left her so manically unsatisfied that she became a minor legend in Russian literature with her salons of young men. They note that the statue of Chernyshevsky in the centre of Saratov, dashingly Romantic in mood and almost lyrical in its physical grace, has about it the lie of a Hollywood screen womanizer who really loved men.

Of deposed heroes like Chernyshevsky racy new biographies will have to be written, to help set Russia on its new cultural path, and Lenin's praise must come down from the museum walls. Yet not everything about Nikolai Gavrilovich was bad, and in his fierce rejection today he seems to me more than ever a martyr to Russian whim. He trained for the Church but switched haphazardly to philosophy and economics. He learned seven foreign languages including, as a good man of the Volga, Tartar. He loved Saratov's Lipki Park, a French creation, and the Volga in the few years he was allowed to live here. Some years ago Saratov went through the complementary temporary madness of wanting to rename itself Chernyshevsk. Tsarist repression came upon Chernyshevsky because he proselytized and simplified Feuerbach's materialism, always to secure a better, more bearable life for Russia. He endured more than twenty years in prison and Siberian exile, and died aged sixty-one a few months after the final repatriation with his home town.

We were thinking about those twenty years this poor man spent in Siberian labour camps as we left the empty red-carpeted house in Chernyshevsky Street. For all its old-fashionedness and our being the only visitors, the museum had put us in a reflective mood. What made twentieth-century labour camps different from those 100 years or even fifty years before? Alyosha mentioned Solzhenitsyn's comparisons of penal servitude in Tsarist and Soviet Siberia. The devilish system was lacking then; some human dignity remained despite the cruelty, police surveillance, poverty and hunger. In our century, how did exile combine with the systematic torture and wilful degradation of human beings en masse? To use Solzhenitsyn's phrase in *The Gulag Archipelago*, what caused out of the cruel tsarist system 'an explosion of atavism'? Human brutality is eternal but the madness, the excess must be laid at Stalin's door. This of course is where modern Russian literature takes its bearings. This is its Holocaust.

That figure of sixty million used by Solzhenitsyn totals the deaths in all Soviet labour camps from their inception, that is before even 1921, and includes those who were moved as whole peoples like the Volga Germans and the Kalmyks. Some camps were close to the Volga: between Rybinsk and Yaroslavl; between Nizhny and Kazan; south of Samara; on the Volga left bank midway opposite Saratov and Kamyshin; southwest of Volgograd close to Sarepta; and inland from the north Caspian shore east of Astrakhan.

Solzhenitsyn borrows the Volga to name one of the many waves of death which swept through Russia between 1921 and 1948.

We lunched in a café of staggering brightness, a former milk bar. Milk bars in Communist countries guaranteed a temporary respite from drunks and smoke. They represented a jolly simplification of life. Real life was so dark that a childish ideology was invented to help people believe the opposite. Ideologically redundant now, our milk bar was half given over to selling tinned food, drinks, pullovers and mechanical spares. The counter showed good food: soup with *pirozhki* (filled yeast pastry), sauerkraut, cutlets, salad. But the look of Soviet things often deceives. We chose the ravioli-like *pelmeni*, but found them filled with high meat or the flesh of an unknown animal. We abandoned them, went on feeling sick and bought some Russian chocolate to kill the taste.

'You know better, Alyosha, than to take our guest there,' Yelena said later, and he looked sheepish. He hadn't wanted to cook. When she had gone he absolved himself by developing our experiences into a lecture on survival. Shopping is more unpredictable than ever in provincial Russia today, and hygiene is not guaranteed. Russians love leaving cooked food standing for hours in warm rooms. They sell roast chickens in sun-baked newspaper kiosks. Alyosha laughs at all this. It surely gives him material for his comic novels, which are so successful. But thirty thousand people in Russia died of food poisoning last year. The figure is official.

After two days of letting Alyosha show me round his usual way of life I decided the whole business must have been infinitely painful for him. This was a forgery that was carelessly done, that was a fake. In shopping at least he had taught himself to read the numbers beneath the bar codes that indicate country of origin. But only eating is proof of which ingredients have been undermined. And only living is testimony for how much old values have lost their meaning and new have not yet taken root. Present-day Russia revels in Western capitalist and democratic vocabulary without the accompanying reality. When old-style Soviet parliamentarians in new democratic clothes provoked street fighting in autumn 1993 they did so in the name of democracy. President Yeltsin had assigned himself temporary sovereign powers. Words in their literal meanings were against him. He was said by men without an ounce of democracy to be undemocratic. I feel Yeltsin was the more sincere, but who can say? In Russia anything significant is quickly reduced to a counterfeit.

There is also much opportunist disloyalty in this turbulent country. 'What do you think of Russia today?' a senior woman reporter from a Saratov newspaper asked me. I made my forty-five-minute speech into her tape recorder as multi-layered as I could. All the while this slender, Western-seeming older woman simpered agreement, sighing as if all were self-evident to her and me, if only the country at large would catch up. '*Diko!*' she uttered from time to time, '*diko!*' which means 'wild'. A week later in Nizhny another Western-seeming TV journalist, dressed in clothes that could have been mine ten years ago, who wanted me to record my perception of Russian women, also kept exhaling that word '*diko!*' as if it were the style-enhancing exhaust of a Hollywood cigarette. The Saratov interview earned Alyosha another rebuke from Yelena. 'Why did you take our visitor there? That woman's a monster.'

We visited the *Volga* office again. Within seconds a huge, powerfully flavoured smoked fish was menacing us with its dead eyes from amidst a pile of pending copy, newspapers and bottles of warm beer. 'Don't touch it,' whispered Alyosha promptly. 'God, it might be from the Volga.' I giggled inwardly thinking of the trouble he would get into if I were sick. Fortunately the hosts were hungry enough to go ahead without us. Then while Alyosha sifted papers I listened to someone on the phone – not what he was saying, just the sheer physical effort needed in Russia to communicate by this early twentieth-century means. 'Hello' is in Russian usage a sustained utterance of mounting volume, midway between a groan and a bellow. This voice was so strained that it suggested a parallel visual situation, where one would need a telescope to see a man across the street. Leaving the office, we narrowly missed the approaching Glazers. God save humanity from so much difficulty! I groaned. And this was not even the climax of the difficulty of my Saratov stay.

For the Glazers actually turned up later, with another critic called Nina, precipitating a chaos which they could hardly appreciate in their drunken state, nor sober next day, since out of discretion no one told them. Police had threatened them with the sobering-up station *en route*. In retrospect the only interesting thing which happened was when they splashed their faces with cold water before setting forth from us at midnight, topped up with whisky and wine. The water left a pool in the hall, and in the night Yelena slipped and fell on it, right down the worn old staircase to the front door. Afterwards, without knowing what had happened, I heard her crying in the night and thought she was crying for Russia. Perhaps, God knows, the human psyche being so complicated, and in this pre-Freudian country, she even fell to make me feel that. What can I say from the suicide hour of 4am? That everything's fine? That everything's ghastly? That I can see this is good and that is difficult? No. Very little is good. It's like being summoned to the bed of a friend who has been disfigured in an accident and hasn't yet been allowed a mirror. I know everyone is unhappy here in Russia and they don't want me to say.

So let me say something else for the time being about Russian dogs. Those I've met on this trip have been strikingly odd. One in Nizhny arrived to help his female owner cope with a divorce and moving house. In the emotional chaos time had lacked to train him, so this poodle, so overgrown he looked as big as a wolfhound, tore about the flat, a huge bundle of uncontrollable Russian energy. Moreover, the moment I set my bare feet out of bed in the morning he would pounce and lick them, having acquired an embarrassing, tickling, finally crippling habit of Christian humility. I came to think of him as the Russian soul unchained. Oh no! I love him sitting with me at meals, I protested, he's a lovely boy, but eventually babushka took him off for a week to the dacha and to get his hair cut, to cool down. He was a true Russian, this dog. (I remembered Peter the Great's Westernization programme involved compulsory hair- and beard-cutting, and true Russians, that is Old Believers, couldn't accept it; they still can't; nor could this canine; afterwards his personality was quite unhinged, but by then I was leaving.)

Now I've been watching Alyosha with his dog, Dzhina. Dzhina gets everything she wants in terms of love and walks and regular food. 'I just want to know someone's OK – why shouldn't it be the dog?' he cries impatiently when I tackle him. Did Nina feel the same way, I wondered, when with a drunk's fixed grin and clumsy hand she fed Dzhina all our household's cheese for the week? Dzhina, bright-eyed, pushed her wet nose into Nina's palm time and again, and next day was ill-mannered and sick. (The dog certainly, and maybe Nina too.) Probably one point about misguided kindness to dogs is that Russians can't or are long past wanting to help each other, but at least they can help animals. I heard a conversation on the boat in which two women said: '. . . Yes, they treated each other Soviet fashion, you know, spat on each other . . .' Kindness has become terribly frustrated in this country, though as a foreigner I have received it generously. (Yelena told me she hated that positive discrimination towards foreigners.)

Last year in Moscow I met a man writing a book about *The Dog in Russian Literature*, and now I understand. Dogs have this unexpected role, to deflect the tension from the national psyche and expose its weaknesses, whether they lie grossmuttishly on your doorstep as in Bulgakov's *Heart of a Dog* and show how easily men can become dogs (a prophetic story about the creation of Soviet Man and real eugenic experiments), or speak to you with a kind of superwisdom in words supplied by Gogol (*Diary of a Madman*) and Pilnyak (*A Dog's Life*), or liaise between illicit bourgeois lovers in Chekhov (*Lady with the Lapdog*). Well, I'm alert to Russian dogs now. I'm also touched by a fashion for pedigrees. The pedigrees were on display in Volgograd market, Alyosha explained to his daughter. He had done some research on prices. Yes, he confirmed to me, we're very concerned with pedigrees in Russia today. And I thought of all those pedigree humans the Revolution shipped out.

Oh, aching unhappiness! I begin to see Saratov like the Symbolist Andrei Bely saw St Petersburg on the eve of Revolution, fractured by myriad dynamic forces threatening destruction, with social surfaces slipping into impersonal collisions of mass and weight and number, and consciousness muddled and frightened by shadows. This is a kind of aesthetic panic I am prone to manufacturing, and it stops me sleeping. But it has at least one real correlative.

An article in a local newspaper asks: 'What is a town?' What should be built in the new free Saratov? Communism stressed communal spaces and in practice killed the public social domain. The arrival of individualism endorsed by private property now inspires fear that the profit motive will wreak havoc with civic areas, since little historical awareness and no civic pride exist. Maybe it is just *The Cherry Orchard* story a hundred years on. But I see it more violently: the anti-garden city, patrolled by gangsters, wandered by unhappy drunks and profiteering, unprincipled dogs.

Some readers may think I am mad. But it is the historically unhinged quality of Russia, that sense of not having a past, which makes it so easy for Russians and Russian observers to find in ordinary urban circumstances instant correlatives for the strained, uprooted, troubled – and withal revolutionary – mind. Alyosha also reminds me, when I gag on being called to testify at the bedside of Russia my disfigured friend, that for this same reason he does not believe Russian literature should reflect everyday life. Therewith it seems to me the writer may reinvent the Russian life around him with the same élan as in the revolutionary era of the 1910s and 1920s. But he has to stay alive to do so. He has not to go mad or, like Mayakovsky and Esenin, principal poets of the era, kill himself. This is a terrifying country to be in, and even worse to contemplate.

23

Under a
German Heaven .

THE GERMANS would have done it differently. I was so determined to see the last traces of their attempts to live on the Volga at towns named Marx and Engels (strictly speaking, Marks and Engyels) that I threatened to go by bus. Alyosha's father stepped in gallantly with the Zhiguli. To cross the Volga we took the three-kilometre road bridge, a 1964 engineering feat less famous than the thirty years older Saratov railway bridge first mooted by Lenin. The Volga's span has produced several contenders for world engineering records over the years. We passed the entrance to a beach enjoyed by Saratovians for generations, despite the risen water level of the Volgograd Reservoir.

Alyosha, Yelena and Ala were picnicking on the Saratov island some years ago when a downpour caused the entire colony of sun-worshippers to want to return home instantly. They surged forward to the quay. The captain of the first boat to dock called through a loudhailer for calm. People would get killed if the crowd did not ease back. He would not lower the gangplank otherwise. Ignoring him, young men began vaulting on to the ship's deck, pulling their girlfriends with them. The scene was chaotic. No one would wait for the next boat. 'I'll always remember that scene,' said Alyosha as we passed. 'It was the day I knew Russia would lose any war with the West.' There were these emotional dates, battles lost in the Cold War. Alyosha told me of another, more public, when a young German called Mathias Rust landed a plane on Red Square in 1987 and Russians concluded that their defences were worthless.

Across the bridge, past a small industrial-cum-residential conglomeration, we travelled for an hour along a straight, flat road flanked by riverside dachas and rows of irrigated black soil fields. Alyosha's suntanned agriculturalist father could not have been a more suitable and amiable guide. 'Rotten road,' he said. 'You have better ones in England, I think.'

I thought of the Volga sand and pebbles that had probably made it. This man reminded me of my father, practical and knowing about cars and places and roads. 'Some of our roads are OK,' I said idly, remembering the day the M4 melted at Heathrow. Actually I just wanted to say the right things and for everyone to be 'happy'. I was getting like Alyosha. I couldn't stand any more confrontation with pain. So we chatted about pensioners in Britain, and anti-theft devices for cars. Fields of millet and sunflowers, of stubble and harvested hay sped past. Beside us a network of fine-gauge pipes sprayed the soil from irrigation canals. An oil pipeline and overhead telephone wires and electric pylons further cluttered the natural landscape. The unforeseen problem with irrigation had been soil erosion. Loss of topsoil had reduced yields and spoilt land. But now I had to ask. Why do mistakes like this befall Russia on such a huge scale? Alyosha's father shrugged. That's how it was. Bad luck.

Now we were approaching Marx, he said, pronouncing it in that resounding Russian way, in which the 'r' resonates like burnished steel, and the 'x' has the crack of a pistol shot.

The Volga 'German' communities were of different religions and German-speaking origins, included Swiss and Dutch and other European settlers, and never looked to one centre. Nevertheless Marx, the nominal capital, appeared to be only a village, reached by another long, straight road of square, well-kept wooden bungalows. At the centre stood a monstrosity, once the Catholic church, then a Communist Workers' Club, now a grey, beached, ugly hulk, towerless, with four barricaded entrances, Doric columns and a red hammer and sickle. The square around, abandoned to cracks and weeds, with a few old parked cars, was forlorn even in sunshine. Lenin still flung out his outstretched arm, but his public had vanished.

Peter the Great's daughter Elizabeth first mooted the idea of inviting Volga settlers, which Catherine then implemented. The first arrivals in 1763 called this town Katrinstadt after her. The

Russians called it Baronsk. Within ten years the colony was growing tobacco and soon became the richest tobacco-growing region in Russia. It also practised over three hundred crafts. But the principal fortune was in wheat. Before the Germans only one flour mill existed. They built two hundred. Wherever Russians and Germans have worked side by side, the Germans have been more efficient. Literature has often commented on the fact. In Nekrasov's epic poem *Who Can Be Happy in Russia?* (1879) the sloppy peasants buried alive their cruelly efficient German estate manager. The French and Dutch and Swedes could equally put the Russians to shame.

The Russian sense of inferiority before foreigners resulted recently in half a century of Cold War tension, so it is useful to look back. The Volga Germans were not trying economically or culturally to conquer Russia. Their life was peaceful and self-contained. The settlers were guaranteed temporary exemption from taxes, and given ready-built homes, tools and freedom of faith in exchange for tithes from the harvest. They applied their talents as the Bible expected. (Only Russians were prodigal.) It was mainly those extreme Protestants called Mennonites, and Catholics and Lutherans, who populated the small German towns, coexisting with a few Russian Orthodox believers. Yields always exceeded the Russian norm, and culture rose above the local *niveau*. Katrinstadt had schools, an opera house, a theatre and a music school, as well as newspapers and a book-publishing press. Not until 1872–4 were its economic privileges and exemption from military service ended. By that time life was well-rooted and flourishing. But by fifty years later the Revolution and the Civil War had almost destroyed it.

Tsar Nicholas II's order that the German community be interned in Siberia would have been executed in 1917 had not the February Revolution, which precipitated his loss of power and abdication, intervened. The politically sluggish Germans formed a National Party of the Volga Germans, largely designed to keep Bolshevik power from touching their lives. A small group of Volga German socialists worked with the Bolsheviks who were fighting to control Saratov. Equally, many White Russian army officers came from Volga German families. In the confusion, the name of Katrinstadt changed, in 1915 to Katerinengrad, then in 1918 to Marxstadt. The

Volga German colonies became an autonomous Volga German district in the new Soviet Union, but the Civil War brought disaster. The Germans, as ethnic aliens with an efficient agriculture, were systematically starved to feed the Red Army. Ravaged, dazed with hunger, Germans were seen wandering about Saratov. According to the new museum of Volga German history in Marx, in 1921, out of an existing 600,000 population 46,000 died and 100,000 emigrated to found another Katrinstadt in Kansas. Those remaining lived in what became under Stalin the Autonomous Soviet Volga German Republic, only to be deported *en masse* to Kazakhstan in 1942.

There was virtually nothing to see. The two-storey brick buildings facing each other through a central avenue of grass and trees contained ragged improvised 'commerical' shops. There was a baker's and a new 'Bank of Marx'. People said the stone buildings were mainly German-built. A Belorussian expressed contentment at living here, though it was not as attractive as Siberia, where you could see your garden grow faster. He had gone east freely, met a Volga German woman, and together they had resettled here. A few Germans were left, he said. They had intermarried, their number was tiny, they spoke Russian and there were few visual clues.

The new Volga German museum was a building site and store of German furniture and ephemera. It smelt of varnish. One display room had a gleaming new parquet floor. A self-confessed lifelong Bolshevik who had edited the Marx newspaper for thirty years, Nikolai Vasilievich Titov, had become curator. He was fourteen in 1942 when the Germans were peremptorily moved on, with their belongings heaped on horse-drawn carts, while their houses were already being ransacked. The experience committed him to his German neighbours, and commitment paid off. This white-haired vital man, with a Japanese copying machine dominating his cheap Soviet plywood office, had an exceptionally lucrative job in retirement and hard times. Since the collapse of Soviet power hundreds of Americans had come here to seek their roots.

In Saratov the regional museum exhibits feather beds, yellowing books in Gothic script, old maps and photographs. Volga German newspapers are busy reprinting documents and oral memoirs. They tell of Volga German river captains, and how the *Tannenbaum* (Christmas tree) was brought to Kazakhstan, and how those deported to become the Siberian Labour Army sang their laments in German to the tune of 'The Ballad of Stenka Razin'. It is all wretched to my mind because the German chapter is only another instalment in the Russian book of waste.

There were Volga German writers, but none of world renown. Boris Pilnyak is most closely associated with the German Volga, but despite being born Boris Wogau in 1894 to a Volga German father and a Russian mother from Saratov, he was a thoroughly Russian artist. Pilnyak's case, though, was tragic, perhaps because subconsciously his psychological and creative preoccupations were European. His story *Mother Earth* gave a vivid, violent picture of Russian peasants and Germans and new Bolsheviks struggling to survive during the Civil War. His Expressionist prose fused nature and psychology. The river and the forest played heightened roles in human lives, and animals observed human behaviour and interacted with humans. Pilnyak expressed an interest in Freud, and his prose did not reflect Soviet realism. He died an early death in a labour camp. Another talent felled. More waste.

Alyosha's father arranged lunch. The café, a few minutes' drive from Marx, was scruffy, but there are not many cafés in Russia, so I wasn't complaining. He ushered us through the public eatery with its concrete floor and indifferent decor, past the kitchen and larder, into a small *cabinet particulier*. A table stood set for four, and as we took our seats, helping ourselves to mineral water and chilled beer, a neat waitress arrived. There was fresh bread, coleslaw salad, a rich, hot soup, freshly cooked pork escalopes in cream with sautéed potatoes, and coffee.

'This was how life used to be,' said Alyosha laconically. He meant not very long ago. There is a new pre-revolutionary nostalgia to do with 1991, not 1917.

The Soviet good life never involved money, but privilege, contacts, access to inner sancta and back doors. Everything was a kind of family affair, and in that sense the real basis of the economy – and of Party political life – did remain the Russian commune. Marxist economics were only a front. But no wonder Russia is economically shattered! Alyosha's father paid a thousand roubles for this meal – barely a dollar.

We returned through Engels, formerly known to the Russians as Pokrovsk and to the Germans as Kozavenstadt. Built to service the saltmines of nearby Lake Elton by rail, and heavily industrialized, it appeared to have more of an independent Russian identity. But we were too tired to investigate. Alyosha's father wanted to swap jokes on the way home. (He was particularly jolly because, supplementing his pension with capitalist experiments, he had sold some cabbages in Marx.) Could I think of a joke? In desperation I adapted the one that Jewish sons tell about their mothers changing lightbulbs. Question: How many Russians are needed to change a lightbulb? Answer: None, because they're happy to sit in the dark. Of course no one laughed.

24

Who Is to Blame and What Is to Be Done?

THURSDAY, 26 AUGUST. I had become used to Saratov, receiving visitors Russian-style in Alyosha's absence, giving up my time to endless talking, and learning to love liquorice coffee out of dirty cups. Now I had the freedom and privacy of a cabin again, where old food was stuck to the bedside table and the whole human cupboard smelt of urine. But it was good to be back on the Volga, on a boat called the *Nekrasov*. Posters on board told the life story of the same Nekrasov who was born on the Upper Volga and spoke in his work of

> . . . Russian thought,
> That chivalrous thought, doomed in fetters to languish
> Which never can die, which can never be slain,
> In which there is so much resentment and anguish,
> In which so much love has been proferred in vain . . .

Nekrasov is the man to consult on eternal Russian patience and passivity:

> You lose nothing by it;
> You just play the fool
> And the Lord will forgive you.
> You know it's forbidden
> To no one in Russia
> To bow and be silent.

Nekrasov was the poet who told of the peasants burying their German master alive. But this came only after they were sorely tried with floggings, as his narrator explained:

> . . . by their patience
> The People of Russia
> Are great, little Grandchild.

Russians could be brutish. Nekrasov almost foresaw the dictatorship of the proletariat:

> The pig has got proud
> Since he's taken to scratching
> His sides on the steps
> Of the nobleman's manor.

But they were people of unlimited potential for the right outsider to help:

> A soil just as fertile
> Lies hid in the soul
> Of the people of Russia:
> O sower, then come!

In Nekrasov's day the Germans were already helping. Lenin came to plough the Russian soul by a new method. Now the Group of Seven developed nations have come to see 'what is to be done'. With potential Western aid and investment has arrived a Western song which rings out from every bar and workshop: 'It's My Life'. Russians may well acquire individualism (though many find it morally ugly). But I wonder if the carelessness and shoddiness will ever end.

This was a difficult day and the Volga, matching our mood, signalling the start of autumn, was choppy, cream and grey. Alyosha was reluctant to start out again and no longer wanted to sunbathe. I had lost the rhythm of the voyage out. In lowered spirits, having watched the boat pass sandy campsites where in previous years Alyosha, Yelena and Ala had holidayed courtesy of Saratov University, where Yelena was then connected and all of which made him nostalgic, we spent the afternoon apart. There was a Green Stop, the stretch north of Saratov being relatively lush, with rolling hills on the right bank sporting here and there a horse and cart, and sandy islands for boating and bathing, but the sun

went in. The shops in Saratov had been full of items for the new
school year starting on 1 September.

The sand was dirty, the people pasty and fat, snacking off dingy
fish and black sunflower seeds. The fatness I collided with on the
gangplank belonged to people who had no palpable muscle or bone,
and their children were as solid and unindented and uncurving in
reality as Seurat's stylized bathers only appear to be on canvas.
Hastening back into my private fastness, hauling down the wooden
blind, I lost a fine pen, a personal present, down the gap between
the blind and the cabin wall. Oh, Lord, everything was wrong.
'Bloody filthy ship! I'm damned if I'm dressing for dinner!' I
shouted to myself.

At lunch we paid the absurd penalty for not having been on
board yesterday to order our food: we were relegated to the lower
deck restaurant. In this dark, windowless, quasi-Victorian parlour,
furnished with dark wood and dirty tablecloths, we received food
dished up from a counter by a disembodied hand which helped to
shape the portions and scrape the serving spoon. A tattered poster
on the wall plugged the merits of bread. 'You have it better upstairs,
eh?' said the pleasant waitress, wondering why we had been sent to
gastronomic Hades. To every repeated misery of the ex-Soviet social
system, still enshrined on the Volga liners, I had to become
reaccustomed.

When I told Alyosha about the lost pen he silently took the
cabin apart with the screwdriver on the Swiss army knife. Even
when we had the window frame off no one passing commented,
though a few children stared. The pen was sighted and almost
retrieved with a stick mounted with wet imported chewing gum.
This I ran to buy for a dollar – the cost of our Marx lunch – at the
kiosk. But then the pen fell to a new, unreachable depth. Thank
God we were only trying to rescue an object, not a life down a
mineshaft. The drama purged us of so much emotion I wasn't sure
whether to laugh or cry.

At dinner in the same infernal floating chophouse we ate some
beetroot and bread and pasta, I had some whisky, then we spent
most of the evening apart. In Alyosha's cabin there was a noisy cold
fan. He was freezing and disturbed by the noise, but the purser
wouldn't turn it off because the weather had been hot last week in

Astrakhan. In my cabin the sink was blocked. I dropped my eye pencil down the wastepipe but it floated back up when I ran the water. The reading lamp was also shooting out its 220 watts like a sparkler.

So I sat in darkness and it was elating to travel with no blind at the window, and no cabin illumination save the vigilant blue spotlight. Scatterings of lights, bonfires on the Volga banks, flashes of greeting from passing vessels provided the setting for two of the best-known first lines in Russian poetry which kept declaiming themselves in my head, Lermontov's *'I skushno i grustno . . .'*, 'the ennui and the sadness . . .' and *'Vykhozhu odin ya na dorogu . . .'*, 'I came out alone on the road . . .'. Suddenly we were passing the cement town of Volsk, which appeared bathed in a milky light. Its tall, thin chimneys were belching dense smoke across the black sky and thick dust was visible in the white and yellow street lights. The scene, void of any human animation, but accompanied by a steady hum of machinery, continued for three-quarters of an hour. I turned up Moscow Radio until the *translator* took it off the air at the ship's eleven o'clock bedtime hour. Since childhood I've loved listening in the dark.

Next day back north past Syzran, an old-fashioned-looking industrial town, with rusty tin chimney pots and brick factories, we were headed for Samara. The radio insisted that God had the answer and I burst into tears. In the afternoon at the rail a kind pensioner donated his Volga map book to me and explained every field and cliff and rivulet that passed. I asked: 'Do you believe in God?' He answered: 'Not as much as I ought to.' His name was Gena and he rode the Volga, 'the best possible holiday', every year. These days he grew flowers in a hothouse on the outskirts of Moscow, having been a train driver. His children had moved away and didn't keep in touch. He, meanwhile, had wasted his whole life on Communism. I liked him for the confession and the lack of bitterness. The sun warmed us again. The river snaking through the green flat country-side was lithe and the line dividing water from bank dissolved in the bright light. There were many small boats. At Novokuibyshevsk we refuelled in midstream from a floating tanker, having been guided to dock by a pilot boat flying a red and white pennant. Alyosha appeared on deck, having slept most of the day.

For lunch, now mercifully back in daylight, in the upper deck dining room, there had been more beetroot, with garlic and cream. It sounds like an insult but I mean it straightforwardly: the Russians are the best beetroot cooks in the world. The meal fuelled our brief expedition ashore at Samara, when against all my instincts I insisted on attending a service in a reopened nunnery. The icons were new and the service took place in what must have been the ballroom of a restored secular house, for the church alongside had been destroyed. In a large upstairs interior painted sky blue the worshippers – young men in jeans, old women in headscarves – stood at equal distances from each other like children at a dance class. The door in the iconostasis opened and towards them walked a bespectacled priest in pale blue brocade, accompanied by a tall, thin, long-haired and bearded helper. In the beginning and repeated now ad infinitum is the revelation of the saving word of God, delivered in the same tone as the old propaganda.

The weather is breaking, rain falls from a grey sky in early evening, tapping on the metal awning covering the deck outside my window, as we sail on. Before the rain the sculpture of a sail on the Samara embankment had stood out in high relief, a beautiful icon of a possible Volga life. Girls sat chattering beside the flowerbeds. Youths were playing basketball. After the rain there was a dazzling orange sunset behind the dark green screen of forest on the right bank, and the air smelt fresh and sweet. The sunset might have been a painting by Rerikh.

In the dining room a new face appeared, another pensioner, another old Bolshevik, who audibly requested to be seated with non-drinkers. Well, they all were except me, surely – except then I noticed two appealingly suntanned young Russian men at the next table with a bottle of vodka. I stole a glance at them and shared a smile. Meanwhile, would anyone put this old man out of his misery? I caught Alyosha's eye. We had to. No one else would. But the new guest had hardly sat down when Alyosha got up, muttering the need to smoke. 'I drink,' I said, left alone with the old man. 'Don't you ever?' He smiled. He did of course, moderately in his cabin, it was just that he didn't want to sit with drunks. Ah. That was OK then. This hypocrite was another retired newspaper editor, this time from Samara. 'Sorry to leave you so soon,' I said. 'I hope we'll have a chance to chat tomorrow.'

Who Is to Blame? Or What? When we called back at Ulyanovsk, Lenin's birthplace, I felt by now I should have the answer, but all I had were hollow facts. Lenin's theory and personality created Soviet Communism. Did that mean, then, that Lenin was to blame? I had not once heard him personally vilified all summer, not privately, nor publicly, nor in the media. I believe he was a vile man, though not personally to blame. Now we were to visit a town which, having acquired his family name in 1924, declines to change it back, despite being free and politically unfashionable.

We docked before 9am at the new anonymous river station and made our way up the imposing hill from the river. Every visitor remembers this hill. A hundred years before Rozanov, Sergei Timofeevich Aksakov passed through. This was the pastoralist who so memorably wrote up his boyhood, youth and years as a young man in the early nineteenth century. The season was also autumn, and his gentry family was crossing from Simbirsk, the pre-revolutionary name of Ulyanovsk, to the family estate at Bagrovo on the left bank.

The descent of the hill at Simbirsk was now infinitely more difficult than the ascent had been; the hill had become a slough, the brakes would not act, and the carriage slipped down sideways at the steep turns. To remain inside was dangerous, and we were all obliged to walk down, in spite of the mud and rain. But the Volga – it is terrible even to think what the Volga was like! The whole of it had turned into hills of water which moved backwards and forwards, yellow and brown over the sandy shallows and black in the centre of the stream. The water was in constant turmoil and commotion, and actually moaned; the waves continually lashed the bank and ran up many feet over it. Over all the expanse of water, and especially in the centre of the river, 'white horses' were running: the crests of the waves, having risen to their full

209

height, suddenly collapsed and were dispersed in broken water and
white foam. Unspeakable horror came over me. . . .

Sergei Timofeevich's father reproached him for cowardice, but in
the event the family nearly drowned. Someone wilfully or with a
grudge against the gentry had bored a hole above the waterline in
their rowing-boat, leaving it safe only in calm water. There was
much talk of the Volga's rages being God's will, but the boy
acquired a lifelong aversion to crossing rivers.

We climbed the hill which the Aksakovs' carriage slid down two
hundred years ago, just as we would slither down the dry, worn
slope four hours later. We made a nineteenth-century entrance to
this old horse-breeding town, to the place where Pugachev was
captured, to the place where Pushkin came to stay to research his
History. There must have been an occasional bus from the river
station, but it didn't occur to us to wait, despite the steep gradient
and my bare legs gored by brambles. Nothing was signposted,
nothing well presented.

Simbirsk is a name of possibly Chuvash origin, meaning 'where
people live', or it may come from the Mordovian for 'green hills'.
The town was founded in 1648 with a hilltop wooden kremlin, but
never possessed strategic importance. The kremlin fell into decay,
and a fire in 1864 destroyed what remained of Simbirsk's older
history. A pre-revolutionary guide said there was nothing here.
The nothing has since yielded to umpteen Lenin memorials, including a statue of mother and son which resembles a Madonna and
Child, and a statue of his father that looks like Marx. There is also
a breathtakingly lovely walk overlooking the Volga, off the ivory-
coloured civic centre. What Ulyanovsk otherwise contains is
obscure. There is a museum devoted to the novelist Goncharov,
whose famous protagonist Oblomov was a quiescent and passive
Russian contrasted with his German estate manager Stolz, whose
name meant 'pride'. Another monument is to the national historian
Karamzin, born here in 1766, who once advised a young idealist not
to let his dreams run away with him in Russia, to be realistic, and
to keep his real thoughts to himself. The monument with a bas-
relief is complex enough to warrant a small explanatory booklet; its
whole has been taken as a symbol of a pro-free market, pro-

European stance by the new newspaper, the *Simbirsk Courier*. Karamzin travelled abroad and, while writing his twelve-volume history of the Russian state, frequently considered the question of Russian backwardness, requiring public refutations of inferiority and private regret. He it was taught Pushkin and Mussorgsky the Boris Godunov story.

The Lenin question dragged us off the sunny hilltop. By 1993 Lenin's popularity in Russia had so diminished that re-examination of his pickled brain revealed no unusual traits. His body, embalmed in a Red Square mausoleum, now faced humble burial. Ulyanovsk – the stress falls on the second syllable – with its four hundred thousand inhabitants, was resisting the tide of change, however. The local authority was pro-Communist. A newspaper called *Homeland of Ilyich* denounced in the old style lazy peasants who wanted land without work and profiled good workers and teachers as 'the sun' and 'fertile ground' and 'instructors in human warmth'. Exceptionally well-stocked shops and subsidized food stood to reward those who still admired the Communist line.

Alyosha gasped. Butter and cheese cost four times less than in Saratov. Undaunted by the ideological spectacle, he became so carried away with shopping possibilities that we almost ran out of time for Lenin. I found my favourite Borodinsky bread to buy for the first time. We came across a pretty *style moderne* fire station and an early cinema, also the late nineteenth-century puppet theatre, but no other buildings of note. The shopping mall in central Goncharov Street reminded me of the eyesore of Paris's Montparnasse, built on the compacted foundations of a more characterful life. Most interesting were the cars parked at the kerb – gracious black saloons from the late 1940s and 1950s, German Fords and early Soviet Pobedas and Moskviches. Neither of us had ever seen so many old-timers in a Russian city. The evidence suggested another perquisite of living in Lenin's shrine – access to spare parts, even their special manufacture in the nearby automobile factory.

The perks remained but the shrine had been desecrated. In the kiosks the Lenin postcards and booklets cost a tenth of a US cent, and the wooden Lenin bungalow and related museums were deserted. The street was immaculate, with grass growing neatly along its tree-lined verges and no access to traffic, but we even had difficulty finding The House. A whole touristic era, its opening marked by John Reed's pilgrimage here to write his eye-witness account of Revolution, *Ten Days That Shook the World*, had ended; all we could do was try to make sense of that end.

Lenin's personality determined events in 1917 to an astonishing degree. To try to understand it, Solzhenitsyn attempted a stream of consciousness account in *Lenin in Zurich*. The book makes dismal reading, for there is no pleasure in inhabiting a narrow, conspiratorial, despotic, intolerant consciousness which never once reaches for a metaphor or expresses joy or sadness or abandon. Solzhenitsyn sees Lenin as less a personality than a brain, and a non-Russian brain at that, dressed up in human flesh to look like a Kalmyk, and applying Germanic ideas like a hook to knead 'sad Russian dough'. 'A quarter of his blood but nothing of his character, his will, his inclinations made him kin to Russia.' Lenin devoted his whole life to world revolution and to revolution in that country where perchance he was born. He wrote in 1902 his own *What Is to Be Done?*, that book being in Solzhenitsyn's words merely 'a scheme for a band of professional conspirators'. He cultivated self-restriction in the name of the cause. The idea was to divide people, split unities, make harmonious parties quarrel. Lenin's politics were designed to lead to war, but chance in the form of the First World War gave him the occasion to practise revolution. The Germans, interested in a destabilized enemy, ferried him back from his Zurich exile to Russia in a sealed train to organize his forces after the February Revolution.

What Is to Be Done? is an extraordinary text to read today, partly for the way it talks to revolutionary insiders, partly for the absurd fictitiousness to which time and political circumstance have reduced it. This badly but spontaneously written tome is the dead body that Communism now bequeathes to outside science for post-mortem examination: a suitable object for post-modern analysis.

Alyosha has rightly been saying throughout our trip: 'All of Russia today is post-modern.' This is a fashionable, suspect term in the West, but Russia might almost define its meaning. It is a society not necessarily facing a new beginning, but certainly one living at the end of an irretrievable past. Anything goes, and outsiders like me and transplanted émigrés and the grandchildren of anti-

Communists like the White general Krasnov and the last prime minister before the Bolsheviks, Alexander Kerensky, come to spectate. The show plays to the neo-Dostoevskian tune of 'if there is no Communist God then everything is permitted'.

What do we see at the post-Leninist spectacle? In its present chaos of multiple enterprises, beliefs, sects, political parties and Mafia clans, Russia, though its society trails half a century behind our own, also seems ahead, a terrible harbinger of what might come if radical pluralism becomes violent. But I think this has long been the case with Russia, that with its early brutal terrorism in pursuit of popular political power and its Third World poverty at the end of the twentieth century, it seems to the West both half-ahead and half-behind, half-prophetic and half-retrogressive.

Lenin is only to blame for the ruthlessness with which the system was contrived and the force with which it was imposed. I say 'only' advisedly. An article in the *Simbirsk Courier*, reprinted from the national *Literary Gazette*, has this week identified 'force' as the phenomenon which post-modern Russia is now living after. Force became a habit. It brutalized Russia, with its inborn tendency towards passivity and quiescence. It allowed the creation and the manning of the Gulag and the destruction of daily civility. That force, conceived by Lenin, was intellectually of German origin, but the ideas themselves were brutalized by application to the Russian soil. And so Fedin was right to call his fundamental Bolshevik by the German word for madness or delusion, *Wahn*, and to make him a German who immigrated to the country of his dreams – subsequently the country of sixty million nightmares.

When Rozanov sailed past Ulyanovsk he was most concerned with identifying the turning-point in the nineteenth century which produced out of Russian society the new kind of intellectuals who were capable of such coercive, narrow theorizing on behalf of the general good, as opposed to the humane, tolerant socialist tradition of the first sixty or so years of that century. It is a question that literary history might toy with on the Volga: when did it become more appropriate to embody the Russian situation in the characters of Fedin's Startsov (one of the old-style intellectuals) and Wahn, rather than Goncharov's Oblomov and Stolz? The latter two were neither of them bad, just different, whereas the former, once friends, became victim and assassin under the merciless pressure of ideological correctness. Was the turning-point a kind of disease that Russia contracted? In *The Gift* Nabokov suggested that a deformity had entered the national genes. The deformity dictated a life short of healthy sexual and emotional drive, short of aesthetic finesse and even lacking in common sense, never mind social accomplishment. In the message Lenin forced on society he was certainly, in some of those senses, one-sided and deformed.

Solzhenitsyn rightly emphasized Lenin's statelessness, which made him cold towards ragged Russian reality, and the German heritage through his mother which made him orderly and methodical, and which might in any warmer human context than revolution have proved a virtue. Reflecting that psychological bias, Alyosha finds many German locutions in Lenin's written language, a tendency away from Slavic syntax and towards borrowed abstractions, as well as the inclusion in *What Is to Be Done?* of many foreign, mostly German, words. The famous pronouncement about Communism being the sum of Soviet power and the electrification of the whole country is one example of a Germanification. To the extent that Lenin's prose is symbolic of the new Russian world that he brought into life, you could see every hydroelectric dam along the Volga as a vast and complex German period trying to harness the careless flow of Russian elemental life. Before this tragic forced marriage came about Khlebnikov tried to insist that the Russian element was quite different from the German; but, in his rarified way, he was not organized to move the masses and his prose was deliberately 'beyond' Russian, whereas Lenin's was functional, pedestrian and for its users an efficient manual.

The text of *What Is to Be Done?* is a testament to how abstractions were forced on to reality, and how by the sheer force of Lenin's revolutionary convictions they were made to live, along with the men representing them, opposing them and contesting them. Thus a whole new imagined world was populated and stirred into civil war. One of the counter-revolutionary phenomena was called 'tailism' (the opposite of wanting to be in the vanguard). Another was *Verballhornung*, which Lenin roughly explained as fixin' somethin' which ain't broke, in this case the theories of the Marxist Plekhanov. Lenin battled against opponents guilty of

Lomonosovism (the pursuit of knowledge in isolation, after the Russian eighteenth-century polymath); against a Menshevik whose pen-name was Narcissus Blunt Snout; against Workers' Causites, economists (who thought the workers should simply strive for a more adequate standard of living, not the annihilation of the bourgeoisie and the seizure of the means of production), Bernstein-ians (followers of a German Communist) and Nozdrevs (characters made in the likeness of a Gogolian invention). Mass spontaneity was another enemy. Every argument was contrived to make Lenin and his professional revolutionaries necessary. The book's authoritarian tone, replete with in-jargon, coarsened political discourse irrevocably. Today it is senseless.

The streets of Ulyanovsk were crowded with queues buying post-Soviet meringues, ice creams, fritters and candy floss produced by enterprising individuals. The new capitalist vocabulary of *biznes* and *sponsory*, *barter* and *shopping* hung like bunting for a fair. In the Russian edition of the *New York Times* for sale in Ulyanovsk John Le Carré argued that the West lacked the moral resources to understand that the economic triumph over Communism was not a victory for materialism. Fair enough. Perhaps venality is now the universal order of the day. But we have to hope not. To promote the universal freedom of individuals to improve on their origins, widen their horizons and generally raise the quality of their experience is the positive moral task for any government. Would that such a well-intentioned government might one day befall Russia!

25

I'm Not Stenka Razin

A HIGH WIND blew and the boat rocked. Some passengers were still sunbathing. Around four the smell of wood sap wafted in through the half-open window of the cabin. Following my nose, I found we had sidled up to a wood barge and were taking on laden sacks. The cleaning ladies in their headscarves, ankle socks and slippers were sitting in a row watching.

'What's in the sacks?'

'Is it any business of yours? Keep your nose out.'

'I'm on the ship too. Why shouldn't I know?' Muttering, I went and asked the sailors. It turned out to be grain. Our crew were doing a private deal with the other crew. It was quite fair and legal these days, only not what the babushki were used to. Smug to have an answer, I trotted back past them in my shorts.

On the radio flashed a welcome snatch of Rachmaninov, introducing a programme about Bunin in Israel. Later there was time for exercises on deck. The river, densely wooded on the right bank, with patches of yellow where the oaks had started to discolour, and patches of red where the marl showed through, was so natural it seemed sublime. But I was still thinking about the crones whose self-appointed job was to stifle human curiosity. I often wonder how I would have fared had I been born a thinking peasant in the midst of Gorky's cruel world.

From before Simbirsk we had entered that zone of many nationalities without states, barely heard of outside Russia, and which is also one of the most appealing stretches of the Volga. Now we could see it by daylight. Cheboksary, the Chuvash capital, lay deeply recessed in a rocky bay, backed by hills with new high-rise apartment blocks. Catherine the Great admired the natural setting, and the higher water level hasn't spoilt it, nor has the long concrete embankment built to contain the Cheboksary reservoir. The port was too small to take more than a few liners, so we had to anchor till a berth became free. A pale neo-classical theatre, the Chuvash national stage, stood midway round the bay, with a single white tower and an onion dome further along the curve. Hydrofoils to-ed and fro-ed to Sosnovka on the far side of the river. Cheboksary, dating from the fourteenth century, became one of Ivan the Terrible's outposts, but it never developed trading nor industrial significance in tsarist Russia, except on a local basis for the exchange of food and timber. The Chuvashes, of Finnish origin, mostly lived away from the town. Some people were Orthodox, but many were pagan. The Troitsky monastery on a hill on the far side of the bay was where all-comers – Chuvashes, Russians and Cheremises – could talk, bargain and settle their differences. Today its Vvedenie church is still busy and well organized, with a notice in fluent English begging for alms. Alyosha didn't want to try to get inside, against the closed doors of a service in progress. Instead we toured high and wide on foot.

Little Cheboksary, quieter than usual on a Sunday, possessed a typical stone Soviet civic centre on an heroic scale and a Lenin statue. The National Theatre, on closer inspection, was decorated with such a crudely hewn bas-relief of massive-limbed dancers and muses that we stood and laughed. The art gallery was full of realistic local landscapes. Nothing suggested that the national artistic life was far advanced. A local museum, olefactorily dominated by its basement lavatories, offered mock-up Chuvash interiors, national costumes with woven lime bark shoes, stuffed animals, maps of the adventures of Pugachev, and a montage of President Yeltsin's visit to Cheboksary in 1992.

The museum pointed out that the Chuvash Republic had recently become independent and was bigger than Kuwait, Cyprus or Luxembourg. But not everyone welcomed independence, to judge by the fresh bouquet laid beneath the Lenin statue. Moreover, the currency was still the Russian rouble and the cultural debt was enormous. In the last century, when the nation emerged, Chuvash literary men all had Russian surnames, because these did not exist in Chuvash. Even the Chuvash language was first written down by a Russian, using a modified Cyrillic script.

'Jeez,' said my companion. 'That was a record. We did a whole museum in ten minutes.'

'I couldn't stand it. It smelt of urine.' Silently I added: *The whole of Russia smells of urine.* Then again out loud: 'Just like my cabin smells of humankind.'

He laughed so long I blushed. He said he would use my funny Russian words in his plays.

Cheboksary was a place to buy handicrafts: baskets, carved wood, jewellery and pottery. The wood carving stood in my mind for all the highly ornate woodwork which decorates dachas and izbas from the Upper Volga down to the central forested region. I bought a tray. Then, rather bored, we bought a cake from a woman with a broad Chuvash face and an accent in Russian, and ate it in riverside gardens aflame with red salvias and a monument to Chuvash literacy. The cake was dry and we fed the remains to a dog of no character. The most amusing incident of the morning had come when a young man, an actor from the National Theatre, pointed out the art gallery. A woman scolded him Soviet-style for speaking to us from the road, to which he replied: 'Mother, I am allowed to get in the way of buses, I am a drunk.'

Is the problem boredom? Alyosha recently sounded a warning for the day when the international drugs market found it lucrative to come to Russia: 'I fear for us Russians. We're a nation of narcomanes.' I agreed with trepidation to the hypothesis that Russian boredom caused first a political revolution, and with the mass resort to drugs might finally destroy the nation.

Back on the boat the sense of numbing isolation from the greater world persisted, though the scenery was fine. We stopped in the Cheremis village of Kozmodemyansk, with a manikin silver Lenin and multi-coloured flowerbeds. Two Russian flowers make up the name of this bridgehead which Ivan established to subdue the once rebellious Cheremises. The town retaliated a century later by supplying Stenka Razin with troops. Today it was proud of its age, with its name and the date 1583 flagged in white letters on the hillside. Kozmodemyansk sat peaceful and twee beside the water, out of touch even with Russia, with no new houses, and only a few paved roads – though I must stress that this was the only view we could have of the Mariel Republic, on a twenty-minute shore leave.

Right to Nizhny the Volga served up a feast of green rolling hills, dense woods, small villages sparkling in the late afternoon sun, gleaming churches. Everything seemed as nature designed it centuries ago, except that the Volga was wider, lapping here and there at the roots of newly exposed trees where the drop from land to water was too abrupt.

Our trip on the *Nekrasov* was drawing to a close. I got irritated with the old editor at our dinner table when in reply to my 'Who is to blame?' and 'What is to be done?' he reiterated that the Russians were a very patient people. 'Good God!' I cried, 'I remember being asked at school aged twelve to consider when it might be wrong to be tolerant. I didn't understand then, but I'm beginning to now.'

'Ah, but you have to pay for education in Britain,' he countered, leaving me the choice of losing the real argument by defending the new allegation, or appearing to avoid the issue and ceding him the moral high ground.

'Not mine,' I snapped. 'Argue fairly or I won't talk to you at all.' I am prim.

'Heavens, heavens, *gospozha*, don't get upset!'

I was on my feet and a few heads in the restaurant turned.

Later my adversary and I took a turn on deck and I asked questions about *farvatery* and buoys. This unwanted old Bolshevik was as tightly wrapped against the wind as once his mother must have swaddled him. Nothing was lost by our making peace.

Alyosha sang to me the rest of the evening, including a song he had made up, inspired by our trip. It was called 'I'm Not Stenka Razin'.

There is a rock on the Volga
All overgrown with fierce legend.
There was freedom there, and merriment and feasting.
I stood out quite odd, disgusted and sad,
Holding back my sense of history.
I didn't paint the town red with a bludgeon
I wasn't on the rock

219

I didn't frighten the princess on the ship.
And my blood was silent, only my brow frowned,
Reflecting the affront to my soul.
I'm not Stenka Razin, not a serf nor a master,
In my thoughts I'm not the least patriotic.
I keep my hand far from the knife.
I'm very different from my ancestors.

What to me are the snares of war and the rotten remains in
     museums
I am another kind and compelled to see of which robber I
     am the agent, spilling the bloody slush of the enemy
     while only half-conscious.
The sunset is a red wave of spent blood and the cliffs grow
     white with bonfires.
Who can say whose fault it is that war follows war with
     children not yet born?
Maybe I will never be able to tell you what I seek like a
     dream. But because Stenka threw his bride into the river
     I can't keep quiet in my heart.

This was one way he reacted to our Volga. He felt quite rightly that
Russia had made progress. I didn't have the heart to keep saying:
'Not enough! Not enough!'
     And with that it was time to part.
     'I wish you success and happiness.'
     'I wish you happiness and good health.'
     'Go carefully.'
     'You too.'
Oh, Russia! Any man, any woman must stand out 'odd,
disgusted and sad' before you. After Alyosha left I even lost, for a
whole morning, my ability to understand your tongue.

It was anyway a ghastly morning. I had wedged a toothbrush
between door and doorframe to stop the cabin squeaking in bad
weather. The ship's juddering in the lock before Nizhny meant
losing several hours' sleep. Not even a drink could be prised from

the restaurant, though with hitherto unsighted Russian efficiency the bedclothes were confiscated at 6.45. At Nizhny my host Masha arrived on board and in winter weather we struggled with my luggage on to a tram. I felt like Tolstoy at his mother's funeral. I wanted to cry but I couldn't.

26

Back in Nizhny and Free to Laugh

I N NIZHNY I was staying with two sisters. There had been many recent family upsets coinciding with Russia's turmoil at large, and the atmosphere was heavy with disappointment and stasis. Irina and Masha, coming to terms simultaneously with divorce and the end of Communism, could not envisage a future, though Masha was less than forty and Irina not yet fifty. Unlike their teenage sons they had no desire to emigrate. Besides a divorce, and the break-up of a second relationship since, Irina had been made redundant as a Russian-language tour guide to Nizhny. Masha, after twenty years' service, faced retirement as a copy typist with the KGB. About her employer her son and nephew teased her unmercifully in my presence.

But the changes disturbed her sister more. We visited the spacious and cosy wooden house where Gorky lived with his grandparents. I spoke of Gorky, for whom I had conceived a great respect, for his books, and for the inspiration he drew from the Volga. But, just as the Volga is now attacked for its toxicity, Gorky is not popular these revisionist days. His critics, including Solzhenitsyn, point out that he approved the White Sea Canal forced labour project, which took many lives. This August the *Literary Gazette* had unearthed an interview with the late Formalist critic Mikhail Bakhtin, aiming to denounce Gorky. Bakhtin did far from that, though he observed that Gorky had been set up by the early Soviet authorities as an ideological model – something he clearly was not, with his vacillations and resort to instinct. Gorky was not to the Formalists' literary taste, but they recognized him as an artist. 'No!'

cried Irina. 'I won't have it said Gorky was easily led. Gorky was a good man, a man who helped people to love the world, a man who noticed everything.' I nodded. I said I loved his writing. Yet what Irina was attached to was exactly that fabricated moral perfection.

We entered Nizhny's other important literary museum, a shrine to another priest's son, Nikolai Dobrolyubov. Another nineteenth-century social democrat, in critical terms he was Chernyshevsky's heavenly twin. Both worked on the journal *The Contemporary*, founded by Pushkin. Before he died at the age of twenty-five Dobrolyubov managed to write enough critical essays to fill nine volumes of sanctified Soviet works, and, in doctored form, to hamper the happiness of generations of Soviet schoolchildren. Yet he was one of the century's most perceptive critics, who first saw the significance of Ostrovsky and his play *The Storm*. About the way in which Dobrolyubov was spoilt by his Soviet reputation I also heard from one of Irina's friends, a professor of physics and a direct descendant of Dobrolyubov. She had never taken an interest in her heritage in Soviet times, but with the arrival of perestroika she had felt differently. She read him in the original, complete versions, became elated and wrote a prize-winning book about Nizhny intellectual life in his day. Irina, though, was a less buoyant character. Her heart could not accept that the private, newly discovered Dobrolyubov was a real minority interest rather than an over-publicized source of mass boredom. When we entered the ground floor of Dobrolyubov's former shrine and found it occupied by the vapid higher consciousness pictures and slogans and medita-tion tapes of a Californian Maharishi, and the upper floor closed, she burst into tears.

In this atmosphere even more so than Saratov, which at least had been drunken, social intercourse was very difficult. There was a material–spiritual circuit I couldn't break into. It consisted in being both exhausted by the barbarity of daily life and at the same time cherishing those moral bastions by which Communism oddly protected the soul – a high moral tone in all the arts and culture. One wept now because there was only barbarity. I backed away from constant heart-rending talk. Masha and Irina decided that Russia had sapped my resources.

One day I met some other Westerners, for the first time in

nearly five weeks, and remembered I was free to laugh. My culture was not so precarious. Irina had some American paying guests with whom I overlapped. What's more, they were real missionaries, except on closer questioning they revealed that they too had come to Russia more out of personal interest than proselytizing passion. One was redundant from the recently defeated Bush administration, another a journalist, the third a trained spy. The spy knew Russian but spoke it with a heavy drawl. I enjoyed sharing a Western perspective on Russia for a few hours, speaking my own language. I felt guilty about my laughter in their company, but I had to let off steam somehow. Later, in the company of Masha, the KGB captain who had been trained to fire a gun, I made a joke about one of the men being a redundant spy. She looked like a bewildered child.

Alyosha had left me on my own and I felt it. I carried Masha's and even more Irina's fate with me as I walked about Nizhny. Having told them that Russia in my view cultivated suffering, revelled in it, something that was impressive in literature but unbearable from day to day, I was determined to wander off alone, despite their dire warnings that I would get lost or stranded. In Mayakovsky Street, jotting down details of buildings which pleased me, or which in some way betrayed a quite different pre-revolution-ary function from their present one, I stared mesmerized at two men fighting. They spilled out of a bar and rolled from pavement to gutter. Hardly able to slug each other for lack of coordination, they were nevertheless soon bleeding profusely and caked with mud and dust. The benevolent bar lady in her white kitchen overall grabbed at them and scolded them, repeatedly beginning to march one or other, whichever promised to stay upright longer, to the police station. A man with a briefcase crossed the street to defend or befriend one of the pugilists. He looked like a pre-revolutionary intellectual populist rushing to the aid of the common people. All the while the blood flowed and there was groaning, and the bar lady shouted like an angry schoolteacher and about twenty of us stared, in a way I would be ashamed to do anywhere else in the world. I hated myself for running away from Masha's and Irina's pain, which was much greater. But I was thinking of myself, thinking that Russian souls squat in that mansion of personal freedom we

224

Westerners assume is our inviolable space, and that they crowd the very space which we believe we cannot live without if we are to be individuals. So I had to get out, to keep my judgement.

A mild emergency later in the week made me sort out my thoughts further. Possibly Russia also exacted its pound of flesh for my desire to remain uncommitted. Irina persuaded me to visit the school where she taught, one of the most progressive and distinguished in Nizhny. The idea was for me to see the first-day induction ceremony for seven-year-olds, to admire the bright, solemn faces of forty miniature adults weighed down with enormous new schoolbags and bouquets of flowers. I was to imbibe a scene set to the accompaniment of mild parental anxiety and exaggeratedly benevolent sentiment on the part of very well-dressed female staff who boomed their welcome and their career prognostications through a microphone. A brass band added to the general melancholy. I was feeling quite sick and agitated when I suddenly heard my name amplified across the playground and saw a hundred and fifty curious faces of all ages turn in my direction. Even the bored, fashion-conscious older classes, joshing each other and even sneaking a quick smoke, stopped talking at the word 'London'. This was the first of Irina's two tricks. I had to say a few words to all the hopeful parents of the new free generation. Then, inside the hall, I was to address the upper school. I spoke up for aspects of the West still alien to Russia. I said there were more important things than *biznes* and *shopping*. Westerners have a less ideal view of each other, I said. Perhaps we are more forgiving. There is a kind of irony at the base of our outlook, which makes moral and political judgements relative. We are not looking for heroes and heroines. I declared I was also worried about the wave of neo-religiosity in Russia. (This was rather bold, because the previous speaker had described the role of religion in his life.) I just want to say, ladies and gentlemen, that to espouse religion is not the only way to be a decent human being. It only sets up new un-ironic values. What we have in the West is a public society which talks back to us about our private failings, and which incorporates those failings, those inadequacies into the fabric of daily life. One of the main institutions to have made private inadequacy acceptable as part of public dialogue has been psychoanalysis. Soviet Russia deprived its citizens of that consolation. We are more tolerant of each other as a result of our sense of psychology. We show less peasant cruelty.

For those high-falutin' words, which I nevertheless meant sincerely, I was ritually fêted with flowers from dozens of uncomprehending children, who had to deliver their bouquets somewhere. We carried them home, strap-hanging in the bus. Irina, who had welcomed me as a Russian woman, now declared, considering my speech: 'It seems to me you have the mind of a man.' But basically we agreed. And she went on to say something about psychology being overdue in Russia, which I found inspiring. She said it was time for Russian psychologists to go to the people and spread happiness as populists a hundred years ago went to the people to spread literacy.

I went out running in the autumn rain. Already there was so much of that mud which blights Russian provincial lives most of the year, the towns being only half-paved; so much of that mud which the idealizing Kustodiev refused to include in his pictures of national life that I could hardly advance through the little park with the rusty, overgrown children's playground without slipping over. On a safer, flatter stretch, where I might have relaxed, a middle-aged man muttered loudly: 'Go home!'

I was less hemmed in along the top embankment of the Otkos, where, not far from Chkalov, young people, the girls in fashionable clothes and heavy make-up, the men in light suits, were drinking wine under a sun umbrella. From a catering caravan beside them came the Beatles' number 'Here Comes the Sun'. I thought it was a crime against Russia that the summer should pass so soon and the climate be so severe. Then I ran past something calling itself the Institute of Traumatology and thought that was about right, until the dictionary forced me to concede I was exaggerating again: it was the injuries clinic, the place dealing with broken bones. Only finally that evening did something unequivocally pleasant happen. I was riding in a trolley-bus back from Irina's when, with a great deal of clanking, we ground to a halt. Every man in the bus except one promptly got off. The one remaining turned round to speak to me. He glowed with health the way I have never seen a Russian glow.

'Something wrong with the bus?' I asked.

'Nothing much. We've come off the overhead rail.'

'So the men are going to put us back?'

'You'll be lucky! They're abandoning the bus.'

We laughed, waited for the bus to start up again, spent the time chatting, and finally got off at the same stop, picking our way in the dark, round the potholes, puddles and raised sewers and pipes which constituted this central Nizhny Street, home incidentally of another Gorky house, his birthplace.

'You know this country,' said the man, a doctor, by Masha's front door. 'But aren't you shocked?'

'Yes. Yes. I was once so shocked I left my job. What will it make me do now?'

'Good luck, whatever it is,' he called in parting. This was a mythical person I met, a reincarnation of Chekhov, a beautiful man whom Russia had made a healer. The meeting really happened, too.

The Nizhny Novgorod Fair across the Oka once received as unlikely a visitor as Lewis Carroll. Given the electronically aided fluency of world trade it is no longer like a vast Russian souk, but simply a standing exhibition centre, which I wouldn't have bothered with had it not been presently showing books. A bus took me over the bridge across the Oka. I silently remembered all those travellers who had once stepped from boat to boat and been desperate for a decent hotel. At the gaudy entrance to the angular, much-modernized, nineteenth-century pavilion the usual state of affairs prevailed: any foreigner could get in, but Russians had to queue and have passes. Inside I browsed, chiefly wondering what I could buy for Irina and Masha, because I had left there, because they were on my conscience. Junk fiction abounded, newly translated from English. But there were also, happily, many reprints of classical literature. Minority publishers were particularly interested in the intellectual period to around 1925. I rooted about. It was a fascinating epoch, little known to contemporary Russians. In 1925 Bakhtin was twenty, studying Kant and the Russian idealist Vladimir Soloviev. For his interest in philosophical idealism he was exiled four years later, after publishing a book on Dostoevsky. In 1925 Berdyayev was also studying idealism and preparing to write about the soul of man under Communism. Later, from abroad, he published a journal called *The Way*. Now post-Communist Russia has resurrected *The Way* to publish for the first time in Russia writings of individualist thinkers like Soloviev, Rozanov and Berdyayev, together with articles reflecting the latest intellectual scene in the West. I found the first number at the book fair; in it editor Anatoly Yakovlev articulated Russia's present intellectual and moral pain, abandoned by a Soviet heritage which was 'The Fabrication of a Tradition'.

> When social and daily reality give a person no hope of support, when objects, people and symbols lose their definition and become unstable and somehow inauthentic, that is the exact moment when thought turns to other criteria, and time finds another measure: then neither days nor weeks, neither months nor years, not even centuries are significant; the human ego strives to find an asylum, an escape from real burdens, in thinking in more universal categories.

Now that was the essay I had to buy for Irina and Masha. A serious present? I'll say. But it's difficult to keep laughing in Russia, unless you're Alyosha. Tucking the book under my arm, crossing back over the Oka, I thought anxiously of the pact he had made with himself to stay alive.

27

The Magic of
the Transvolga

THIS NEXT chapter is about magic. It is perhaps the only chapter in the whole book an intending tourist should read, for only briefly, in Transvolga folklore, is it possible to forget the grinding misery of contemporary Russia.

The Makariev monastery is where the Fair was held for two hundred years before moving to Nizhny. Makarievo has since dwindled to a village, but the monastery is a legendary sight, a grand, fortified, high-walled, white corral with thatched squat Russian towers resembling chimneysweeps' brushes stowed stick first into tall chimney pots. In its original state it was depicted on two famous icons. The whole stands on an isthmus where the river Kerzhenets enters the Volga.

The Volga–Kerzhenets junction was a meeting point for ships. At the monastery pilgrims offered and traded goods. From these activities arose an annual fair which received the tsar's warrant in 1641. Makariev was adopted as patron saint and his day, 25 July, taken as the start. A German visitor in 1804 described the Leipzig and Frankfurt fairs as barely deserving the name by comparison. Here were erected some four thousand wooden stalls beside stone walls and the *gostinny dvor*. The Makariev Fair flourished until a fire in 1816. The site then moved so quickly that it caused Pushkin to introduce a minor anachronism into his novel in verse, *Eugene Onegin*.

The monastery was founded on the Yellow Lake, since swallowed by the Volga. The power of Makariev to attract followers led the Tartars to burn it down in 1439, but the monastery was revived in the seventeenth century, after Ivan had subdued the Tartars. It stored merchandise and provided accommodation. From 1883 it became a nunnery, and Rozanov tells a parallel story of another Makariev monastery in Reshme which suggests why: the number of monks having dwindled, the remainder became so lazy and drunk that the Church closed the place down. The Bolshevik state seized the Makariev nunnery, but briefly let the nuns stay on. The nuns allowed Church valuables to be sold to buy food abroad during the 1921 famine.

Today from Nizhny the 100km (60 mile) journey south to Makarievo takes two hours by hydrofoil; the stop is new. The alternative is a difficult route overland. It is an isolated spot, often hit by storms and floods. When Peter the Great visited in 1722 he had the high-water level of 1709 marked in his name. In 1926 Makarievo struggled to breathe above flood waters which rose another 13.5 metres (44 ft) higher. By the same token it is a wonderful place to escape: indeed the only such countryside I have ever seen in Russia.

The beauty of the area, particularly inland up the Kerzhenets river to Lake Svetloyar, helped inspire a legend which moved Rimsky-Korsakov to write an opera, a sweet-onerous national lament called *Tale of the Invisible City of Kitezh and the Maiden Fevronya*. It was said that between Makarievo and the lake there was a town, Bolshoi Kitezh, which when threatened by the Mongol Batu was swallowed by the lake and became invisible, thereafter continuing its existence underground. If the traveller put his ear to the ground between Makarievo and Svetloyar he would hear the bells of Kitezh pealing below.

I was an unexpected traveller on the local *meteor* or hydrofoil, and the collective farm deputy manager in the next seat offered me cucumbers and tomatoes and lots of personal enthusiasm for the Volga. Then he asked: 'Are you married?' I suppose he thought why would any woman give her passionate, undiluted attention to a river? Married to Russia, but on the verge of divorce, I thought, but otherwise shook my head.

The sharp-prowed hydrofoil swished up to the wooden pontoon beneath the monastery wall and turned to halt like an ice skater in slow motion. All around for miles was blue water and wooded land, with a few haystacks and a single human figure along the riverbank. I said goodbye to the farmer, and our barely sprung, worn seats. A former English teacher in a bobble hat, an audible lover of English phonemes, addressed me caressingly in my own language, then hastened off to see a sick friend. She was going to walk the seven kilometres, she wanted me to know. While we talked, some young men set sail from beside the station using an improvised boat with a sapling for a mast.

Once the noise of the *meteor* receded, the silence resounded. I crossed the dry, reedy grass to the monastery's twenty-foot-high wooden front door, and pulled the bell tug. A vile hooter broke the silence but provoked no answer. The sunshine just lacked the power to summon forth an Indian summer.

Makarievo was an entrance into Old Believer country, which stretched up the Kerzhenets river. The early nineteenth-century historian Pavel Melnikov-Pechersky, whose work re-created the intricate, half-buried past of his native Nizhny and its surroundings for later generations, wrote two long tales about the lives of these fundamentalists, which he called *In the Woods* and *In the Hills*. Both the collective farmer and Irina mentioned that I should read these huge volumes. Perhaps one day. Then I will return to glide up the quiet Kerzhenets in one of its typical flat-bottomed boats, half-punt, half-canoe, and here and there examine a gravestone. I have seen pictures of the boats, called *botniki*, and they look as if they have been hollowed out of tree trunks and have not changed for a thousand years.

I hooted at the front door of the monastery a second time. A young nun answered. Beneath her dusty black habit she wore a red pullover, a skirt and thick woollen stockings. Her hair was dragged back by a woollen headscarf exposing an expressive, high-cheek-boned face and full, shapely lips. Her hands were rough and her breath smelt of sausage. Inside the kremlin a mare and her foal and a few sheep grazed. There was a kitchen garden. Thousands of visitors from many countries have come since the nunnery reopened in 1990, and that has provided money for repairs. Some workmen, making as if to mend the summer church, looked up: 'Heh, Yelena, have you got a visitor?' Their voices were lurid, and Yelena lowered her eyes. I wanted her to talk about herself, but she refused. She must have practised keeping her voice so steady and calm as she declaimed the monastery's history. The vast, tall, bare and damp interior of the Troitsky, regarded as the winter church, was no happy place to stand with its faded frescoes and cracked walls and memories of wealth. In 1838 the Chernetsov brothers estimated the weight of silver used on the jewel-studded icon covers at over 400 kilos (nearly 900 lb). Yelena spoke scornfully of Soviet desecration: the way the monastery was turned into a children's home in 1927, and after the war was entrusted to a veterinary institute whose director let animals loose in the frescoed church and left cabbages to rot there. Water, though, wrought the main damage. The Troitsky frescoes, executed in natural pigments, were almost obliterated. Before the completion of a restoration project under Stalin, war intervened and Makariev became an evacuation hospital.

I was interested in how today's twenty or so nuns had been so ready to take up their vocation when freedom came. Yelena said they had prepared themselves for many years through the underground Church. Now I think it is possible that in the whole world it was only the Church in Russia that was ready for the end of Communism.

On the return *meteor* I found a deckchair seat in the lounge. From there the history of the *raketa*, the *meteor* and the *sputnik*, the various sizes of Soviet hydrofoil designed by Rostislav Alexeev (1916–80), dominated the view forwards. Alexeev and his team changed the daily life of the river from the late 1950s, making the Volga at all points an efficient local transport route with these rapid and until recently inexpensive ferries. Thank you, Comrade Alexeev. They're fun. Even glamorous with their long foamy wake. Not much in the country is. Or perhaps I'm just going soft.

Together Irina and I did one other trip by *raketa*, 55km (30 miles) in the opposite direction upstream from Nizhny, to the ancient town of Gorodets. The boat was smaller and seemed faster. On deck was a small terrier who rode the *raketa* as a way of life. Yes, I am right, it is fun! In our wake a youth in a rowing boat is riding the waves like surf. At last! Something to do in Russia.

We passed at close hand the Sormovo shipyard, a power station releasing dense white smoke into the pale blue autumn sky, then Balakhna, a small town with a salt industry which by some accounts predates Nizhny and may have been a Bolgar trading town. Gorky's grandmother admired its famous lace-makers. Near the old town stands a huge 1930s' paper mill at Pravdinsk, which makes, you've guessed, the newspaper for *Pravda*.

After these sights on the right bank, the view became green and flat and rural either side. Gorodets appeared to be a beach of mud beneath a sheer cliff. Any obvious path had vanished, leaving only a few planks and corrugated sheets to bridge the mud, but there were two snakes of people from the river station, one taking the invisible low road, one approaching an apparent high road via a long, steep wooden staircase. This was of the rough-hewn kind, with a rail and slightly crooked, the kind which so often occur in prints of traditional Russian villages. The crookedness gives the picture a quality somewhere between the daemonic and the simple-minded, like a village by Chagall.

We climbed these steps to the town of Gorodets, looking back down through dense treetops to the water, where barges laden with timber passed. A few hundred yards upriver stood the huge Gorky hydroelectric station with its lock and weir. Across on the right bank of the river new motor industry was concentrated at Zavolzhe. What contrasts! Here were the epitome of dirty Soviet industry, high engineering ambition, the slow chug-chug of barges closer in their speed and ambition to ordinary life, and eternal mud. The brow of the hill suddenly levelled to give a flat green space. Midway along what might have been an esplanade, but was no more than a hilltop with houses, some workmen were digging, and others readying a stone pedestal. On the latter rested a bottle of vodka, but this was soon to be replaced with a long yearned-for statue of Alexander Nevsky.

Nevsky, Prince of Vladimir, died here in 1263, when Moscow was still a backwater and Gorodets the eastern outpost of the Russian principalities of Vladimir and Suzdal. He had been away paying the required tribute to the Golden Horde, which included a winter in harsh conditions at Sarai-Berke. On Nevsky's death his youngest son Daniel became ruler of Moscow, which doubled in size during his forty-year reign. So Nevsky gives Gorodets a hint of past grandeur and status. That may be why the Communist authorities always refused to erect a statue.

We dropped in on the editor of the local newspaper, housed in a wooden villa on the esplanade. The hole-in-the-ground conveniences, my main reason for suggesting the diversion, couldn't have changed much since the days of Nevsky. The editor with his droopy moustache, like the Beatle George Harrison transplanted in space and time, was welcoming though not very helpful. The money for the statue was coming 'from a Mamontov', but who knew which. Sergei Mamontov, industrialist and financier, was Shalyapin's early patron. Post-Communist Russia now falls over itself to remember families like this, who, quite unlike the Communist picture painted of their greed, used their wealth to build churches and hospitals and factories and to fund theatre and ballet.

Prince Yury Dolgoruky, son of the last man to unite the medieval power of Kiev Rus, founded Gorodets in 1152. Still visible is part of a ravine dug for fortification. In 1238 the Mongols razed the town, and a layer of ash is the geological testament; more recently cleaved skeletons, crushed skulls and a Russian helmet have been unearthed. The city revived, and experienced its finest years as a medieval administrative centre and Volga trading post. It even minted its own silver coins, and there is evidence of a high standard of literacy. But everything was lost in the second Mongol obliteration of 1408. Gorodets ceded its importance to nearby Balakhna, and did not recover its status as a town until 1921.

Today Gorodets, its Lenin small and gold, half-hidden by trees, glows with new whitewash and blooming geraniums in anticipation of the possible visit of President Yeltsin to unveil the Nevsky statue. In the upper town, the mid-nineteenth-century part, arranged concentrically, almost every house is in the decorative wooden style, the façades and window frames and eaves worked into a pageant of carving. The subjects are mythological and classical. Some of the houses are so overladen that they seem to be dripping wooden lace. I wonder if this little town does not have a guaranteed quota of varnish and paint, whatever Alyosha might say. Since before the Time of Troubles Gorodets has betokened favour and received it. Ksenya Godunova, Boris's daughter, owned it, then Shuisky's wife.

The houses of Gorodets and elsewhere along the Volga led Igor

Grabar to see decorative domestic architecture as the genius of the nation. House decoration and domestic artefacts are certainly a way into that colourful, pagan mind. Decorative moulds are special because Gorodets was famous for its *pryanik*, a holiday cake packed with spices reflecting the wealth of trade with the East; beloved by children, it was sold as a local speciality at the Nizhny Fair. By the mid-nineteenth century the stylized illustrations on the moulds included goods trains and Volga steamboats.

Fabric is another Volga treasure. The Gorodets weavers produced prized linen tablecloths with decorative borders. The town still claims distinction in fabric-making, though Irina and I found nothing of the kind in the dark draper's shop in the lower town which reminded me of my Welsh childhood. Nor did we find any *pryanik* at the baker's.

Still, this is a tourist paradise, and when the port is improved the liners will stop and people will realize.

When the tourists come in greater numbers, then will be the time to relish the story of Little Kitezh, a town in legend which seems to have been based on Gorodets, once called Kideshka. The action of Rimsky-Korsakov's opera of 1904, *Tale of the Invisible City of Kitezh*, begins here. In Little Kitezh the maiden Fevronya and Prince Vsevolod were enjoying their wedding feast when the Tartar army arrived to besiege the town. Vsevolod was killed and Fevronya taken prisoner. Meanwhile a Judas from Little Kitezh, Grishka Kuterma, offered to show the Tartars the way to the capital, their most desired prize, Great Kitezh. This was the town midway between Makarievo and Lake Svetloyar. As in the legend, so in the opera: Great Kitezh disappeared under the water rather than let itself be taken. At the sight of this magic the Tartars dispersed in fright. The traitor Kuterma, full of remorse, fled to the forest and went mad. Which left only Fevronya to see good in the magical vision. At the lakeside she slipped under the water to be reunited in a paradisical life with Vsevolod. The music emerging out of this action is of that colourful folk song-and-dance variety beloved by all the nineteenth-century Russian composers, married to a nostalgic, impressionistic evocation of steppe and forest. The battle against the Tartars at the traditional Russian wedding feast makes a glamorous and afterwards brooding centrepiece.

There is this magical quality about the Volga, and its history, which spawns such legends and begs for a musical representation, and the magic seems especially strong near Nizhny. For here, where the Volga embraces her sister, the Oka, Tchaikovsky too set an opera. *The Sorceress* (*Charodeyka*) tells of a beautiful fallen woman, Kuma, who works in an inn and exercises her magic over first the Prince and then his son, Yury. Morally tarnished, as the saying used to go, she is redeemed by her true love of Yury, even while she is poisoned by the Prince's wife for her less commendable seduction. The tale unfolds against a background of memorable local colour, for Kuma works in an inn where there is much imbibing. The opera, Tchaikovsky's penultimate and rarely performed, ends with a grand, *Lear*-like scene. The Prince roams the forest in a storm, mad with grief. Kuma is dead, his wife is a murderer, and he has killed his son.

In Gorodets, on the surrounding Kirillov hills, exists yet one more legend. This is also magic, but this time it connects the mystery of one part of the Volga to another. It was said that if a ship passed Gorodets at dawn, the hills would open and sacred elders in white robes would emerge to send a greeting to their brothers in Zhiguli. And similarly in Zhiguli the old monks of the hills would hail their northern brethren. The Volga thus keeps its identity over two thousand miles and through fifteen degrees of latitude. It is the one Russian mother, and a cultural mother above all.

28

Reasons for Pessimism

THE *Chernyshevsky*, which I had reboarded, was a kind of home. But it was also draughty, bare and understaffed at the end of the season. Some Belgian tourists seemed charmingly exotic. I had been away long enough to feel an exaggerated, detached fondness for Western ways. The bar took over from the sundeck. We drank Moldavian brandy and many small strong black coffees made with real coffee beans, and ate chunky Russian chocolates with soft centres, which doubled as small change. The six Belgians dressed nicely for dinner, a different outfit for the women every night, and afterwards they danced and were jolly, though they had to make their own company. Most other passengers comprised Russian friends of the staff, intent on disco-ing.

My companions were a man and wife whom I presumed to be Russian, until I noticed that the man was translating everything into English. Peter was twenty-two when his family was expelled from Russia in a spectacular prisoner exchange across the Berlin Wall. His father, one of five exchanged, was a dissident Baptist. Peter too had spent a year confined for the same cause. Now he was back in Russia, in the shipping business. His American architect wife was supporting him and gleaning experience for the day when she hoped to enter US politics. What fine companions they were! We talked non-stop the three grey, blustery days back to Moscow. Peter, prematurely grey – thanks to his time in prison, perhaps – was good with people, quietly spoken and fearless. I learned from him how to deal with Homo Sovieticus. We were lunching when Pavarotti came on the radio. Lord, music at last! Russians, despite being on their way out of the dining room, kept reaching up and switching these lovely arias off, something they never did with pop.

Each time Peter patiently switched on again. The lovely tenor voice then seemed all we needed to make the autumn Volga lovable.

It's not the same, of course, to see the river without sunshine, and I wonder how different would have been my impressions had I, at least part of the time, looked on the ice-bound Volga from its snowy banks in winter. In winter pictures of Nizhny and Astrakhan the great liners berthed together seem to have an almost animal nature, suggesting patience, stoicism and nobility. Now is the season when the captain and his seamen rest at home after their five summer months away, and the ships are painted and repaired. The Upper Volga is normally frozen from the end of October to mid-April. As far south as Volgograd the ice season has shrunk to November–March, and in Astrakhan it is the shortest, only beginning in December. The winter of the battle of Stalingrad was one of record cold, and tanks manoeuvred on the ice. From the same latitude there are accounts a hundred years ago of camels and sleds travelling over the ice. Mariengof remembered horse-drawn sleds elegantly traversing the river at Nizhny, and of course the ice was always thick enough for skating. Only these days, perhaps because of a relatively warm period on the earth, Russian winters are not what they used to be, nor the ice reliable. Or perhaps people have become more sensible. Mrs Atkinson in 1863 described being required to set out from Nizhny for Kazan with all her luggage on a sled, and soon passing another such vehicle half-submerged and deserted.

Upriver from Nizhny forest dominated the red soil of the right bank, with trees and their exposed roots again showing at the water's edge. The right bank trees were turning, with now and again an entire yellow dress hung in a wardrobe of greens and rusts. The left bank, green, flat and constant, was still of an Alpine sharpness and stillness. The day, 4 September, had been dark, cold and grey, but at 7pm the sun shone, clearing and brightening the evening. Farms and fields on the left bank slotted neatly into place, and there were occasional woods on that side of the river too.

Between roughly Nizhny and Tver, in just this kind of landscape, with the historical memory of battles against Mongols and Poles and Lithuanians, and the dominant economic force of merchants who traded along the river, so much Russian literature and poetry and music has been inspired and created that it might be called the first cradle of Russian art, home of traumatic drama and lacquered spoons side by side. The satirist Mikhail Saltykov-Shchedrin came from an old family which bore a Tartar name. He was born in Tver, and worked as a government official. But of far more intimate connection with the Volga were Nekrasov and Ostrovsky. Closest to where our ship was passing now, 100km (60 miles) before Kostroma, Ostrovsky lived at Shchelykovo, 17km (10 miles) inland from the left bank of the Volga at Zavolzhsk, opposite Kineshma. His father, an archpriest, came from Kostroma.

The Volga is such a powerful force in *The Storm*: in no other Russian written work is the river harnessed more effectively. Leos Janacek turned the play into the mighty opera *Katya Kabanova*. The Volga expresses the elemental freedom to which Katya and her lover Boris Dikoi are fatally attached, in contrast to the dark, repressive, narrow world they come from. Katya's hateful, scheming mother-in-law, who only wishes unhappiness and destruction upon all around her, who does her best to stop life blossoming, is unrelentingly evil. About Boris and Katya two motifs play, which subtly reiterate the bond with the river: one is the feeling of being free as a bird, the other is the sense of being in the grip of an uncontrollable power. Katya is possessed of a headlong passion for living which gives her a blazing vision of sin and a morbid awareness of immanent death. Boris's surname means 'wild'. The bird motif, linked to the river, recalls those folk songs which the singers on the *Chernyshevsky* explained to me on the journey out. Here is the quintessence of human life, and there in the water that the bird skims across is universal nature. That is the folk plane, which operates powerfully in the play, with songs being often and repeatedly sung and quoted.

But also on a broader, social level, the symbolism of which proceeds directly from the layout of all the small Volga towns that Ostrovsky knew, from Tver to Kineshma, the wide river contrasts with the narrow venality of the mercantile town, and the darkness and poverty and monotony of lives stifled in stuffy dark wooden houses. The frontier between two kinds of life, one repressed and mean, the other wild and free, is the Promenade. In *The Storm* we are told directly that the good aspect of the Promenade, its power to

239

exercise and refresh, has been neglected. Kulygin, the bystander who gives the play its moral orientation, observes that the poor have no time to take the air, that the middling people only come to show off their clothes; meanwhile the rich bully their servants and each other, shunning the air to promote the cause of darkness. Only drunks cross the Promenade by accident. Then the storm brings people out of their houses like a minor apocalypse. That night Katya appears on the embankment and throws herself into the Volga. The Volga is the only home for this bold, restless, modern spirit, struggling against wilful destructiveness.

Ostrovsky studied the obscurantism, the domestic tyranny, the unusually cruel sexual customs around Tver which allowed girls great freedom before marriage, but kept them in purdah ever after, and he looked at the causes of poverty. He might have been writing of the economic problems of 1993 when he noted the relentless desire to buy and sell, rather than work hard on the river. He made his 1856 journey from Tver to Nizhny as part of a government economic survey at the beginning of Alexander II's reign, prior to the Emancipation of the Serfs. Later he published twenty-five pages of elliptical travel notes, essential background to *The Storm*. Curiously for the Volga, they end with the words 'like the Nile . . .'. Fifty years later Rozanov would write up his notes as *The Russian Nile*. Ostrovsky then mooted a cycle of plays headed 'Nights on the Volga'. *Kozma Minin* appeared in 1862 and *The Voevoda* or *Dream on the Volga* in 1865 (the basis for Tchaikovsky's opera *The Voivoda*). Years later, in 1879, Ostrovsky finished *The Woman Without a Dowry*. He loved the Volga region, with its fairy-tales and folk wisdom and dark woods; he sensed the river's potential on stage as a presiding god or a mute Greek chorus.

Kostroma itself is not only a backdrop to Ostrovsky's life and work but enlivens so much Russian literature. The critic Yevgeny Belov suggested that this was where the townspeople might have prepared for Gogol's government inspector to visit, and where the same author's Chichikov traded in dead souls. It is where a quaking boy of seventeen was chosen to be the first Romanov tsar, and where the last Romanovs, Nicholas and Alexandra, celebrated the tercentenary of the dynasty in 1913. It is where a peasant who saved the life of the first Romanov tsar-elect, Ivan Susanin, inspired the lovely Italianate opera by Glinka now performed in the open air here. Everyone in the arts used to frequent Kostroma before the Revolution: Kustodiev, Blok, Rerikh, Meyerhold and Alexei Tolstoy were among them. The paintings in the town's art gallery include some of the Volga at last, with an example of the Chernetsov brothers' naive work, a number by Kustodiev, and one of men on a Volga ferry in the mid-nineteenth century which might perfectly illustrate Chekhov.

We found the silvery and whitish-yellow neo-classical stone town full of literature and echoes of Ostrovsky. But first the parody: to the row of wooden landing stations that the *Chernyshevsky* joined were anchored so many great names: the *Feodor Dostoevsky*, the *Mikhail Lomonosov*, the *Maxim Gorky*, the *Vissarion Belinsky*, the *Leo Tolstoy*. And the temptation: we watched people breakfasting on the other ships and envied them their orange juice and rolls. I have gone this whole trip without explaining a technicality: the Volga ships moor parallel and passengers go ashore by crossing through the middle of one or two other ships. Each ship is a mirror image of the next, so it is easy to compare conditions and even to get lost. Another technicality is that if you miss your boat you may take any other river craft to rejoin it at the next port – but only the insane would voluntarily test this rule.

In Kostroma Rozanov spent his impoverished, semi-orphaned childhood watching the rain. He would run barefoot on to the porch in the morning and see that it was raining, as almost always. The unyielding greyness inspired a metaphysical rebellion. He remembered: 'Why should I be a good boy if everywhere the world is as ghastly as this?' To his physical introduction to the world in Kostroma, aged five, Rozanov directly linked his later intellectual pessimism.

Our weather was dry but unpredictable. Russians donned mackintoshes, headscarves, tights and sandals. Peter's wife lent me a pullover. I'm a rotten traveller. I have a Freudian inability to pack a suitcase. The guide was gloomy and intractable. 'Speak a little slower!' I begged, to which she snapped: 'I know how to do my work.'

Stone shopping arcades from the late eighteenth and early nineteenth centuries are the Kostroma centrepiece. But as usual trading was happening outside, on the walls and on the ground, and comprised the familiar jumble of souvenir books and postcards, newly translated *bestsellery* and imported tinned goods. A black-moustachioed man, bare-headed and wearing trainers, rode up on a chestnut thoroughbred, offering rides behind his saddle. I wanted to go but didn't dare deviate from the motorized tour which was the only way of seeing the area.

A passenger who was an art historian told me she would buy linen here. Kostroma factories have produced it for more than two centuries. Pavel Mikhailovich Tretyakov, the private collector who founded the national art gallery in Moscow, made his fortune that way and his *style moderne* house is a minor attraction. The barmaid on the *Chernyshevsky* had promised her mother pasta from Kostroma. Ostrovsky quoted Pushkin, who committed to verse that a nearby Volga town, Torzhok, excelled in macaroni. Kostroma was also known for its fish cookery. Ostrovsky noted that the fish were so thick in the river here they were caught with sacks. But everything changes, not just in Russia. Touristic purchases look back to an unverifiable golden past. Rousseau first described the romantic habit when the difference between regions, and their remoteness from each other, still justified it. Now in Europe just the time-wasting habit remains. You see I'm not much of a shopping tourist. Though Russia, like its September weather, is unpredictable. For Russians to visit a place where this or that manufacture originated is still a treat, notwithstanding that today neither linen nor pasta would be found.

Our guide hauled us all off to see the Lenin memorial. The Kostroma Lenin is odd for being crudely superimposed on the 1913 monument to the same man's enemies 'Romanov and Co.', as if one culture could supplant another so directly. 'Phui! Wretched Communists with no aesthetic taste!' said the guide, describing how the Romanov detail on the monument had been erased, leaving a monstrosity. I could have done without her tendentious guidance.

The same Yury Dolgoruky of Suzdal who laid the foundation of Gorodets founded Kostroma in 1152, and like its downstream neighbour it was twice wiped out by the Tartars, reaching in the meantime a position of eminence in Rus. Some thirty churches destroyed by a fire in 1413 were a benchmark of Kostroma's medieval importance. The next two hundred years saw it develop and flourish as an east-west trading centre. Fish, flour, salt, icons, iron and furs changed hands in its markets, while Kostroma soap, jewellery and fabric were prized. The English, following their first contacts with Ivan, established a trading station here. On account of the Romanov connection, from the seventeenth century the best architects and builders in stone in Russia came from or were associated with Kostroma. Led by Gury Nikitin and Sila Savin, Kostroma icon painters frescoed churches with unsurpassed skill. Kostroma retains from its wealthy days 328 manuscript books, including the *Ipatiev Chronicles* which told the tale of Prince Igor, the basis for Borodin's opera, and a Godunov family Bible.

The old boyar families competed to invest in the town. Legend told that the Godunovs' Tartar ancestor Chet had a vision while taken ill at the Ipatiev monastery. On his recovery he converted to Christianity and blessed the holy place in eternity. This was the monastery where the Godunovs subsequently invested their wealth, while the rival Saltykovs endowed the Bogoslavsky monastery, now the oldest building in Kostroma.

Like all Russian provincial towns, Kostroma has lost hundreds of buildings to fire over the centuries, but there is still a preponderance of stone buildings. Townspeople say today that Nicholas II asked to move to Kostroma with his family after his forced abdication; he always loved its atmosphere and traditions. Catherine called here in 1767 on the same pale green ship, the *Tver*, which carried her on to Makarievo and Kazan and Cheboksary. She was followed by Paul I (he who proposed the Russian conquest of India in concert with Napoleon against the British, until his reign was brutally curtailed by murder). The main square, named after Susanin, with the tag 'Revolution Square' already in its past, is chiefly impressive for being old and all of a neo-classical piece. The ochre and white stone Russian Fire Tower resembles a lighthouse in an architectural style from Ancient Greece. Nearby stands the Guardhouse, also built in the mostly outward-looking reign of Alexander I. Now it is the Wedding Palace. Close by, a score of solid, official-looking nineteenth-century buildings, some with attractive curved frontages, include the one-time Hotel London where Nekrasov used to stay, and the former Communist Party headquarters, before that the Gentry Assembly, where each tsar had a commemorative room. Near the Volga, meanwhile, stand two columns which used to designate the Moscow Gate, the river tradesmen's entrance into town. The pillars each bore a bronze double-headed Romanov eagle. Today without the eagles, they are barely noticeable.

Finally there is the Susanin monument to observe. The story is gripping, because it reinforces the Romanov connection, gives the local people a vital role in Romanov well-being against the Polish/Lithuanian enemy, and has left a curious legacy in architecture and a beautiful one in music. In a story which reverses the treachery of Gury Kuterma in Kitezh, Susanin led the Poles astray in local woods but sacrificed himself. The town gave Susanin the original monument in 1851 – a red granite pedestal with a bas-relief showing his death by Polish sabre. A kneeling statue of him as a bearded and learned-looking elder with his hands folded in prayer topped the pedestal. Beside him rose a tall, slender column holding a bust of the angelic young Romanov. The entire monument was destroyed in the Revolution or after. When Soviet Russia built a new one, of yellow sandstone, in 1967, it depicted Susanin alone. Thus officialdom did for the monument exactly what it did to the opera when it removed from Glinka's own change of title, *A Life for the Tsar*, all trace of the monarch and insisted on calling the opera just *Ivan Susanin*.

We went out to Ipatiev to inspect the Romanov chambers and the Troitsky church with the Nikitin and Savin frescoes. The white fifteenth-century monastery with its fortified kremlin wall and gold cupolas sits regally at the confluence of the Kostroma and the Volga. In the village by natural survival and inside the monastery grounds, many having been brought on purpose to form an open-air museum, are striking wooden buildings, churches built without nails, and village bathhouses on stilts rescued from the path of the Great Volga. Inside the monastery the Troitsky frescoes, in deep blue with red and gold, are splendid. To assess their artistic merit one would need hours in their presence, and the time would be absorbingly spent.

Under Alexander II the Romanov chambers were remade in seventeenth-century style. They comprise a modest two-storey oblong building reached by a solid stone staircase, and with a heavy porch shaped like a keyhole forced apart. Since 1990 an exhibition has been mounted here. The documents include Nicholas II's unpublished love letters to Princess Alix of Hesse (the granddaughter of Queen Victoria who became Tsarina Alexandra). Nicholas's English is movingly perfect, though he insists on writing his endearments in his own tongue, even if unintelligible, so the letters are peppered with Russian too. It is probably a characteristic of cross-linguistic love affairs everywhere. The photographs show the room in Sverdlovsk in the Urals where the family and their servants were massacred. I toured the exhibition alone. Russians, though this newly permitted aspect of their cruel history fascinates them, probably could not have afforded the one dollar entrance fee. The immediate beneficiaries of the display were the babushki attendants who swaddled each exhibit with excessive tenderness and rote learning.

It's strange to be in a country which so recently killed its king, and to hear that 'king' speak through his letters with terms of passion and fondness familiar from one's own life. In the early days after the Revolution the violence was justified in so many Russian and international minds by the idea that justice was finally being done, after decades of tyrannical tsarist rule and mass social hardship. In de Mille's *The Volga Boatman* the aristocrats, still in their evening finery, were fastened into *burlak* harnesses and made to pull a ship. Their new masters flogged them. Yet the morally exceptional boatman only asked that they should work alongside him and know his lot, and begged for them not to be killed. Played by William Boyd he looked like an heroic Jesus, as Tuzhansky's Stenka Razin did.

By contrast revolutionary violence in the round was simply violence, often for its own sake. Bely's *Petersburg* hummed with that raw and directionless violence, like electricity in the air, so we can still know what it felt like.

Rozanov wondered what came over Russia. He asked of a whole generation, his generation: where did the stubborn dedication to the cause, and the certainty, and the revolutionary passion, come from? He set down his answer in middle age while cruising the Volga. The men of the 1860s and 1870s were 'reborn' when they severed links with the Christian tradition. They concerned themselves exclusively with an ethnographical reality, which excluded from significance friendship, forgiveness, non-resistance to violence, and charity. They resembled the Ostrogoths barbarizing the Romans, said Rozanov. Turgenev drew his portrait of such a man with more pathos in *Fathers and Sons*.

Monks in gold robes were processing up the stone-canopied staircase into the Troitsky. They had left a bus like ours, and had come from where we had been, at the Bogoslavsky nunnery, officiating at the service as the Orthodox Church requires male priests to do. The Troitsky bells rang, their tuning dissonant and wild like faith wrestling to contain the mystery of life. The Ipatiev bells were famous in the seventeenth century – which didn't stop them being melted down to finance Peter I's war with Sweden. They were restored in the 1960s. In Yaroslavl Rozanov met a blind bellringer who helped him understand the art. He concluded that the sad vespertine bell of Russian churches deterred sceptics and satirists from travelling further along their paths of criticism and protest, and that perhaps for that reason Russia never produced a Voltaire or a Renan. Perhaps. But what resulted were violent anarchists and nihilists instead, and the damage they did is incomparable.

29

The Cachet of an Ancient Russian Town

THE *Chernyshevsky* was headed for Yaroslavl, on the right bank of the Volga, 80km (50 miles) on from Kostroma and our final stop. We arrived next morning in heavy rain, serenaded by a professional jazz band from the quay. None of the players, in shabby raincoats and trainers, was less than fifty. Beside these talented musicians young men sold postcards and books and Chaika pocket watches for dollars. The younger generation seemed trivial.

Yaroslavl takes its name from the eleventh-century Prince Yaroslav the Wise of Kiev Rus, who wanted free passage here for his merchant ships. In the battle against local plunderers he killed a bear loosed on him, and this animal became the symbol of a city whose early concentration of wealth and monasteries made it one of Russia's very few great centres of beauty and learning. It suffered under the Mongols, and the 'Grieving Hill' battle site became a natural monument to that enslavement. Yaroslavl also became the centre of Russian opposition to the Poles and Lithuanians. From here Minin and Pozharsky marched with their Volga army to liberate Moscow.

Baron Haxthausen observed the two hundred spires and cupolas of his day and suggested that Yaroslavl bore comparison with Hamburg, except that it had scarcely twenty-five thousand inhabitants. Gautier wrote of the same epoch: 'Yaroslavl certainly has the cachet of ancient Russian towns, if the name old can be given to something in Russia where whitewash and colourwash doggedly cover up every trace of age.' Today Yaroslavl still has many spires and cupolas, a modest amount of whitewash, and six hundred and forty thousand inhabitants, but many modern visitors pass through feeling that they have found less than they expected.

This is a pity. Yaroslavl is a relative of Nizhny Novgorod. The splendid once-private town houses along the Volga esplanade as far as the confluence with the Kotorosl, and that esplanade itself, with the wrought-iron railings, the globe lamps, the elegant statue of Nekrasov, and the bridge over the gully from river to town centre, together with many small churches, all contribute to a still potentially graceful existence. Prince Andrei Bolkonsky from *War and Peace* died in Yaroslavl in a rented merchant house on the Volga embankment, surrounded by Natasha and the other Rostovs and his son Nikolai and his estranged wife Lisa. Near Yaroslavl was a hospital for real victims of the battle of Borodino. Where the Kotorosl meets the Volga are fine views of the colony on the far side that was once famous for its leather and its churches. Soviet Yaroslavl preserved forty-three out of its hundred extant churches after the Revolution, a little over double the national average. Each one amplifies upon the town's rich trading past, when merchants founded churches and stored their goods in the basements. We walked from one to the other in the rain.

Yaroslavl's Golden Age was the seventeenth century. It came next only to Moscow in importance and wealth, followed by Kostroma. The port handled grain and salt and cargoes going east from western Europe. Yaroslavl was famous for its glazed tiles made with Volga clay, and other applied arts. One of the first textile mills in Russia opened here in 1722. The railways expanded the port's activity. The Nobels had a storage depot here, laying the foundations of a Soviet oil refinery. Mayakovsky addressed the citizens of Yaroslavl as 'butter makers and weavers', but that was rather old-fashioned even in 1927. They were already on their way to becoming chemists, petrochemists, tyre manufacturers and makers of diesel engines: the automobile industry would depend on their products.

Yaroslavl town centre has rows of stone trading arcades like those of Kostroma, and a *gostinny dvor*. The white Spas monastery, where the most important manuscript in Russian literature before Pushkin, *The Lay of Prince Igor*, was found before it was lost again, is like a great kremlin of snow on a wet September day. Everywhere on a Monday morning there is bustle and trams and cars and trucks. Yaroslavlians are famous in Russia for their uncommon enterprise and hard work. We were invited across the diesel-belching lanes of cars to admire a statue of the actor who founded the first Russian national theatre here in the mid-eighteenth century, Fedor Volkov.

Our Yaroslavl guide was larger and kinder and less angry than her Kostroma counterpart. In her commentary on churches and monasteries and renamed streets she bemoaned the barbarism of Soviet days, and explicitly spoke of a country which had murdered its past. She seemed to do this less to confess her guilt, more to express authentic incomprehension. She meanf, in part: 'How could I have done that?' Before retirement she had been a secondary school teacher. I heard her talking to another Russian woman when the microphone was off; she was wondering whether in these inflationary times she could afford her own funeral.

The Yaroslavl agenda is churches, galleries, monasteries: a demanding programme when compressed into less than a day. The history of the Tolga monastery, not far from where the tiny Tolga joins the voluminous Volga, shows many signs of the Polish/ Lithuanian nearness. For ages the only access here from Yaroslavl was by the Volga, since the land was densely wooded. After the Second World War this graceful monastery became a home for delinquent children, which resulted in wilful damage, but slowly today's vegetarian community of a hundred and thirty nuns is restoring it as a religious and cultural centre and a place where old crafts are revived. The accent is on healing. It is said that Ivan the Terrible toured the monasteries of his day seeking a cure for a bad leg, and that he found it at Tolga. There is accommodation for visitors who would dare seek a modern cure. From somewhere as we stood in the drizzle (Russian women took it in turns to hug me under their umbrellas) came the encouraging smell of bread. There was an overgrown orchard, where a solitary figure was working, and a horse and a cow.

Back in the town the seventeenth-century redbrick church of Ilya Prorok, Elijah the Prophet, was less restful, being already given over to the nascent, hard-nosed tourist industry. But still it was a marvellous sight, with its interior of glazed tiles and frescoes painted by Nikitin and Savin, which Igor Grabar compared to those of the Early Renaissance. Yaroslavl has managed to retain the distinctive blend of aristocratic classicism and Russian mercantile colour and solidity which characterized the nineteenth-century life of these Upper Volga towns. Then suddenly came Bolshevism, to which there was fierce resistance here. It culminated in a two-week battle in July 1918, in which the Tolga monastery was implicated for counter-revolutionary activities, and which the White Guards lost.

Just off the Volga Embankment the local history museum has some evocative photographs. One shows students in 1905 waving red flags from their rowing boats on the Volga. The notoriously fanatical professional revolutionary born in Nizhny, Yakov Sverdlov, was active for about a year in Yaroslavl and it was he who organized that day of protest on 1 May 1905 along the Volga Embankment. Solzhenitsyn accuses Sverdlov of direct involvement in the Romanov murders, though most historians place him only on the Moscow end of the telephone to Ekaterinenburg (later Sverdlovsk). This pretty embankment where Sverdlov mobilized the Yaroslavl students became known, after his terrorist ambitions won through for Russia, as the First of May Boulevard. Another renaming, then.

Why do I find the renaming business so disturbing? I think it is simply the naive desire for language to be used in a morally responsible way. Because it often isn't, anywhere in the world, one must travel and try to see and feel for oneself, and also look: at buildings, paintings, artifacts.

The Yaroslavl art gallery is just such a wordless and more trustworthy place, well endowed with modest canvases, the paintings themselves rich in the old mercantile spirit and in more recent evasions of Soviet orthodoxy. There were postcards and books on sale inside the entrance to this atmospheric eighteenth-century house with a magnificent ballroom full of Karelian birch furniture. I must have all of those, I observed to myself greedily. Like all commodities here, you never know when information and publications will appear again. Moreover, the prices are negligible for a foreigner. The women at the desk cried: 'First see the pictures! Then you may buy a postcard.' They still have culture here, you see. Blending it with shopping fills them with distaste.

My eyes roamed over Kuinzhi and Rerikh and Korovin and Kustodiev. Not on display to me, but apparently held by the museum, were elegiac Volga scenes with which Savrasov, Levitan's teacher, consoled himself after the death of his daughter.

I made most of the still-lifes, since this was a suspect genre in high Soviet days. The world of such small-scale creations is private. They deal in the publicly unspoken. They express domestic intimacy and the satisfaction of simply living. They depict a world to which ideology can contribute nothing. So here are the pleasures of summer life, a kitchen table in a dacha, with an old *kuvshin* (a jug shaped like a hollow duck) of *kvas* (rye bread beer), spring onions with their roots freshly torn from the soil, a dark loaf, a painted *khokhloma* spoon, and dried fish in a string on the wall. In the kitchen and in the country Russian traditions at least tried to evade the proletarian new broom. The painting entitled *Nile Flowers*, showing tiger lilies in sinuous and regal splendour inside a Russian interior, with guitar and fruit and candles, shows the kind of aesthetic transformation of prosaic reality which was possible every moment, even in Soviet Russia.

Through the ruched curtains at the first-floor windows was a grand view of the Volga. The decorative black wrought-iron balustrade figured in the foreground, and the view was filtered through lime trees. The fluidity of the trees and the water, the concertina-ed white satin and even the turns in the wrought iron all contrasted lyrically with the flat wet black asphalt, a gift of Soviet modernization as late as 1961. Outside, a man and a woman in early middle age were slowly collecting fallen leaves from the limes in white enamel buckets. I had passed them outside. As the rain fell, they kept asking each other the time. Behind them the embankment broadened into a semi-circular belvedere on which stood a white-columned rotunda. The street had no shops and no traffic. Russia is funny like *Waiting for Godot* is funny, I remembered. And perhaps the renaming business is funny in the same way. Yaroslavl, with its acute awareness of history, is the only town where I have found an openly mocking attitude to renaming. Our good guide, the one worried about the cost of her funeral, pointed out the folly of one street with four names: Rostov Street, Khrestyanskaya (Peasant) Street, Andropov Street and Katerinenskaya (Catherine) Street.

I spent the rest of our short day in Yaroslavl walking through its muddy streets, buying an ice cream, getting swept along by shoppers under the arcades, walking back through a well-kept park to the Alexandrine Esplanade. The only blight to this lovely part of town, from where, moored, we took our farewell, was the crumbling concrete hinterland to the 1960s' river station. Deserted at twilight, and slippery in the wet, its crowning spiral staircase was dangerously loose, like the Chkalov Steps in Nizhny.

30

Russia, Literature and Travellers

OVER DINNER we argued about how to treat the Soviet past. 'What do you do about the offspring of rape?' asked Peter, who wanted to cast 'it' out wholesale (though to perpetuate the metaphor by personalizing the 'offspring' would make his argument seem more inhuman than intended). I felt there was something to be salvaged; something which was in the Russian tradition. We couldn't agree, but dinner itself was very good: chicken with garlic sauce, followed by leavened *oladi* pancakes and honey.

The *Chernyshevsky* rocked on the Uglich reservoir, though it did not creak like the *Nekrasov*. I toyed with thoughts of slow, painful Russian progress. Germane to the theme seemed to be Peter's wife's professional observation, when she had picked up some building bricks at the Tolga monastery yesterday, that those Russian bricks were soft. The art historian said Russians were either Oblomovs or Foma Gordyeyevs. The reason might be ease or debauchery; the result was no one wanted to do anything. In Nizhny Irina had spoken of a nation of Sharikovs, after the dog who in Bulgakov's story was metamorphosed into a sub-human person without any refinements of the higher species. I noticed that these were all women talking about Russian men.

We copied the Belgians and got our hair cut, then sat in the chilly bar again. The barmaid suddenly changed the exchange rate, seemingly to squeeze a last profit from the season, though she claimed world markets had shifted. She tried it on with the Belgians, but they were alert, having already been robbed while the

Chernyshevsky was moored in Nizhny. One had held out a fifty-dollar note to pay for drinks and a stranger whisked it away. Except that the stranger wasn't a stranger to the barmaid, according to what Peter and I overheard in Russian. An atmosphere of unease and faint suspicion added to the barometric chill in the bar.

The cabins were warmer, if isolated. The radio concluded an instalment of *Dom Syem*, a series about Moscow low life contrived with BBC help. There was the tinkle of knives and forks and the hum of surrounding diners as a group of people went out for a celebratory meal. When it got to such lines in Russian as 'I'll have the fish', and with so many Anglo-Saxon social niceties being observed, I burst out laughing at the implausibility of this being Moscow. Beyond the rain-streaked cabin window odd wild blazes of orange foliage shot into view, offering more excitement than in a month of Russian life.

Late in the afternoon we made a sanitary stop in Kimry. All the returning Volga liners have their water checked for contamination. Kimry, an old craft town famous for its shoes, is close to where the Volga rejoins the Moscow canal. Its citizens had lined up their wares, though no one was allowed to disembark and any trading took place from the lower deck. The air smelt of flowers. Someone said that Kimry had made all the boots for the army Brezhnev sent to Afghanistan in 1980, the last act of Soviet foreign aggression before the unstoppable decline of the empire.

A voice beside me at the top rail shouted down: 'How much are the carrots?'

'A hundred roubles,' replied the babushka, and the nicely made-up, nicely dressed questioner drew a sharp breath.

'Is that expensive?' I enquired.

For a moment she took me for a Russian. 'Lord, what do you think?' she retorted angrily.

I found myself talking to the ship's book-keeper, and took the opportunity to make a few suggestions about the restaurant. These were dismissed with a breathtaking frankness about human nature which these days would be almost criminal in the West. There could be no self-service at breakfast because the first people would eat everything. The cultural level of customer was not high enough.

The book-keeper also maintained that Russians would complain if, as I had also suggested, they received less meat. I wonder. They don't complain when mealtimes are arbitarily changed or whole meals are suddenly not offered.

One of those changes, made because the staff wanted to go off early, found us dining at high-tea time in broad daylight on our last evening. The Vuchetich statue of Lenin was clearly visible at the head of the canal, and, on the far side opposite, the pedestal where Stalin had stood. The Belgians popped out to snap Lenin in the evening sun, while Peter provoked the waitress into saying it was high time Lenin went too. In chatting we frittered the evening away and turned off the Volga in the night.

The boat was stationary at Khvoiny Bor, waiting for clearance through a narrow part of the canal. I looked at my watch and felt that odd sprightliness at 7am which told me I was both relieved and sad to have left the great river. Beneath our bows the water was clear and still. A green and yellow birch forest rose up from the red sand beach. Out of pure water like this, the pure forest stream, ideally vodka is made, with the grain of Russian fields, and purified through the white silver bark of these slender trees. In the pure water I saw mirrored the nostalgia I couldn't express. A man from the United Nations Association in Moscow, another early riser, came on deck to test the soft, damp weather and greeted me.

There had not been a single dangerous moment. Through Russia over two thousand miles and back I had been passed from hand to hand like a child. How could I not be grateful and even awe-struck? The fact that this legendary Russian caring exists side by side with the dehumanized cruelty of the Gulag and one of the most negligent and destructive forms of government in history is more than intellect can deal with. The communal tradition encourages passivity but also upholds secret values smothered and buried in society at large. The visitor to Russia is left juggling with passivity and dehumanization, soulfulness and the good life.

*

Volga travellers through the ages have not always had it as physically easy as I have. Ibn Fadlan or Fosslan journeyed in 921–22 through Bukhara and Khorezma as Abassid ambassador to the Volga Bolgars, and left vivid descriptions of peoples including the Russians and the Bashkirs, and of their folklore and way of life. In 1324 the Arab writer Ibn Battuta mentioned the Volga on the journey he undertook to New Sarai. Next century Afanasy Nikitin exposed the great political and economic potential of the Volga at a stroke. 'Pagan' Tartars made Nikitin's journey more colourful by turning pirate and stealing all his belongings after the first easy stops at Uglich, Kostroma, Nizhny and Kazan. The complete voyage to the Indian Ocean and back via the Black Sea took six years, from 1466 to 1472. With the kind of symbolism which seems so often to occur in Russian history, it was the patriotic Karamzin, some of whose precious *History of the Russian State* perished in the Moscow fire of 1812, who first found Nikitin's manuscript more than three hundred years after it was written.

Then came the turn of the Germans, keen for Oriental trade, and the British, likewise with their eyes on the Volga route to the East. Jenkinson, Muscovy Company agent and ambassador of Queen Elizabeth to Moscow, described his several Volga journeys including ones to Astrakhan undertaken between 1557 and 1572. He drew a map of the Caspian. Adam Olearius, born in 1599 in Saxony, travelled to Russia and the Volga in 1633 and 1635–8. A court mathematician and librarian, Olearius observed the country around him, leaving behind valuable accounts, and also drew maps. He took with him a German poet, Paul Fleming, whose verses are still quoted in guides to Astrakhan. Fleming himself became the subject of a novel in 1842; thus Volga travelling again entered literature. Other sixteenth-century British travellers included Merrich and Chardin.

The most interesting book, though, was John Perry's, published in 1716 as *The State of Russia under the Present Tsar*. The shockwaves after the Bulavin Uprising in Astrakhan in 1703 reached Britain in the form of gruesome accounts of how foreigners in the city had been hacked to death. Peter the Great tried in vain to have English workers recruited to tend Astrakhan's vines three years later. But Perry was braver, accompanying Peter to Holland, working on his Kamyshin canal and leaving a grand account of

Peter's good instincts in developing shipping, expanding Volga trade and trying to cultivate good relations with the Tartars. He said of the Volga that it was probably stocked with more fish than any other river in the world.

In the next century travellers became more political and eventually, with Romanticism, individualistic. Enlightenment shone the light of reason over much of Europe, but in Russia its progress was obscure. The Industrial Revolution was slow to commence, almost a century behind England. Outsiders travelled to Russia now not so much for uncharted lands (though this was Humboldt's brief) but for political curiosity. Here was a backward place. I have mentioned Oliphant and Spottiswoode (who travelled to Volga towns, but mostly overland), and the Frenchmen Gautier and Dumas *père*. Gautier's was the slightest journey, inspired by the music of the name Nizhny Novgorod. Still, I have never mentioned that name to anyone who did not also warm to its lovely timbre and elegant cadence.

Dumas, meanwhile, was fun and I wish he had written in more detail of how it was to re-encounter after thirty years the characters out of whose youthful fates he had woven a romantic tale. He had written of the love affair of the Decembrist Muraviev-Apostol and a French princess. When they met again the couple were married and middle-aged, and the Decembrist was governor of Nizhny. Mrs Atkinson traipsed after her husband to Siberia via the Volga and Kama in 1863, while Kate Guthrie went with her daughter initially to see the art of central and eastern Europe. The Victorian ladies were seduced by Russia, venturing further and further into the interior until their journey reached an apogee of torment in a two-day dust storm in Tsaritsyn, where they were locked up with a mute Russian stranger.

Baron Haxthausen was a German traveller in a higher intellectual class. It was his intention to recount the sights and say what he had for breakfast only insofar as they shed light on the economic, social and political condition of Russia. The result was a magnificent analytical account in 1847 of his two-year Russian journey, which included the Volga. He made the point which undermines any travel book, but which must be made, that 'whoever would travel in Russia, earnestly to study the condition of the country, and observe its national life with unprejudiced eyes, must first of all forget everything he has read in other countries upon the subject'. His fundamental understanding of Russia was as a patriarchal, not a feudal, state. Always there was a sense of the people as family, with the tsar as father and the land shared in a commune, which was 'almost sufficient of itself to explain the whole social and political condition of Russia'.

Haxthausen has such a fine sympathy for the Russian condition. His words still describe the bind in which the Russians are caught:

> The Russians who have acquired the usual West European cultivations are called lacquered barbarians; this is inaccurate: they are no barbarians, but a healthy, vigorous intellectual people, of noble race, religious and moral; if however they are brought suddenly into contact with and receive the taint of modern culture, their natural virtues vanish, their religions and morals, simplicity and honesty are destroyed, and nothing remains but the animal nature common to man. The Russian then becomes worse than those who bear the poison of civilisation more easily, from its having been longer united with their existing manner.

For the British the writer, businessman and Slavist Maurice Baring left a slight, engaging account of his journey down the Volga in 1913. In Baring the broad Haxthausian view was implicit; and had it been voiced, overcoming British reticence, it would have been much better. Then the Haxthausen voice disappeared altogether.

So what now, post-Communism, post yet another discarded set of forms, after another revolution, for the Russia traveller? For the last six decades this great river has hardly been the object of Western travel. The cities of Nizhny, Samara, Saratov and Astrakhan were closed until 1992. What a shameful waste! I would say. Yet you might go there and counter: but there is nothing anyway to offer, nothing to see!

While I was travelling I sometimes thought of Napoleon, who is supposed to have cried out with disappointment before Moscow: 'I haven't come all this way to conquer a pile of shacks.' That typical impatient, practical view made me laugh and feel at home in Russia when I needed to invent some mental comfort. Dumas took a more imaginative approach. He said that the man who came to Russia and looked for something behind the façade was like a cat expecting to meet another cat on the other side of the mirror. Haxthausen contented himself with saying that the external boundaries and outlines were always set in Russian towns; they just needed filling in. Now it is true that though the Volga is beautiful there is little to see, except the water, and everything to fill in with the mind. But that perhaps is the clue to Russian travelling.

Or I mean I cannot understand the Volga without literature, and that Russian literature exactly fills that void which bewilders outsiders. Russian literature answers the long-standing need to flesh out the invisible and create traditions. It has kept alive that vast world of correspondences and supports which Chernyshevsky could not understand and Soviet reality tried to banish. Khlebnikov took this to the limits of comprehension when he longed 'upon the proud vessel of minus-one to sail across Razin's soul . . . to choose as my Volga his destiny'. The poet wanted to cross his life with Razin's, to blend their two experiences of the Indo-Russian river linking Russia north to south, east to west, and Russia to the East. 'He [Razin] was seeking out the structural axes of the human world, the central pilings of his own belief, which he later drove like powerful pilings deep into the ancestral homeland.'

When Shalyapin sings the Stenka Razin ballad he chuckles bitterly, as if to say: men cannot live by imagination alone. But read Gorky and you will see in the Volga the sluggish but beautiful Russian soul, never quite realizing its potential. Read Khlebnikov to redeem the story-book heroism which makes Stenka Razin and the Romantic river of pirates and primitive social justice seem otherwise brutal and irrelevant (Alyosha's view). Read Boris Pilnyak to feel with the creation of the Great Volga and the emotional consequences of Bolshevism.

The Volga Flows into the Caspian Sea, finished in 1929, is a neglected, prophetic novel. It described the project of one Professor Poletika to create a new river from the Oka to Moscow and to make the river Moscow flow backwards. Before building even began on the Great Volga Pilnyak's novel set hydro-engineering in the brave new spirit against good and bad forces of tradition. Professor

Poletika – politics – replaced eternity with courage and construction. The new river meant destroying old villages and rebuilding Russia on European lines. It would save Russia from its advancing deserts. Yet was the effort worth it when, after the Civil War and the Bolshevik takeover, society was descending into ever deeper chaos and worthlessness? Pilnyak took the idea of the imminent Great Volga as a metaphor for the state of Russia under Communism. He showed the good intentions and the real destructiveness of the abstract idealists in a land already suffused with endemic confusion and unhappiness.

Yet, still, if only the economic dream, Sadko's dream in Rimsky's opera of Russian waters, could become true! If only a giant open waterway could lead to a rich Russia! If somehow, too, the northern spirit that Russia shared with the melancholy Varangians could be married to the charm and lightness of the Eastern world, Russia's other heritage! Listen to those two siren songs in Rimsky-Korsakov and you will understand the strains on the Russian heart. The *Sadko* fairy-tale yielded in time to a dream of Stalinist industrialization, the same dream which was epitomized in Plyos on the Kholui box showing a tractor at the centre of the ideal, beautiful life for Russia. In Alexandrov's film *Volga Volga* that dream was also as really embodied as I have ever seen it: in the then magical new architecture of the Moscow-Volga canal and the river station. As the liner *Josef Stalin* approached Khimki in 1938 this might have been Atlantis or a new Sarai, or Kitezh returned to the visible, or Sadko's homecoming with stacks of treasure from overseas and the prospect of eternal co-existence with love and beauty in Russia, under the water.

Today at 11am it is the post-Soviet, cosmopolitan, economically polarized and violent city of Moscow. A queue forms to make telephone calls at Reception, yellow Volga taxis and Zhigulis drive over the wharf, no one cares except a passing outsider for the cracked icons of the River Station, and the Amazon with the boat has lost her mystery: we have been there.

Gorky's Volga remains in the mind:

The beautiful and mighty *Yermak*, Gordyeyev's steam tow-boat, was rapidly floating down the current, and on each side the shores of the powerful and beautiful Volga were slowly moving past him. . . . The broad-bosomed river stretched itself majestically between the shores; noiselessly, solemnly and slowly flowed its waters, conscious of their invisible power; the mountainous shore is reflected in the water in a black shadow, while on the left side it is adorned with gold and with verdant velvet by a border of sand and the wide meadows. Here and there villages appear on mountain and on meadow, the sun shines bright on the window-panes of the huts and on the yellow roofs of straw, the church crosses sparkle amid the verdure of the trees, grey windmill wings revolve lazily in the air, smoke from the factory chimney rises skyward in thick, black curling clouds. Crowds of children in blue, red and white shirts [the colours of the Russian flag], standing on the banks, shouted loudly at the sight of the steamer, which had disturbed the quiet of the river, and from under the steamer's wheels the cheerful waves are rushing toward the feet of the children and splash against the bank. . . . From the shore a melancholy song is heard:

'Oh, o-o-o, once more!'

The steamer passes many rafts, splashing them with waves. The beams are in continual motion under the blows of the waves; the men on the rafts, in blue shirts, staggering, look at the steamer and laugh and shout something. The big, beautiful vessel goes sidewise on the river; the yellow scantlings with which it is loaded sparkle like gold and are dimly reflected in the muddy, vernal water. A passenger steamer comes from the opposite side and whistles – the resounding echo of the whistle loses itself in the woods, in the gorges of the mountainous bank, and dies away there. In the middle of the river the waves stirred up by the two vessels strike against one another and splash against the steamers' sides, and the vessels are rocked upon the water. On the slope of the mountainous bank are verdant carpets of winter corn, brown strips of fallow corn and black strips of ground tilled for spring corn. Birds, like little dots, soar over them, and are clearly seen in the blue canopy of the sky; nearby a flock is grazing; in the distance they look like children's toys; the small figure of the shepherd stands leaning on a staff, and looks at the river.

The glare of the water, freedom and liberty are everywhere,

the meadows are cheerfully verdant and the blue sky is tenderly clear; a restrained power is felt in the quiet motion of the water; above it the generous May sun is shining, the air is filled with the exquisite odour of fir trees and fresh foliage. And the banks keep on meeting them, caressing the eyes and the soul with their beauty, as new pictures constantly unfold themselves.

Everything surrounding them bears the stamp of some kind of tardiness: all – nature as well as men – live there clumsily, lazily; but in that laziness there is an odd gracefulness, and it seems as though beyond the laziness a colossal power were concealed; an invincible power, but as yet deprived of consciousness, as yet without any definite desires and aims. And the absence of consciousness in this half-slumbering life throws shades of sadness over all the beautiful slope. Submissive patience, silent hope for something new and more inspiriting are heard even in the cry of the cuckoo, wafted to the river by the wind from the shore. The melancholy songs sound as though imploring someone for help. And at times there is in them a ring of despair. The river answers the songs with sighs. And the treetops shake, lost in meditation. Silence.

This is how it feels to love a river and be dwarfed by it. And love counters the meaninglessness which bedevils Russian existence.

Bibliography

The literature of the Volga is vast, though little of it is concentrated in single books in English. The volumes listed here helped to shape my journey and may suggest some further reading.

Adelung, Friedrich von *Ubersicht der Reisenden in Russland vor 1700* St Petersburg 1846

Ahmad Ibn Fudlan *Puteshestvie Ibn- Fadlana na Volgu* Leningrad 1939

Aksakov, Sergei *Years of Childhood* tr J. D. Duff Oxford University Press Oxford 1983

Astrakhan: Literaturny khudozhevstvenny sbornik Astrakhan 1958

Astrakhan: Putevoditel Astrakhan 1979

Astrakhanskaya Oblastnaya Kartinnaya Gallereya Moscow 1990

Atkinson, Mrs *Recollections of the Tartar Steppe* London 1863

Baedeker K. *Russia 1914*

Baring, Maurice *What I Saw in Russia* London 1913

Belov, Evgeny *Kazan Nizhny Novgorod Kostroma* Moscow 1913

Bely, Andrei *Petersburg* tr Robert A. Maguire and John E. Malmstad Harvester Press Sussex 1979

Birkos, Alexandr S. *Soviet Cinema* Connecticut 1976

Bogolyubov, N. P. *Volga ot Tveri do Astrakhana* Sanktpeterburg 1862

Bol' i Beda Rossii Moscow 1989

Borovikov, Sergei *Xamerzshie slova* Saratov 1991

Borovsky, Viktor *Chaliapin* London 1988

Bremmer, Ian and Ray Taras *Nations and Politics in the Soviet Successor States* Cambridge University Press Cambridge 1992

Brown, Edward J. *Russian Literature since the Revolution* London 1969

Bunin, Ivan *Long Ago* selected storied tr David Richards and Sophie Lund Angel Books London 1984

Carroll, Lewis *The Russian Journal* New York 1935

Chatwin Bruce 'The Volga' in *Great Rivers of the World* ed Chekhov, Anton *Pis'ma* [Letters] *Polnoe sobranie sochinenii* t. 15 Moscow 1944–51
    Lady with the Lapdog and other Stories tr David Magarshack Penguin Harmondsworth 1964
Chernetsov, Grigory and Nikanor Chernetsov *Puteshestvie po Volge* Moscow 1970
Chirov, Dmitry *Pisateli nizhnei Volgi* Volgograd 1973
Conquest, Robert *Lenin* Collins London 1972
Cooper, Joshua tr: *Four Russian Plays* Penguin Harmondsworth 1972
Demidov, Andrei and Irina *melodii staroi Samary* Samara 1992
Dokuchaeva, V. N. *Boris Kustodiev: zhizn' v tvorchestve* Moscow 1991
Dontsov, E. K, G. I. Karas'kov and P. P. Shcherbinin *Kostromskaya rez'ba* Yaroslavl 1991
Dumas, Alexandre *De Paris à Astrakhan nouvelles impressions de voyage* Paris 1862
Fedin, Konstantin *Sochineniya* Moscow 1952–54
Figes, Orlando *Peasant russia, Civil War The Volga Countryside in Revolution 1917–21* Oxford University Press Oxford 1989
Fisher, H. H. *Famine in Russia* New York 1927
Galai, Yu. *Makarevsky monastyr* Nizhny Novgorod nd
Gautier, Theophile *Voyage en Russie* Paris 1867
German, A. A. *Nemetskaya avtonomia na Volge* Saratov 1992
Gilbert, Martin *Russian History Atlas* Weidenfeld London 1972
Golomshtok, Igor *totalitarian Art* London 1990
Goncharov Ivan *Oblomov* tr Nathalie Duddington Dent 1932
The Voyage of the Frigate Pallada tr N. W. Wilson London 1965
Gorky, Maxim *The Artymonov Business* tr Alec Brown London 1948
    Chaliapin An Autobiography as told to Maxim Gorky London 1968
    The Man Who Was Afraid [Foma Gordyeeff] London Fisher Unwin 1905
    My Apprenticeship tr Ronald Wilks Ronald Harmondsworth 1974
    My Childhood tr Ronald Wilks Penguin Harmondsworth 1979
    Through Russia. A Book of Stories tr C. J. Hogarth Dent London nd
Gorodetskaya starina Vypusk 1 Gorodets 1992
Grechukhin, V. A. *Derevyannye khudozhestva* Yaroslavl 1991
Groushko, M. A. *Cossack Warrior Riders of the Steppes* Cassell London 1992
Guthrie, Kate *Through Russia* London 1874
Haxthausen, Baron *The Russian Empire* 2 vols. London 1856
Hayward, Max *Writers in Russia 1917–1978* Harvill London 1983

Hingley, Ronald *Chekhov* Unwin London 1950

Humboldt, Alexander von *Reise durchs Baltikum nach Russland und Siberien 1829* aufgezeichnet von Hanno Beck Stuttgart 1983

Kapuscinski, Ryszard *Imperium Sowjetische Streifzuge* aus dem Polnischen von Martin Pollack Frankfurt am Main 1993

Karelin, A. O. Creative Heritage Nizhny Novgorod 1990

Khlebnikov, Velemir *Collected Works* tr Paul Schmidt, ed Charlotte Douglas 2 vols London 1987

Kochan, Lionel *The Making of Modern Russia* (Penguin Harmondsworth 1963)

Kozlov, P. I. and V. F. Marov *Yaroslavl* Yaroslavl 1988

Kublitsky, Georgy *Volga* Moscow 1978

'Kustodiev i Astrakhan' in *Volga* 1978 No 3

Lenin, Vladimir Ilyich *What is To be Done?* tr Joe Fineberg and George Hanna Penguin Harmondsworth 1988

Lepeshinskaya A., and B. Dobrinin *Volga* Moskva 1911

Lincoln Fitzpatrick, Anne *The Great Russian Fair* London 1990

Mamaev Kurgan Volgograd 1989

Marlowe, Christopher *Tamburlaine* ed J. W. Harper London A & C Black 1971

Materikin, A. V. *Volgograd v nazvaniyakh ulits* Volgograd 1992

Medvedev, Zhores *Soviet Agriculture* London 1987

Mel'nikov, A. *Nizhegorodskaya starina* Nizhny Novgorod 1992

Mirsky, D. s. *Contemporary Russian Literature 1881–1925*

Moskva – Astrakhan – Rostov- na- Don7u Turistskaya Karta -Skhema Moscow 1986

Nabokov, Vladimir The Gift tr Michael Scammell Penguin Harmondsworth 1981

Nekrasov, Nikolai Alekseevich *Who Can Be Happy and Free in Russia?* tr Juliet M. Soskice London 1901

Nekrasov, Viktor *V okopakh Stalingrada* tr David Floyd as *Frontline Stalingrad* London 1962

Nikitin, A. *Khozhdenie za tri morya 1466–1472* [Voyage Beyond three Seas] (Russian, Hindi, and English texts) Moscow 1960

Nikitin, V. P. *Astrakhan i ee okrestnosti* Moscow 1981

Oliphant, L. *The Russian Shores of the Black Sea in the autumn of 1852, with a voyage down the Volga* Edinburgh and London 1853

Ostrovsky, A. N. *Polnoe sobranie sochinenii* 12 vols Moscow 1975

Ostrovsky, Nikolai *Kak zakalyalas' stal'* tr Alec Brown as *The Making of a Hero* London 1937

Pal'kin, Nikolai *O, Volga!* Moscow 1985

Perry John *The State of Russia under the Present Czar* London 1716

Pilnyak, Boris *Chinese Story and Other Tales* tr Vera T. Reck and Michael Green University of Oklahoma Press 1988

The Volga Flows to the Caspian Sea London 1932

Petrov, Vladimir *Isaac Levitan* St Petersburg 1992

Petrova, Evdokia *Shchelykovo* Moscow 1982

Pushkin, Alexander *Polnoe sobranie sochinenii* 12 vols Leningrad 1977

The Captain's Daughter tr Paul Debreczeny London 1992

Eugene Onegin tr Charles Johnston Penguin Harmondsworth 1979

The History of Pugachev tr Earl Sampson Ann Arbor 1983

Priestley, J. B. *Anton Chekhov* London 1970

Razumovskaya I. M. *Kostroma* Leningrad 1990

Richardson, Joanna *Theophile Gautier* London 1958

Rozanov, V. V. 'Russky Nil' in *Novy Mir* No 7 Moscow July 1989

Ruhle, Jurgen *Literatur und Revolution Die Schriftsteller und der Kommunismus* Koln/Berlin 1960

Russell, Betrand *Autobiography 1872–1914* London 1967

The Practice and Theory of Bolshevism London 1920

Ryan, Frank *Tuberculosis The Greatest Story Never Told* 1992

Saratovsky gosudarstvenny khudozhestvenny muzei Moscow 1991

Schlogel, Karl *Das Wunder von Nishnij oder Die Ruckkehr der Stadte* Frankfurt am Main 1991

Seaton, Albert *The Horsemen of the Steppes* London 1985

Sholokhov, Mikhail *And Quiet Flows the Don* tr Stephen Garry Penguin Harmondsworth 1967

Simmons, E. J. *Russian Fiction and Soviet Ideology* New York 1958

Solzhenitsyn, Alexander *The Gulag Archipelago 1918–1956* abridged in one volume tr Thomas P. Whitney and Harry Willetts Collins Harvill London 1986

Lenin in Zurich tr H. T. Willetts London 1976

Spottiswoode, William *A Tarantasse Journey through Eastern Russia in the autumn of 1856* London 1857

Stin, Irina *Kostroma Pamyatnik arkhitektury* 1974

Tarasov, L. K. *Ot rasshivy do krylatykh korablei* Gorky 1988

Tolf, R. W. *The Russian Rockefellers* Stanford 1976

Tolstoy, Aleksei *Darness and Dawn* [includes *The Sisters* and *1918*] tr Edith Bone and Emile Burns London 1935

Nikita's Childhood tr Violet Lansbury London 1945

The Road to Calvary [includes The Sisters, *1918*, both revised, and *Bleak Morning*) tr Edith Bone Hutchinson London 1945

A Week in Turenovo [stories] ed George Reavey New York 1958

Tolstoy, Leo *War and Peace* tr Rosemary Edmonds Penguin Harmondsworth 1957

Travels of Ibn Battuta London NKP 1929

Trotsky, Leon *The Young Lenin* tr Max Eastman Penguin Harmondsworth 1974

Troyat, Henri *Maxim Gorky* London 1991

Twain, Mark *Huckleberry Finn*

Valkenier, Elizabeth *Ilya Repin and the World of Russian Art* New York 1990

Vinogradova. T. P., *Nizhegorodskaya intelligentsia vokrug N. A. Dobrolyubova* Nizhny Novgorod 1992

Volga [guide with foldout map] Moscow 1903

Yashin, A. I. *Sto stranits o Saratove* Saratov 1990

Zamaytin, Evegeny *The Islandersu Salamander Press Edinburgh 1984*
    We tr Bernard Gilbert Guerney Penguin Harmondsworth 1972

Zaripov, M and Zh. Mindubaev *Ot Ulyanovska do Kazani* Moscow 1976

Zorkaya, Neya *The Illustrated History of Soviet Cinema* New York 1989

Zvanstev, M. P. *Zavolzh'e* Moscow 1972

Index